INTELLIGENCE-LED POLICING

Leadership, Strategies & Tactics

THOMAS E. BAKER

43-08 162nd Street
Flushing, NY 11358
www.LooseleafLaw.com
800-647-5547

Library of Congress Cataloging-In-Publication Data

Baker, Thomas E., 1941-
    Intelligence-led policing : leadership, strategies, and tactics / Thomas E. Baker.
        p. cm.
    Includes bibliographical references and index.
    ISBN 978-1-932777-75-8 (alk. paper)
    1. Law enforcement. 2. Crime prevention. 3. Police administration. 4. Crime analysis. 5. Leadership. 6. Intelligence service. I. Title.
    HV7935.B35 2009
    363.2068--dc22

                                                            2008050220

Cover design by *Sans Serif, Inc.* Saline, Michigan
Cover Photo by *Gary Maio*

Table of Contents

I

INTRODUCTION

Purpose and Direction

Intelligence-Led Policing: Leadership, Strategies and Tactics bridges the gap between strategic leadership, intelligence, and crime analysis operations. Intelligence-Led Policing is the management system and philosophy that coordinates the sharing of criminal information.

  (a) This book is primarily for police leaders and officers seeking promotion to command positions.
  (b) A secondary audience would include students of criminal justice, criminal analysis, intelligence, and Homeland Security programs.
  (c) The goal is to teach policing strategies and tactics, but does not suggest that every police agency is a mirror image. Leadership strategies and tactics are adaptable and flexible in response to the size and mission of individual police departments.

A Special Tribute

Sir Arthur Conan Doyle, author of the Sherlock Holmes detective series, was a source of inspiration for this book. His mastery of inductive and deductive reasoning would serve any analyst well. Moreover, his powers of observation and critical thinking skills were the kindred spirit of modern law enforcement analysts.

DEDICATION

This book is dedicated to:

The men and women of law enforcement who risk their lives everyday to protect us, especially the NYPD, who found a lost five-year-old boy and changed his life and destiny forever. That child was the author of this book and that positive legacy will never be forgotten.

and

Officer Michael Paturzo and Helen McGrath

ABOUT THE AUTHOR

Thomas E. Baker, Lieutenant Colonel, MP

Tom served as a Lieutenant Colonel with United States Army Reserve Military Police Corps, Special Agent and Commander with United States Army Criminal Investigation Command. Moreover, his service includes three years in the regular Army. His civilian experience includes: former police officer for Henrico County Police, Richmond, Virginia and Montgomery County, Maryland. He served in the Vice, Organized Crime Intelligence Unit as an undercover and intelligence specialist. In addition, he is a member of the International Association of Law Enforcement Intelligence Analysts. Tom is presently serving as an Associate Professor of Criminal Justice at the University of Scranton.

PREFACE

In solving a problem of this sort, the grand thing is to be able to reason backwards. That is a very useful accomplishment, and a very easy one, but people do not practice it much. In the everyday affairs of life, it is more useful to reason forward, and so the other comes to be neglected. There are fifty who can reason synthetically for one who can reason analytically.
— Sir Arthur Conan Doyle

The need for accurate police intelligence and analytical reasoning rings like burglar alarms at midnight in an unoccupied downtown warehouse. The cases are far too many to cite where intelligence analysis could have saved the lives of police officers and the citizens they were striving to protect. Many perform heroic police acts, but few have the training and expertise to reason analytically. Law enforcement agencies need to stay ahead of the curve, and focus intelligence requirements on criminals and terrorists. An Intelligence-Led Policing philosophy, supported by professionally trained intelligence analysts, protects society and saves lives.

Intelligence-led Policing (ILP), based on the United Kingdom's National Intelligence Model (NIM), is dramatically sweeping the nation. The International Association of Chiefs of Police (IACP) embraces this new philosophy and intelligence management approach. Their proactive advocacy has enhanced the ILP Model and brought it to the forefront of the new intelligence requirements.

ILP has become the new organizational nomenclature that assists in incorporating the flow of intelligence information that is on the cutting edge of future intelligence requirements. Moreover, it is congruent with coordinating a host of federal agencies, including the National Criminal Intelligence Sharing Plan (NCISP), The FBI Intelligence Plan, and the Department of Homeland Security Intelligence Requirements.

The last decade of terrorist and criminal activities has placed global intelligence requirements on State, Local and Tribal Law Enforcement (SLTLE) agencies. Research conducted by the Federal Bureau of Investigation reveals that the average police department employs less than 50 officers. Moreover, 75% of police agencies have less than 25 sworn officers. Future intelligence requirements will dictate increased cooperation and coordination of SLTLE agencies. Therefore, resources addressing Intelligence-Led Policing assist in filling the escalating demand for adequate law enforcement expertise and training requirements in many of these smaller agencies.

ILP philosophy integrates with community-oriented policing, problem-oriented and CompStat policing strategies as foundations for collecting accurate criminal intelligence. Moreover, ILP is a collaborative means of organizing intelligence data and information. ILP assists in writing intelligence policies, guides procedures and describes information sharing. In addition, the legal safeguards protect citizens from intelligence abuses.

Intelligence-led policing (ILP) serves as the foundation for effective leadership, decision-making, crime prevention and intervention strategies. Accurate criminal intelligence provides and guides transition points for effective police executive, middle manager and supervisory decision-making. Intelligence-led policing (ILP) and computer applications assist strategic and tactical strategies. Intelligence analysis, GIS crime mapping, and frequently emerging analysis technologies serve as basic tools for preventing crime and terrorism.

ILP and criminal intelligence are indispensable to thriving crime intervention and prevention strategies; this book maximizes those objectives. Intelligence analysis employs a variety of strategies to analyze criminal patterns commonly used by organized criminals, terrorists and other criminal conspiracies. For example, collection techniques, intelligence analysis and targeting strategies provide an excellent foundation for prosecuting criminal organizations and their conspiracies to violate the law.

Analytical methods and data collection serve prevention strategies that look into the future and examine trends. The application of analytical techniques provides new investigative leads and possible crime solutions. *Why is ILP important?* The answer is uncomplicated. Organized and other criminals find fewer opportunities to initiate crimes and victimize the public. Intelligence analyst solutions, in concert with excellent criminal investigators, increase opportunities for effectiveness, and promote justice in the communities they serve. The consolidation of crime/intelligence analysis, CompStat, and other police strategies under ILP management, unifies crime-fighting potential.

Target Audience

Intelligence-Led Policing: Leadership, Strategies & Tactics serves the needs of readers interested in pursuing the field of intelligence analysis, and related law enforcement careers. The book targets multiple audiences, based on intelligence theory and practice as applied to ILP and strategic planning. The author seeks to serve the needs of academic criminal justice majors, law enforcement leaders, police officers, and future police intelligence analysts.

Intelligence-Led Policing: Leadership, Strategies & Tactics integrates many progressive educational practices, principles and concepts. Law enforcement practitioners and students of ILP may benefit from the book's design. The themes serve as a reference and inform from a teaching and learning perspective. The emphasis is on intelligence analytical concepts, intervention strategies, and technological applications.

Universities and community colleges are initiating intelligence analysis certificates, associate and bachelor's degree programs. Graduate certificate programs are emerging to meet vastly expanding needs of field practitioners. *Intelligence-Led Policing: Leadership, Strategies & Tactics* would serve as an appropriate required text for intelligence analysis curriculum or reader for related courses.

Intelligence-Led Policing: Leadership, Strategies & Tactics, makes an excellent contribution to national and international libraries; community colleges, colleges and universities would welcome the text for interested readers. The content and foundations serve as a resource document for federal, state, and local tribal law enforcement agencies.

Further research and literature will assist in expanding the field of Intelligence-led Policing. Resource materials are limited, primarily due to the recent revolution in police intelligence. The integration of intelligence analysis and technology represents a major developmental evolution.

Intelligence-Led Policing: Leadership, Strategies & Tactics serves an expanding literature market for academia. Police intelligence is a relatively new requirement with diverse specialties that perform unique intelligence tasks. The field of Intelligence-Led Policing continues to evolve, and the associated literature is rapidly launching to address those requirements.

Educational Philosophy

Intelligence-Led Policing: Leadership, Strategies & Tactics is organized and presented in a reader-friendly format, which does not require learners to have prerequisite knowledge in the field of intelligence analysis. An insightful avenue of exploring intelligence analysis for experienced police officers is an additional intention. The pursuit of knowledge is an honorable goal and that premise serves as the foundation for this book.

Intelligence-Led Policing: Leadership, Strategies & Tactics emphasizes critical thinking, problem solving and an active approach to learning. The philosophical and educational approach is dynamic and action-oriented, incorporating critical thinking as the ILP foundation. Critical thinking requires organizing information and applying concepts to new and unique situations.

Crucial to the ILP philosophy and intelligence analysis, is the synthesis of raw data into a meaningful format, for decision-making applications. The educational philosophy seeks to educate so that the reader can appraise criminal and terrorist criminal patterns, think beyond the mere facts, and reach out to the outer boundaries of the human mind.

Structure and Features

The purpose of the text is to support the reader with interesting analytical solutions to dangerous and everyday law enforcement problems. However, the writing seeks to avoid a thesis approach and attempts to dissect the content down to basic intelligence components. In addition, case studies illustrate analytical applications.

The paragraphs and sentences are deliberately short and to the point. The text addresses diverse learning styles; case illustrations and concrete examples clarify concepts and maintain reader interest. Intelligence-led policing can be multifaceted; consequently, the text and illustrations enhance learner understanding and retention.

Limitations: This book was written from a law enforcement and intelligence perspective, intended for university students and police officers interested in the field of ILP and intelligence analysis. A derivative audience would include libraries and police trainers; however, it is not proposed for advanced practitioners in the field of ILP.

Some areas of expertise were not included in the text because of space considerations and related themes. However, this does not imply that omitted areas are not important. Readability, clarity and consistency of themes enhance retention and the learning process. The text strives for clarity in writing and excellent learning progressions.

Instructor Materials

The book incorporates an extensive variety of illustrative materials:

- This text presents considerable analytical concepts; therefore, numerous illustrations, models, charts and tables supplement the text.
- Visual components assist in active explanation of text concepts.
- Subheadings and short paragraphs enhance transition, coherence and clarity for the learner.
- Large fonts enhance reading under poor lighting conditions, an important consideration for law enforcement officers in the field.

Special Note: The accompanying instructor manual and PowerPoint presentations support classroom endeavors. The instructor manual highlights learning objectives and recommends student assignments. Essay and objective questions support student review and instructor examinations. The questions measure theories and concepts, in an attempt to determine understanding rather than a learner's memorization of facts.

Scope and Organization

Intelligence-Led Policing: Leadership, Strategies & Tactics applies analytical methods to crime and attempts to produce practical crime prevention and intervention strategies. This text emphasizes basic strategic leadership and tactical analysis concepts and explores intelligence-driven policing.

Preface: The Preface introduces the text and addresses where the reader is going, how they are going to get there, and discusses support materials for instructional objectives.

Part I
INTRODUCTION: INTELLIGENCE-LED POLICING

Prologue: Critical Thinking and the Intelligence Analyst defines Intelligence-Led Policing and describes the role of the intelligence analyst and foundations of intelligence analysis. **Chapter 1: Introduction to Intelligence-Led Policing** describes basic intelligence concepts and the Intelligence Cycle.

Chapter 2: Intelligence-Led Policing: Organizational Strategies describes the blending and integration of an ILP philosophy and police organization.

Chapter 3: Crime Analysis Strategies integrates street crimes and intelligence-led policing.

Chapter 4: Problem-Oriented Policing and CompStat Integration describes the need for integrating, collaboration and coordination of the planning process.

Part II
STRATEGIC LEADERSHIP

Chapter 5: Intelligence-Led Policing: Leadership and Communication addresses strategic leadership, communication, and intelligence feedback applications.

Chapter 6: Intelligence-Led Policing: Leadership and Planning describes the need for police planning synchronization, fusion centers, and intelligence targeting.

Chapter 7: Intelligence-Led Policing: Analytical Products describes analytical reporting and the staff recommendation process.

Part III
TACTICAL APPLICATIONS

Chapter 8: Intelligence-Led Policing: Analytical Models and Charting describes support documents, conceptual models, and visual diagrams that support the strategic and tactical planning strategies.

Chapter 9: Intelligence-Led Policing: Investigative Strategies describes enterprise conspiracy crimes, informants, and electronic surveillance strategies.

Chapter 10: Intelligence-Led Policing: Tactical Leadership Training describes front-line leadership and tactical planning.

Epilogue: Concluding focus points reiterate and further explain basic strategies of intelligence-led policing. The Epilogue explains the arrival of the content and text, and re-orients the reader to essential theories, concepts and future applications.

Conclusion

The purpose is to write a book that students and law enforcement practitioners will find interesting and enlightening. Analytical foundations support critical thinking and problem-solving skills that enhance intervention, prevention and law enforcement solutions. Learning progressions enhance the academic process, and build prerequisite fundamentals for essential concepts. The text emphasizes the need for accurate criminal information to engage in strategic ILP strategies and positive enforcement and community outcomes.

Increase your understanding with the
Test Preparation Guide and Instructional Strategies for Intelligence-led Policing

---

ACKNOWLEDGMENTS

I would like to thank Jane Piland-Baker, my wife and partner. Her assistance in the area of editorial and graphic illustrations has made an immeasurable contribution to the text. To the staff at Looseleaf Law Publications, Inc: Mary Loughrey, Editorial Vice President; Maria Felten, Production Editor; Michael Loughrey, President and CEO.

PART I

INTELLIGENCE-LED POLICING
INTRODUCTION

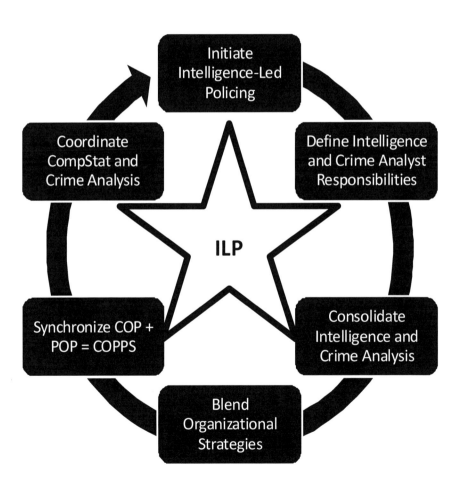

PART I: LEADERSHIP FOUNDATIONS

Leadership Foundations	Guidepost Behaviors
❖ Initiate the intelligence-led policing philosophy	❖ Appoint an intelligence ILP manager and define the role of ILP.
❖ Define intelligence and crime analyst responsibilities.	❖ Hire intelligence and crime analysts.
❖ Consolidate intelligence and crime analysis.	❖ Improve information sharing, collaboration, and co-locate the analysts.
❖ Blend and integrate police organizational strategies.	❖ Integrate and consolidate: ILP + COPPS+ Crime Analysis+ Intelligence Analysis+ CompStat = Police Excellence
❖ Synchronize community oriented and problem oriented policing.	❖ COP + POP = COPPS Coordinate long term and short term planning. Synchronize crime analysis and CompStat functions.
❖ Coordinate CompStat and crime analysis functions.	❖ Maximize sources of information: Information + crime and intelligence analysis = actionable criminal intelligence.

PROLOGUE
Critical Thinking and
the Intelligence Analyst

It is a capital mistake to theorize before one has data.
— Sir Arthur Conan Doyle

The popular culture myth recounting exploits of intelligence analysts conjures up images of a perilous "hero" engulfed by beautiful young women. James Bond films and Ian Fleming's books generate images of danger lurking in dark passageways and international intrigue. The reality is far removed from idealistic scenes depicted in the film entitled, "The Spy Who Loved Me." Ironically, men and women served with distinction in intelligence capacities for thousands of years.

Field agents and international informants contribute in dangerous assignments; however, the vast majorities are bookworms swimming in a sea of paperwork. The 9/11 attacks demanded an immediate call for field agents, better human intelligence in the field, and hazardous assignments.

The classic "cloak and dagger" stereotypes do not accurately portray police intelligence analysts who serve in staff capacities, as sworn police officers or civilians. One advantage of hiring civilian personnel is the achievement of considerable experience and expertise over time. Police officers often rotate or transfer out of intelligence assignments, while some earn promotions. The Prologue attempts to eliminate myths and describes intelligence analyst responsibilities.

PROLOGUE FOCUS

Criminals demonstrate considerable cleverness, operational strategies and planning. Therefore, intelligence data and analysis admirably serve the law enforcement mission. The threat of terrorism and diminished homeland security has driven Intelligence-Led Policing (ILP) center stage. Occasionally, ILP is referred to as intelligence-driven policing; ILP forms the basis for formulating strategic intelligence. Strategic intelligence may lead to operational tactics, which target specific criminal activities and organized criminal enterprises.

Defining an analyst's role is complicated because the associated professional discipline continues to unfold. An analyst's position is associated with a variety of professional skills and talents. The development of Intelligence-Led Policing (ILP) mandates reorganization of law enforcement procedures, and analyst role requirements. The Prologue addresses fundamental intelligence analyst roles and organizational responsibilities.

INTELLIGENCE ANALYST

The analyst's role requires multi-tasking and thriving performance in a rapidly changing environment. The new role under ILP philosophy suggests escalating responsibilities and collaboration throughout the law enforcement agency. Coordination requirements with commanders, middle management, sergeants, officers and detectives have increased considerably.

Analysts are primarily responsible for developing intelligence products, which coordinate information needs of internal and external customers. Strategic and tactical products require decisive thinking across staff and line operations. Intelligence products that assist in meeting tactical, operational, and logistical requirements must be succinct and timely.

A formidable test requires converting data into a useful format, and convincing others of the significance and merits of ideas. Moreover, supplying intelligence to rightful customers is the eventual objective. Analysts refine the intelligence product, and determine the needs of consumers through consultation and feedback. In addition, they brief commanders with reference to operational areas of criminal activity, and possible strategic and tactical outcomes.

Basic intelligence analyst responsibilities include collecting information or data from open and closed sources, followed by targeting known criminal organizations and criminals. Raw data or information is not police intelligence. The *collection process* is the initial step, followed by *critical analysis*, conducted by a trained professional capable of critical thinking. *Problem solving* is the third step, and the final step is proper *dissemination* of intelligence, to those who have the need and right to acquire such data. Refer to Table P-1, for additional information concerning intelligence and analyst skills.

Table P-1   Staffing Requirements

Staffing and recruiting requirements include:	Intelligence analysts' skills and abilities include:
❖ Ability to work independently ❖ Persistence ❖ Good communication skills ❖ Thorough knowledge of police practices ❖ Being well-read on world affairs ❖ A four-year bachelor's degree ❖ Possible post graduate degree ❖ Varied work experience	❖ Excellent research and writing skills ❖ Computer literacy ❖ Creativity ❖ Ability to work independently ❖ Logical thought processes ❖ Persistence ❖ Ability to think critically ❖ Willingness to make judgments ❖ Visualization skills

Previous analytic-based work experience could be in:	Analysts must be:
❖ Law enforcement ❖ Journalism ❖ Research ❖ Social sciences ❖ Another related field	❖ Self-directed ❖ Intellectually disciplined in their work habits ❖ Initiating lines of investigative inquiry ❖ Identifying resources that will assist the investigation or study.

Source: Adapted from International Association of Law enforcement Intelligence analysts (IALEIA), *Intelligence-Led Policing: Getting Started*, 2005.

The analyst position requires computer skills that enhance access to numerous national databases. Analysts collect and collate data, then validate information through successful queries of accessible databases. In addition, analysts confirm, identify conflicts, or refute contradictory information. Expert analysts employ information databases, think critically, organize reports, and present concise criminal information.

CRIME ANALYSTS

Crime analyst responsibilities vary according to the local needs of police agencies. The local community's crime problem and emerging crime patterns may require overlapping functions with intelligence analysis. The mission and size of the police department, is significant in defining crime analyst role requirements and responsibilities.

"Crime analysts routinely collect, synthesize, and supply information to officers and their managers. Providing the police officer, detective or administrator with crucial information helps them make better decisions. It enables the individual to react more rapidly and wisely, and it decentralizes information to the end user." [1]

CRIMINAL INVESTIGATIVE ANALYST

Criminal Investigative Analysis (CIA) is a separate violent crime investigative strategy; the analyst performs psychological profiling and crime scene reconstruction. The purpose of CIA serves to investigate serial crimes; i.e., serial rape, arson and murder. CIA analysts and investigators focus on criminal typologies, to develop their related profiles of violent serial offenders. The Modus Operandi (MO) may be similar, but trademark and signature clues offer the best opportunities for case linkage.

CRITICAL THINKING AND ANALYTICAL SKILLS

Critical thinking skills are essential intelligence analyst proficiencies, concepts difficult to define. Critical thinking concepts offer great promise, even with definition limitations. Successful intelligence training stresses critical thinking skills as vital components of the field. Moreover, ILP requires analytical capabilities. Refer to Table P-1 for the critical thinking, and ILP process of analysis.

PROFESSIONAL ORGANIZATION

The requirement for accurate police intelligence represents an expansion industry. Homeland security issues accelerate the demand for intelligence analyst positions. Historically, the International Association of Law Enforcement Intelligence Analysts, Inc. (IALEIA) remains the pioneer organization. The organization supports intelligence analysts in the field of law enforcement, and the goal, as with most professional organizations, is to network, exchange ideas and encourage/facilitate sufficient training opportunities. [2]

Table P-2   Critical Thinking and Intelligence-Led Policing

Critical Thinking	Intelligence Analysis
❖ Identify central issues and define the problem	❖ Distinguish between verifiable and unverifiable intelligence data ❖ Problem-oriented
❖ Recognize underlying assumptions or unstated assumptions	❖ Distinguish between the relevant and the nonrelevant intelligence data or information

❖ Evaluate evidence or authority by:
  ❖ Recognizing stereotypes and clichés
  ❖ The ability to select pertinent information
	❖ Recognize data adequacy
	❖ Distinguish between the essential and the incidental
	❖ Verify information sources
	❖ Corroborate facts and raw data

❖ Recognize bias and emotional factors in presentation ❖ Integrate thinking ❖ Define Knowledge ❖ Impose criteria ❖ Intellectual standards ❖ Recognize stated and unstated assumptions	❖ Planning process ❖ Start the intelligence cycle ❖ Intelligence analytical strategies ❖ Quality analysis ❖ Analytical techniques ❖ Determining the facts ❖ Support a generalization ❖ Avoid drawing false conclusions
❖ The ability to draw conclusions ❖ Judge validity of information ❖ Share findings	❖ Collaborative coordination ❖ Intelligence protocols ❖ Information sharing ❖ Dissemination
❖ Feedback and recycle the thinking process	❖ Repeat intelligence cycle

Intelligence-Led Policing

INTELLIGENCE ETHICAL RESPONSIBILITIES

Police intelligence analysts are apprehensive about violating dissemination protocols and civil liberties. There exists a delicate balance of constitutional rights, in a democratic society, regarding citizen protections versus criminal activity. The release of final intelligence assessments can create embarrassing publicity and legal consequences. Intelligence sharing is essential to successful police operations; however, potential litigations escalate amid improper disseminations.

INTELLIGENCE SHARING

The ILP management approach offers an information sharing advantage over the former traditional intelligence approach. ILP made its first policing appearance in the United Kingdom. The 1990's UK Intelligence-Led Policing innovation made the transition from business and management theory to policing.

According to *Intelligence-Led Policing: Getting Started*, an IALEIA publication, "Intelligence-Led Policing (ILP) is the model that brings intelligence and analysis to the forefront of police operations. It promotes the efficient use of resources, the production of workable crime prevention strategies, and the successful completion of investigations and prosecution. The ILP management approach has translated into the National Intelligence Model, and into the National Criminal Intelligence Sharing Plan (NCISP) in the United States." [3]

The NCISP recommends every law enforcement agency incorporate the minimum standards for policing. The NCISP plan provides guidance for intelligence sharing, and a blueprint for building an intelligence system. In addition, the plan provides a model for intelligence policies.[4] NCISP recommends that the chief executive officer or appointee who is responsible for intelligence functions, implement the following management of intelligence operation recommendations listed in Figure P-1.

Figure P-1   Figure Created from NCISP's Recommendations

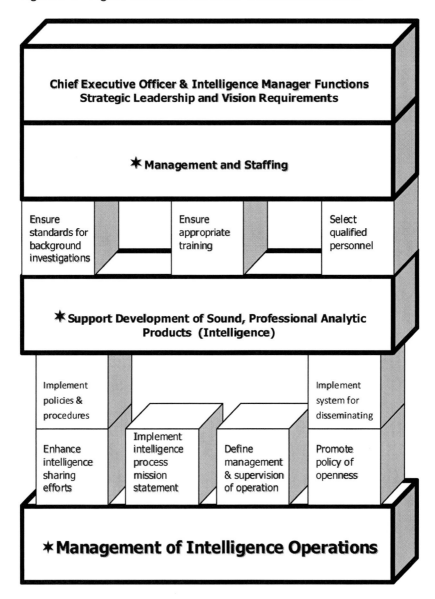

STRATEGIC LEADERSHIP AND VISION

Strategic leadership does not designate micromanagement and control of personnel. This leadership style is concerned with a few conceptual decisions that have maximum impact on the intervention, and prevention of criminal activities. The executive decision-making process revolves around the ILP management model, and strategic critical thinking. The goal is to develop an organizational and community vision, which targets crime with maximum personnel and logistical resources.

The concept of *vision* applies to law intelligence analysis, strategic and tactical planning. Commanders, middle managers and first-line supervisors require intelligence analysis to enhance leadership decision-making. Vision, strategic and tactical planning remain core requirements for police leaders.

Critical thinking, intelligence and crime analysis provide direction. Leaders supply officers with a map and compass for getting there. Intelligence analysis assists in answering three basic direction questions: Where is the law enforcement agency going? The next step in the intelligence planning process is how will the law enforcement agency get there, assess, and evaluate its arrival.

ILP and intelligence analysis is the primary method for the development of vision, to execute meaningful future-oriented decisions. Accurate intelligence analysis ensures that valid and reliable criminal intelligence serves as the foundation for plotting the department's future course. The key to establishing vision and strategic planning is the ILP analysis process.

ILP helps chart the course, defines strategic goals, and assists department members in their search for the right course of action. Objectives and action plans provide procedures for reaching the law enforcement agency's destination. The assessment phase evaluates arrival achievement, revises the department's vision, and suggests an appropriate future destination.

Focus Points: Defining the Destination

An ILP management organizational strategy provides vital information for strategic police planning. Timely criminal intelligence is essential to excellent police leadership performance. ILP collects raw data, coordinates the flow of accurate information, analyzes, and disseminates intelligence to those who have a need and right to know. Therefore, the accurate flow of information and channels of communication must remain open to the law enforcement community.

The intelligence dynamic requires criminal information to circulate from citizens and officers, to senior leaders, middle managers and sergeants. The centralization and coordination of intelligence, permits chief executives and senior leaders to establish the vision, and accomplish the mission. The intelligence then flows laterally and vertically within the police organization, and down the chain of command, to officers in the field. The following ten intelligence-coordinating strategies assure that the flow of criminal information/intelligence, reaches community, regional, state, tribal and international (SLTLE) agencies.

Strategy 1: Strategic Leadership

The Chief of Police, an important strategy initiator, determines strategic planning and forecasts future department requirements. However, senior leaders, middle managers and first-line supervisors, have important roles in the process. They determine the department's vision, goals, objectives, and future destination. ILP provides criminal intelligence for strategic planning. Moreover, ILP is the means for achieving successful crime prevention and crime control strategies.

Strategy 2: Intelligence-led Policing

ILP is the master organizational strategy that guides the collection of raw data and criminal information in law enforcement organizations. The administration and centralization of raw intelligence data, requires liaison activities that accomplish synchronization and proper dissemination. The information sharing process is expansive and coordination mandated. Collation and targeting processes demand excellent analysis, improved strategic tactical planning, and command decision-making.

Strategy 3: Removing Barriers

Assessment of an agency's existing organizational structure and its relationship to intelligence infrastructure is required for improved ILP intelligence. Organizational realignment and innovative architectural strategies should remove barriers to gathering intelligence, and encourage intelligence and information reciprocity.

Innovative ILP adaptations promote superior responses to Homeland Security, natural and person created disasters. Infinitely diverse criminal activities remain the major priority. Reorganization should improve coordination with Federal, State Intelligence Systems, Regional Operations, and Intelligence Centers. SLTLE agencies should encourage an active exchange of intelligence, that facilitates cooperation and related mission requirements.

Strategy 4: Synchronization: COP & POP

Community-oriented policing, problem-oriented policing (COPPS) and CompStat leadership strategies require intelligence and crime analysis capacities. In addition, ILP maintains the management and intelligence analysis requirements. CompStat and problem-oriented policing provide mission objectives, tasking, and remedial actions that drive street and crime analysis operations.

Strategy 5: Strategic Planning

The ultimate goal of strategic thinking and planning, is to look into the future, and calculate goals and objectives necessary to arrive at the destination. The proactive approach moves to offensive maneuvers calculated to win, and create a threatening presence to criminals and their organizations. The threatening presence of effective law enforcement is the best deterrent to crime.

Strategy 6: Intelligence Analysis

Intelligence analysis is a sub-discipline of the ILP management philosophy. This form of analysis involves the systematic collection, analysis and dissemination of criminal information, to those who have a need to know, and have the proper security clearance. Intelligence analysis focuses on enterprise crime criminals, and their illegal syndicates.

Strategy 7: Crime Analysis

The ILP model primarily focuses on cross-jurisdictional conspiracy crimes. Criminal enterprise crimes and terrorism are oriented toward threat analysis, and are strategic assessment driven. Therefore, the ILP approach cannot serve law enforcement without incorporating crime analysis, into the department's organization, operations and planning requirements. The twin processes of intelligence analysis and crime analysis merge to generate successful outcomes.

Crime analysis analytical processes provide timely and pertinent information fundamental to crime patterns, and trend correlations. In addition, crime analysis supports department functions including patrol deployment, special operations, tactical units, and investigations.

Strategy 8: Criminal Investigative Analysis

Criminal Investigative Analysis (CIA) begins with a premise that the analyst's task is to organize information concerning the social behaviors of suspects. The premise or classification identifies signs, behavioral clues, or other information that may lead to the offender's identification, and arrest. Psychological profiling clues, crime mapping, and computerized profile classifications, assist investigators in solving serial murder and rape crimes.

Strategy 9: Analytical Reporting

The flow of accurate critical information is the essence of intelligence. Intelligence information sharing is contingent on enhanced communications and networking. Fundamental intelligence requirements for collecting, analyzing, and sharing essential information, include the development of analytical documents and briefings. Analytical reports incorporate models and charting strategies.

Strategy 10: Intelligence Sharing

The Regional Information Sharing System (RISS) represents a national network of six regional state centers. Moreover, it provides an interstate network for investigating trans-jurisdictional crimes. RISS offers support, and information sharing services for law enforcement investigative, and prosecution requirements across the nation. For example, the Middle Atlantic-Great Lakes Organized Crime Law Enforcement Network (MAGLOCLEN) includes eight states, the District of Columbia and member agencies in England, Canada, and Australia.

There are many computer centers that support law enforcement operations: (1) Anti-Terrorism Information Exchange (ATIX), (2) Law Enforcement On-line (LEO), (3) Law Enforcement Intelligence Unit (LEIU), (4) Joint Regional Information Exchange System (JRIES), and (5) other points of intelligence exchange. Computer network systems continue to expand and provide additional services.

CONCLUSION

In conclusion, excellent strategic thinking has numerous applications, and principles; ILP serves the foundation for strategic policing. Strategic thinking starts with understanding the basics of Intelligence-Led Policing, and considering how to apply related intelligence concepts, strategies and tactics. Innovative strategic leaders improve crime prevention and intervention efforts by initiating the basic ten strategies.

The ten strategies are interactive, an action plan for the ILP management philosophy. This book encourages police leaders to think strategically and convert the theory of ILP management into activities that fight crime. The text is written specifically for police officers, supervisors and commanders who aspire to higher levels of responsibility and promotion. The emphasis is on strategic leadership strategies, and police tactics.

ENDNOTES

1. Susan C. Wernicke and Mark Stallo, "Steps Toward Integrating Crime Analysis into Local Law Enforcement," The Chief of Police (July 2000), 57.

2. International Association of Law Enforcement Intelligence Analysts, Law Enforcement Analytical Standards, November 2004, 3.

3. International Association of Law Enforcement Intelligence Analysts, Booklet Committee, Intelligence-Led Policing: Getting Started, January 2005, 3.

4. Global Intelligence Working Group, National Criminal Intelligence Sharing Plan, October 2003, 2.

CHAPTER 1
Introduction

Crime is common; logic is rare. Therefore, it is upon the logic rather than upon the crime that you should dwell.
— *Sir Arthur Conan Doyle*

Intelligence-Led Policing (ILP) derives power from logic that supports the philosophy. The emphasis on logic allows police leadership to envision effective solutions to crime patterns. Solutions become possible once the leader's responsiveness moves from criminal outcomes to analysis and logic.

Police leadership, logic, and effectiveness represent essential ILP components. The ILP evolution offers opportunities to achieve proactive police goals and objectives. Logic and knowledge correspond to powerful tools in the implementation of effective crime prevention, intervention, and crime control strategies. ILP provides commanders, supervisors, and officers with timely criminal intelligence that leads to effective decision-making.

CHAPTER FOCUS

The ILP management philosophy is now an essential component of police organizational structure. The chief executive should define ILP as fundamental to the organizational climate. Senior leaders, middle managers, and supervisors require diverse ILP techniques to function effectively. Intelligence analysis and accurate statistics assist in formulating critical thinking and vision for future planning. Refer to Table 1-1 for the Chapter Focus, concepts, and terms.

Table 1-1   Chapter Focus

	ILP Intelligence Concepts	ILP Intelligence Cycle
Intelligence-Led Policing	❖ ILP Intelligence Reorganization ❖ Intelligence Defined ❖ Intelligence Analysis ❖ Strategic Analysis ❖ Tactical Analysis ❖ Crime Analysis ❖ Criminal Investigative Analysis	❖ Requirements & Collection ❖ Planning & Targeting ❖ Collection & Collation ❖ Processing & Analysis ❖ Evaluation & Production ❖ Dissemination ❖ Intelligence Products
	ILP Sources of Information	**ILP Information Sharing**
	❖ Legal Requirements ❖ Open Sources ❖ Closed Sources ❖ Databases ❖ Media Reports ❖ Internet Searches ❖ Business Directories	❖ Premonitories ❖ Strategic Assessment ❖ Intelligence Estimates ❖ Vulnerability Analysis ❖ Aggressive Analysis ❖ Intelligence Reporting ❖ Interdiction

Defining intelligence is an elusive concept because of overlapping jurisdictional qualities and perspectives. National security and military intelligence combined with a myriad of governmental agencies add complex dimensions to the proliferation of intelligence definitions. ILP has multiplied the *intelligence* definition discussion, because of the overlapping confusion associated with intelligence analysis. This chapter reaffirms prior definitions of intelligence analysis; however, not all possibilities.

This chapter focuses on ILP and related concepts that form the basis for accurate criminal information. The role of the intelligence cycle and the related dissemination process receives specific attention. The chapter describes various types of threat analysis performed by intelligence analysts: (1) intelligence analysis, (2) strategic intelligence analysis, (3) premonitories, (4) threat assessment, (5) vulnerability assessment, (6) aggressive analysis, and (7) warnings.

INTELLIGENCE-LED POLICING REORIENTATION

ILP addresses management coordination of raw data, collected at all levels of the law enforcement organization, and serves as the driving component of the police business of intelligence. Intelligence analysis involves *collection, analysis, and dissemination.* There is a clear delineation of both intelligence definitions, because both differ conceptually, and eventually merge. ILP is an intelligence driven philosophical approach to policing at every level of the law enforcement organization.

The United Kingdom's National Intelligence Model (NIM) advocates the concept of applying a business management model to law enforcement. The following questions require answers: (1) What is an accurate picture of the business? (2) What is actually happening on the ground or in the environment? (3) What is the nature, and extent of the problem, (4) What are the trends, and (5) What is the main threat. [1]

The NIM approach recommends that intelligence-led policing abide by the following objectives: (1) establish a task and coordination process, (2) develop core intelligence products to drive the operation, and (3) develop systems and protocols to facilitate the intelligence cycle. In addition, ensure successful training protocols for all levels of policing. Refer to figure 1-1 for an example of the basic elements of the NIM approach. [2]

Source: National Criminal Intelligence Service (NCIS), The National Intelligence
           Model, The National Intelligence Service, London, 2000.

Figure 1-1   United Kingdom's National Intelligence Model

In contrast, the Bureau of Justice Assistance (BJA) defines ILP in the following manner: "Intelligence-Led Policing (ILP) entails the collection of information by law enforcement, the analysis of that information, and conclusions based upon the analysis. This process provides law enforcement agencies the ability to prevent crime, plan operations, and allocate resources. Today, law enforcement agencies must proactively bring together information gleaned from their own personnel with intelligence and information garnered from other agencies." [3]

On the state level, the New Jersey State Police's definition of ILP advocates: "Intelligence-led policing is a collaborative philosophy that starts with information, gathered at all levels of the organization that is analyzed to create useful intelligence and an improved understanding of the operational environment. This will assist leadership in making the best possible decisions with respect to crime control strategies, allocation of resources, and tactical operations. The adoption of ILP processes requires a concerted effort by all parties, including analysts, operators, and senior leaders. For analysts, the key components of this process include the creation of tactical, operational, and strategic intelligence products that support immediate needs, promote situational awareness, and provide the foundation for longer-term planning." [4]

INTELLIGENCE ANALYSIS DEFINED

Analysis resides at the nucleus of the intelligence process. Information does not become intelligence without analysis to derive meaning from data. Intelligence summaries and reports become products of analysis. Strategic and tactical intelligence products are most effective when completed by professionals trained in analytic techniques.

"Intelligence analysis as the systematic collection, evaluation, analysis, and dissemination of criminal information, especially related to their associations and identification with organized criminal activity." [5] "Intelligence analysis focuses on enterprise crime, including: major rackets controlled by a syndicate, auto theft rings, fraudulent credit card operations, land swindles, and other criminal organizations." [6]

"Crime analysis focuses on the correlation of certain elements of crime and criminal intelligence concentrates on names of individuals and organizations. Therefore, crime analysis attempts to tie a link between such elements as suspect description and modus operandi with a series of offenses, whereas intelligence analysis attempts to develop information and establish links between known or suspected criminals and other suspected criminals or organizations." [7] Refer to Table 1-2 for additional order of analysis concepts.

Table 1-2   Determining the Order of Analysis

Defining the Problem:	Assistance:
❖ What part of the analysis can be strengthened by what is learned in another aspect of the analysis? ❖ What do I know about the problem? ❖ Who should be consulted to gain better understanding of the problem?	❖ What type of assistance and expertise is needed in analyzing the findings from each activity? ❖ Who should implement each activity? ❖ At what point will initiating each activity complement the analysis plan?
Type of Analysis:	**Data Analysis:**
❖ What type of analysis activities must be conducted (i.e., surveys, interviews, etc.)? ❖ How time-intensive is each activity? ❖ What type of assistance and expertise is needed in designing, administering, and managing each activity?	❖ What data (police department data or data from external agencies) are available to develop a better understanding of the problem? ❖ How accurate are the data? ❖ Do I need assistance from anyone to gain access to the data and to analyze the data?

Source: Adapted from Timothy S. Bynum, U.S. Department of Justice, Office of Community Policing Services. Using Analysis for Problem-Solving: A Guidebook for Law Enforcement (Washington, DC: GPO, 2001) 6.

Intelligence analyst recommendations may assist police senior leaders and commanders with a range of decision-making parameters concerning strategies and tactics. Intelligence Cycle planning provides the means for leaders to assess criminal activities and allocate resources. "The Intelligence

Cycle and analysis can support the operations of law enforcement agencies and should be viewed as 'mainstream' within the department. Effective intelligence operations receive raw data from all sections of the department and provide knowledge products in return." [8]

INTELLIGENCE CYCLE FOUNDATIONS

The Intelligence-Led Policing/Intelligence Cycle includes procedures and protocols. Guidelines ensure that gathered information is valid, reliable, and trustworthy. The Intelligence Cycle provides the means for collecting, targeting, collation, evaluation, and dissemination that provide precise criminal information. The product is often a logical, informed judgment. Refer to Figure 1-2: Intelligence Cycle and Figure 1-3: The Six-Step Process to Effective Dissemination of Intelligence Information and Products.

The Intelligence Cycle is not a linear model, in practice; it consists of many cycles. Analysts may return to an earlier level for reevaluation anytime during the cycle. Steps may vary as new raw data becomes available, i.e., field intelligence reports or investigator updates. Therefore, the steps are not automatic procedures and final products are subject to revision. Analysts apply the cycle as general procedural guidelines and remain receptive to new information or perspectives.

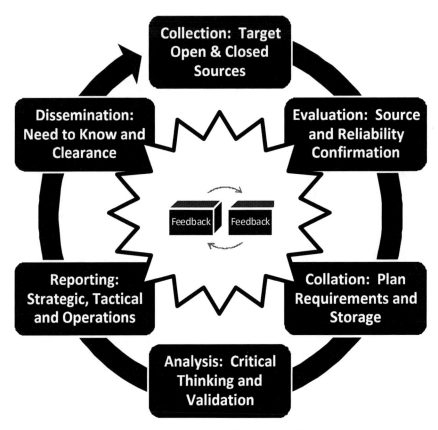

Figure 1-2   Intelligence Cycle

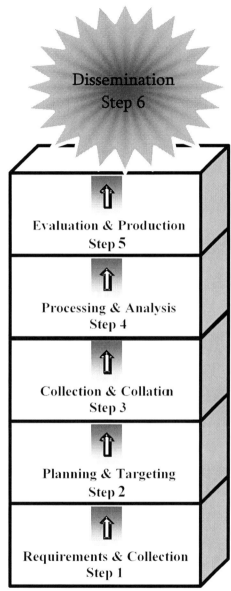

Figure 1-3   The Six-Step Process to
Effective Dissemination of Intelligence
Information and Products

STEP 1: REQUIREMENTS & COLLECTION

The analyst or investigating officer initiates the collection process. Information is regularly updated to reflect realistic intelligence requirements and objectives. This process ensures that information gaps are quickly reconciled, and the intelligence is collected according to basic investigative requirements.

Collection methods address two general areas: (1) *overt collection* and (2) *covert collection*. Overt collection, including newspaper articles, library resources, and public records offer many open sources of valuable information. Open and available sources help develop data on criminal activity.

Analysts often underestimate and do not highly acclaim open sources because of uncomplicated availability. Paid informants and physical or electronic surveillance can make covert collection expensive. Analysts may miscalculate the benefits of covert sources because of the classified status and secrecy connotations. Refer to Figure 1-4 for examples of open and covert sources of criminal information.

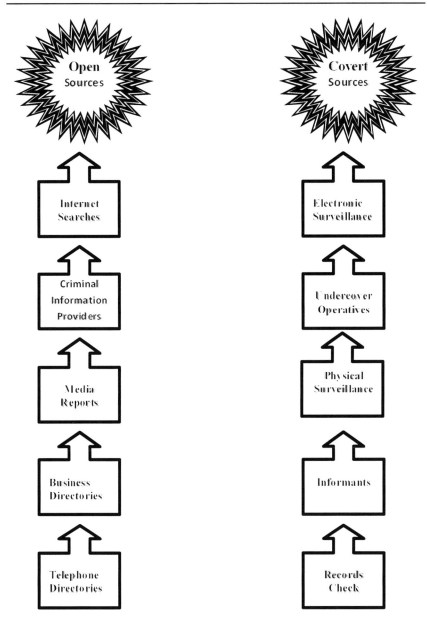

Figure 1-4   Open and Covert Information Sources

Legal Regulations

In the United States of America, the goal must remain the protection of citizens' rights. The danger is always present that we may become a force of oppression, instead of freedom. Remaining committed to that goal is particularly difficult when freedom and citizen lives are at stake. Citizens should remain free from oppression and government surveillance unless there is at least a reasonable suspicion and preferably probable cause that criminal or terrorist activity is apparent.

Federal regulations provide the following mandates on intelligence collection and exploitation of information sources: 28 CFR, part 23, "Operators shall collect, and maintain criminal intelligence information concerning an individual only if there is reasonable suspicion that the individual is involved in criminal conduct or activity and the information is relevant to that criminal conduct or activity. In addition, an operator shall not collect or maintain criminal intelligence information about the political, religious or social views, associations, or activities of any individual or any group, association, corporation, business, partnership, or other organization unless such information directly relates to criminal conduct or activity and there is reasonable suspicion that the subject of the information is or may be involved in criminal conduct or activity. Reasonable suspicion or criminal predicate is established when information exists which establishes sufficient facts to give a trained law enforcement or criminal investigative agency officer, investigator, or employee a basis to believe that there is a reasonable possibility that an individual or organization is involved in a definable criminal activity or enterprise." [9]

The Collection Plan

The analyst's collection plan coordinates the data and serves as the focus of collection resources. A collection plan should flow logically from the statement of the problem. It does not have to follow any prescribed format; it may range from one sheet to an extensive and detailed plan. [10] However, a collection plan includes: (1) a description of the data; (2) sources of the data; (3) steps to secure the data; and (4) target dates for each stage of the data collection phases. [11]

The absence of trained analysts diminishes the value of collection and computer storage systems. Analysis results in the production of "intelligence products," which lead to suspect linkage. Experience, training, and expertise enhance the accurate and timely identification of criminal patterns. Three prerequisites facilitate effective intelligence production: (1) *understanding* organizational goals, objectives, operational procedures and routines; (2) *access* to information appropriate to the assignment; and (3) *availability* of resources, trained personnel, equipment and funding. [12]

STEP 2: PLANNING & TARGETING

Primary information sources include the victim, neighbors, informants, and complainants. Supporting law enforcement agencies provide meaningful exchanges of invaluable criminal information. Essential Criminal Intelligence (ECI) information is exchanged on a regular basis; however, the rules for dissemination are established and followed on a "need to know" and security clearance basis.

Targeting Information

The targeting system collects and stores information concerning a target. Targets vary according to the community's crime problems, for example, specific criminal activities housed in identified buildings or businesses. The target collection folder is a management tool used to identify, track, record, analyze, and manage information about specific targets. This target folder information ensures that timely analysis is available to police officers and field investigators.

Target Selection and Evaluation

Key to successful target selection and evaluation is focusing on a narrowly defined target area, a particular business, rather than an entire community. Analysts prioritize targets according to probable criminal threat. Debriefing and follow-up questioning of target area criminals for supplementary offenses enhance the development of essential information.

STEP 3: COLLECTION & COLLATION

Collation is the first step in the process of translating raw data into criminal/intelligence information and includes the removal of useless or incorrect information. It also involves the orderly arrangement of collected material, concepts, and data so that it forms connective relationships to establish patterns or modus operandi information. Basic to the collation process is an organized system for filing and retrieval of gathered information.

STEP 4: PROCESSING & ANALYSIS

Central to intelligence is the analysis system, an important phase directly related to collation. Analysis requires the ability to think critically and develop stated and unstated assumptions. The analyst studies fragments of criminal information and attempts to assemble them into logical patterns.

Constructed fragments of information form a hypothesis or logical guess to test tentative conclusions. In addition, the analyst may develop several alternative hypotheses. The analyst must understand how to conduct applied research and evaluate all available information. The formation of patterns or hypotheses forecasts potential criminal activities, which may lead to new strategic and tactical objectives.

STEP 5: EVALUATION

Evaluation consists of two basic parts: (1) a *judgment* of the validity of the information, and (2) an *assessment* of the truthfulness and reliability of the source and its pertinence, accuracy and corroboration. Intelligence analysis units develop prescribed methods for incoming information reliability and validity assessments.

STEP 6: DISSEMINATION

The ultimate value of criminal intelligence is to assist police officers in the field. The speed and accuracy of its dissemination to those who legitimately need it is the main effectiveness requirement. However, dissemination must respect the privacy of individuals and safeguard its ethical release on a right and need-to-know basis.

The Global Intelligence Working Group (GIWG) has established a visualization of the National Criminal Intelligence Sharing Plan. The plan provides a blueprint for leaders to follow. The plan provides guidance on model policies and standards for developing local intelligence units. Moreover, the discussion and recommendations emphasize methods for developing and sharing criminal intelligence. Refer to Figure 1-5 for additional information on shared intelligence.

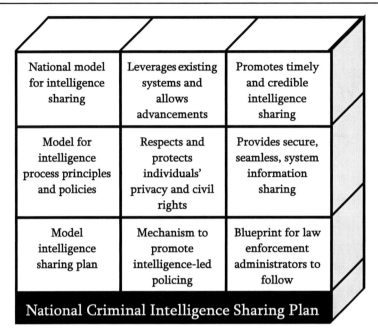

Figure 1-5   GIWG's Vision for the National Intelligence Sharing Plan

STRATEGIC ANALYSIS STRATEGIES

Intelligence systems comprise capabilities to identify criminal patterns, and forecast trends through the collection of criminal information and systematic analysis. The potential exists for advanced computer technology to collect and store additional criminal information. Qualified personnel to accomplish the analytical work necessary to maximize those opportunities are in diminutive supply.

Intelligence analysis has a long-term, strategic value; however, law enforcement officers have difficulty envisioning the future. "Strategic analysis is conducted a priori (before the commission of a predicted or expected crime) and outside the general course of an investigation. Its purpose is to provide decision-makers with predictions about future crime occurrences and trends. Recommendations follow concerning long-term strategies for dealing with offenses effectively and efficiently." [13]

A natural conflict exists between strategic and tactical intelligence, the temptation is to sacrifice the future for immediate results. Investigators may feel pressured to produce short-term tactical results, i.e., case prosecutions and convictions, creating opportunities for criminal leadership to learn from mistakes and avoid prosecution. Time and patience enhance law enforcement initiatives; short-term tactical results should not sacrifice positive future strategic outcomes.

PREMONITORIES SOLUTIONS

"Premonitories are short-range assessments that bridge the gap between tactical and strategic intelligence; they use a strategic approach to generate investigative targets. The distinction between this and other types of strategic analysis is the time-period. Premonitories target potential subjects of investigation immediately, before initiating an investigation, whereas other forms of strategic intelligence products are long-range." [14]

THREAT ASSESSMENT STRATEGIES

Threat assessments analyze what enterprise crime groups and operations cost the community. Groups or operations that most threaten the peace and stability of the community directly and indirectly influence expenditures. This type of analysis can be proactive when it attempts to predict the vulnerability of a community to enterprise crime. Vulnerability analysis assesses the internal characteristics of the enterprise for points of vulnerability and interdiction. [15] Refer to Table 1-3 for illustrations of strategic analysis.

Table 1-3 Threat Analysis Strategies

1. IDENTIFYING THE THREAT	2. ANALYTICAL ASSESSMENTS
Major functions of a threat assessment program include the reduction and prevention of the risk of violence and organized crime posed by a given group(s) at a given time, and the risk that terrorists or organized crime group(s) present to a given target. The process of identifying a potential terrorist organized crime group involves: (1) defining criteria that could lead to the group becoming a subject of a threat assessment collection, analysis, and investigation; (2) determining the areas within the law enforcement or other agency that will be responsible for receiving or sharing information and intelligence about threat assessment investigations; (3) and searching multiple open and closed sources of information to provide data about a group's behaviors, interests, and modus operandi.	The primary objective of strategic risk analysis is to gather information on the group's potential targets, criminal activities, and threat(s) presented to the community and nation. General strategic assessments present a document and overview of the available information about a terrorist or enterprise group. Strategic assessments rely on past and present criminal information or intelligence to forecast future activities. Aggressive analysis quantifies the aggressiveness, adventurousness, and expansionist tendencies of the criminal group or enterprise. The emphasis is on operations, the use of force, power, and control themes.
3. THREAT ANALYSIS	**4. STRATEGIC ANALYSIS PRODUCTS**
An analysis process evaluates information gathered about the groups(s) and the potential target(s). In the first stage, information is collected and evaluated for evidence of conditions and behaviors that would be consistent with an organized crime investigation or criminal violations. The second stage of evaluation seeks to determine whether the terrorist or criminal group(s) appears be moving toward or away from former or new criminal violations. Analysis concerns the group's goals, objectives, and criminal procedures. The focus is on criminal targets, offenders, victims, and social environment. Moreover, organizational structures, social histories, and group allegiances are important considerations.	Estimates are useful from an interdiction point of view. Estimates are a compilation of data, which measures the historical occurrence of criminal activity, trends, and forecasts of historical data. Strategic intelligence analysis products may include information on drug supply, routes, prices, source country production, availability, and future trends. Threat assessment products include: (1) threat assessments, (2) vulnerability assessments, (3) aggressive analysis, (4) and warnings. Other products may include models, statistical analysis, association analysis, biographical sketches, commodity flow analysis, and financial analysis.

While the following case study is dated, it remains an excellent model for effective threat assessment. A threat assessment is a strategic document that emphasizes a group's tendency for violence, aggressive criminality, or possible occurrence of criminal activity in a certain time and place. Refer to the Jamaican Posse case study for an integration of the abovementioned threat assessment concepts.

CASE STUDY EXAMPLE: JAMAICAN POSSE

Pennsylvania Crime Commission: Strategic Threat Assessment

Criminal Jamaican posse activities in the United States were recognizable as a threat in the 1970s, but it is only in the 1980s that they have become a major threat. The basic estimate is that there are 30 to 40 posses with about 10,000 to 13,000 members active in the United States. Accurate estimation of membership is difficult because the lower echelon workers of posses are transient and shift from one organization to another. The largest posses have nationwide organizations with branches in many cities and states.

In the Commonwealth of Pennsylvania, at least ten different posses have been active, particularly in the Philadelphia area; but they also have a significant presence in Pittsburgh. Jamaican organized crime groups target the York and Harrisburg areas, Scranton/Wilkes-Barre, Allentown-Bethlehem, and to a lesser extent, Williamsport and areas in the Poconos region. For example, the Shower Posse and the Spangler Posse are the oldest, the best organized, the largest, and the most violent of the posses. Investigators know of other "spin-off" posses. The Shower posse (allegedly named for their practice of spraying their rivals with a "shower" of bullets) and the Spangler posse are the two dominant posses in Pennsylvania.

In some cases, posse leadership has a high level of insulation from actual drug transactions and incursion into new territories. In other cases, the leadership plays a "hands-on" role in establishing a presence in new territories. They may be intimately involved with various parts of the operations, including the actual processing and transporting of drugs and the acts of violence. Moreover, the trend in this country is toward a less structured relationship between the national leadership and local groups, with frequent formation of local splinter groups with unclear loyalties.

In Pennsylvania, while the posse organization has dominated, several of the large posse gangs have dissolved or are dissolving, and are becoming more independent, loosely affiliated groups that center on one or more male entrepreneurs. These new Jamaican operations rely on domestic-kin and friendship ties and somewhat resemble Black drug groups.

...Police infiltration is frustrated. Jamaican nationals recruit in the home neighborhoods of leaders, and through an elaborate system of safe houses, stash houses, heavily fortified gatehouses, and other checkpoints...

Source: Adapted from Pennsylvania Crime Commission, Organized Crime in Pennsylvania: A Decade of Change 1990 Report, 1990, 239-247.

Aggressive Analysis

Aggressive analysis quantifies the aggressiveness, adventurousness, and expansionist tendencies of enterprise crime groups and their operations. The use of force and intimidation is an index of power and control themes. Analysis includes examining the use of lethal violence by a group. [16] When corruption and compromise fail, violence is the likely course of action.

The following citation illustrates the aggressive analysis connection of the Jamaican Posse organization: …"Jamaican members who have demonstrated ability, and who desire a greater share, may be permitted to establish their own operations in new territories, but still obtain their drugs from the posse leader to whom they return a share of the money. This "franchising" provides for expansion of posse activities; but as posse affiliates move into new areas, disputes over drug territories have involved posses in considerable violence vis-à-vis rival posses and Black drug organizations." [17]

Note the propensity for violence and the aggressive nature of the Jamaican Posse: "…Jamaican posses are heavily involved with firearms, and have a well-deserved reputation for brutal violence, even by standards of an unusually violent business. Brutality stems in part from cultural tradition and belief that violence is an occupational necessity. The name 'posse' testifies to their fascination with the Hollywood image of the Wild West outlaw 'gunslingers.' Their attitude toward the Jamaican police is to kill and eliminate incorruptible officers. They take pride in their criminal identity and in being 'macho gangsters.'" [18]

Intelligence Estimate

Estimates are a compilation of data, which measure the historical occurrence of criminal activity and include trends and forecasts based on historical data. Strategic intelligence estimates include information on drug supplies, routes, prices, source county production, availability, and future trends. [19] Estimates are useful from an interdiction point of view.

The following citation illustrates the strategic intelligence estimate connection of the Jamaican Posse organization:

...Although posses are responsible for a sizable share (roughly 20 percent) of the marijuana that is brought into this country, Jamaican posses have been involved increasingly in cocaine trafficking (particularly crack). The established marijuana smuggling routes facilitated this expansion. Cocaine brings higher profits and is harder to detect than marijuana because of its lighter odor and more compact size. Jamaican groups are especially associated with the distribution of crack cocaine; and according to some federal officials, they control as much as 40 percent of the crack trade in this country.

Jamaican trafficking activities have begun to show greater diversification. Recent Jamaican government crackdowns on marijuana have contributed to increased posse activities in the production of hashish and hashish oil, which is popular in Canada. There are also recent reports of Jamaican involvement with trafficking in heroin and in methamphetamine. In addition to their drug trafficking, Jamaicans have also been involved in trading firearms for profit by taking advantage of state differences in price and availability. [20]

Assessment Process

The following paragraphs illustrate the assessment process and future role of the Jamaican Posse: ...Jamaican organized crime groups pose a continuing and serious threat within the United States and Pennsylvania. Combinations of strong organization, aggressive marketing, and ruthless violence have enabled Posses to expand rapidly throughout the country and to capture a major share of the market for crack cocaine and marijuana.

Their involvement in high levels of violence and their cultivation of a "gangster" image has brought intense law enforcement scrutiny. Successful RICO prosecutions have brought about the demise of several major Jamaican drug rings in Pennsylvania. However, the Jamaicans have shown themselves to be resourceful and adaptive. They appear to be aiming for a lower profile and less visibility to law enforcement.

The fluid structure of national organizations makes it relatively easy to shift personnel and start new operations. Widespread poverty on the island of Jamaica, coupled with the lure of easy drug money, ensures a ready supply of new recruits. Law enforcement will need to monitor, investigate, and prosecute Jamaican crime groups whenever possible. Cooperation and coordination among federal, state, and local enforcement agencies remains essential. [21]

In summary, strategic analysis has different types of analysis: (1) threat assessments, (2) vulnerability assessments, (3) warnings, (4) aggressive analysis, (5) general assessments, and (6) premonitories. Strategic analysis and threat assessment reports are predictive and future oriented. The Intelligence Cycle serves as the means to manage data or criminal information for strategic analysis and threat assessment strategies. There are numerous potential sources of information, i.e., law enforcement records, employment, financial and public records.

The threat assessment may take the form of a warning. The assessment concerns data on the possibility or degree of present threat that target(s) will seek involvements in criminal act(s). Eventually, the threat assessment merges into a vulnerability assessment. Historical antecedents may also precede the threat assessment report. [22]

FOCUS POINTS: INTELLIGENCE-LED POLICING

Critical thinking and logic represent foundations for the ILP management philosophy. Excellent logic and strategic planning leads to calculated goals, objectives, and tactical action plans. Proactive ILP intelligence gathering procedures provide support for intelligence and crime analysis strategies.

There are many intelligence analysis definitions and facets of meaning. The fundamentals include *collection* of raw data, *analysis*, and meaningful *dissemination*. The essential quality is *analysis* of the information; otherwise, it is merely a collation of facts or raw data.

The six steps of the Intelligence Cycle offer the systematic collection of pertinent data and criminal information. The process of collection, analysis, and dissemination provides the means for law enforcement leaders to make excellent and timely decisions.

Efficient planning for collection focuses on the target. Collection planning requires that at different phases of the investigation, methods of collection are coordinated according to the specific target. The proper coordination of collection avoids the use of numerous logistical resources by avoiding duplication of effort. In addition, it provides the correct distribution of personnel resources.

Federal regulations provide legal mandates on the collection of raw data or criminal information on citizens. The two guiding principles for agents are "reasonable suspicion" and "definable criminal activity." The basic standard is a "reasonable suspicion" of criminal behavior for targeting persons or organizations. There must exist, at the moment of intrusion of privacy, "reasonable suspicion" that criminal activity is eminent or has occurred. Government agents must have a definable criminal activity or criminal enterprise as the basic criteria for the evasion of privacy and collection of information.

Generally, threat assessment concerns criminal activity, followed by recommendations and remedial solutions. Analysts inspect data and historical facts, predicting future crime patterns. Threat assessment represents one of many intelligence products available for analyzing criminal behavior. The final intelligence product may include an assessment based on human expertise that includes conclusions and recommendations.

CONCLUSION

ILP philosophy eventually improves leadership effectiveness and criminal information applications. This management approach is a powerful and pragmatic apparatus of law enforcement that offers leaders opportunities to make informed decisions. Moreover, ILP strategic intelligence strategies form the ideal foundation for successful policy and strategy development.

Sound policies that enhance positive crime prevention, intervention, and crime control outcomes evolve when leaders incorporate sound social science and statistical information in the decision-making process. These considerations suggest the possible synchronization of ILP management, strategic and tactical planning.

ENDNOTES

1. National Criminal Intelligence Service, United Kingdom, The National Intelligence Model (London, England, 2000), 8.

2. National Criminal Intelligence Service, 8.

3. Bureau of Justice Assistance: Solutions for Safer Communities, Intelligence-Led Policing: (http://www.ojp.gov/BJA/topic/ilp.html).

4. Joseph R. Fuentes, et al., and New Jersey State Police: Practical Guide to Intelligence-led Policing, the Center of Policing Terrorism at the Manhattan Institute, September 2006.

5. Program Brief: Integrated Criminal Apprehension Program, U.S. Department of Justice, Office of Justice Programs, Bureau of Justice Assistance, Washington, D.C., February 1985, 2.

6. Timothy D. Crowe, SHOCAP Program Implementation Guide: Law Enforcement Organizational Development and Productivity (McLean, VA: U.S. Department of Justice, Office of Juvenile Justice Programs, and Public Administration Service, 1992), 33.

7. Crowe, 34

8. Booklet Committee, Intelligence-Led Policing: Getting Started, January 2005, 3.

9. United States Department of Justice, Title 28, Code of Federal Regulations, Part 2, "Criminal Intelligence Operating Policies." Washington, DC: GPO.

10. Paul P. Andrews, Jr., "Collection and Analysis Plans," Criminal Intelligence Analysis, Paul P. Andrews, Jr. and Marilyn B. Peterson, (eds.) Loomis, (CA: Palmer Enterprises, 1990), 43.

11. Marilyn Peterson, "Law Enforcement Intelligence: A New Look," International Journal of Intelligence and Counterintelligence, Volume 1, No. 3, 1986, 34.

12. Don McDowell, Strategic Intelligence in Law Enforcement: The Development of a National Capacity for Production of Strategic Intelligence on the Criminal Environment in Australia. (Australia: Canberra, Attorney General's Department of Australia, 1991).

13. Crowe, 34.

14. Peterson, "Law Enforcement Intelligence: A New Look," 18.

15. Peter A. Lupsha, "Steps Toward a Strategic Analysis of Organized Crime," The Police Chief, (April 1980), 38.

16. Lupsha, 38.

17. Pennsylvania Crime Commission, Organized Crime in Pennsylvania: A Decade of Change 1990 Report, 1990, 239-247.

18. Pennsylvania Crime Commission, 241.

19. Peterson, 19.

20. Pennsylvania Crime Commission, 241.

21. Pennsylvania Crime Commission, 243-344.

22. Marilyn B. Peterson, Applications in Criminal Analysis: A Sourcebook (Westport, CT: Praeger Publications, 1994), 56-57.

CHAPTER 2
Organizational Strategies

When you have eliminated the impossible, whatever
remains, however improbable, must be the truth...
— Sir Arthur Conan Doyle

The Intelligence-Led Policing (ILP) philosophy suggests targeting specific organizational components to meet new intelligence sharing requirements and initiatives. Successful reorganization eliminates non-functional organizational structure, what remains must be the truth. ILP commitment encourages creative global and proactive avenues to obtain and share intelligence.

CHAPTER FOCUS: REORGANIZATION

Chapter 2, Intelligence-Led Policing: Organizational Strategies describes ILP philosophy integration. This chapter discusses advantages of synchronizing current policing strategies, including: Community-oriented Policing, Problem-oriented Policing, and CompStat, in a complementary approach. The successful formula achieves a more powerful combination than each component could realize independently.

The ILP approach requires integration and consolidation of present strategies, offering police service uniformity. This approach recommends nomenclature standardization, and adopting ILP intelligence and related strategies. Smaller police agencies may not require implementation of some formal and organizational components. Less urban agencies regularly rely on regional, state, federal, and other database support systems. Refer to Table 2-1 for additional information on the chapter focus.

Table 2-1   Chapter Focus

Intelligence-Led Policing	ILP Management Philosophy	ILP Policing Strategies
	❖ ILP philosophy ❖ Policy development ❖ Consolidation strategies ❖ Reintegration & organization ❖ Organization strategies ❖ Blending strategies ❖ ILP defined	❖ Community-oriented policing ❖ Problem-oriented policing ❖ SARA planning strategies ❖ CompStat strategies ❖ Homeland Security ❖ Focused policing ❖ Holistic approach
	ILP COP philosophy	ILP CompStat Leadership
	❖ COP direction ❖ Citizen interaction ❖ Attitudes & values ❖ Police cooperation ❖ Civic cooperation ❖ Decentralized ❖ Citizen feedback	❖ Empowers commanders ❖ POP & CompStat ❖ SARA planning process: ❖ Scanning ❖ Analysis ❖ Response ❖ Assessment

Leadership addresses intelligence procedures and operational priorities. Successful ILP implementation requires acceptance, cooperation, and commitment from all agency levels. Gateposts open and organizational change becomes instrumental in achieving successful ILP execution. The starting point for developing the ILP management philosophy is an organizational definition.

POLICING STRATEGIES: SYNCHRONIZATION

ILP reflects an evolutionary strategic shift toward the development of a future-policing archetype, a holistic or blended paradigm. The present multiplicity of overlapping police strategies requires organizational realignment to achieve intelligence-driven policing. Homeland security and accurate criminal intelligence planning serve the core of law enforcement operations.

Peterson defines ILP from a management perspective: "Intelligence-led policing is a collaborative enterprise based on improved intelligence operations and community-oriented policing and problem solving, which the field has considered beneficial for many years. To implement intelligence-led policing, police organizations need to reevaluate their current policies and protocols. Intelligence is part of the planning process, and reflects community problems and issues. Information sharing must become a policy and practice. Most important, intelligence must be contingent on quality analysis of data. The development of analytical techniques, training, and technical assistance needs to be supported." [1]

The combined components of ILP offer a criminal information framework for community crime problems, and homeland security solutions. **ILP + COPPS + CompStat = Intelligence Strategies and Tactics**. Moreover, this formula offers focused policing that is target specific to particular crimes, and threats to homeland security. The holistic approach, including the sum of its parts, equals more than the whole. The COP philosophy remains indispensable for all related strategies.

COMMUNITY-ORIENTED POLICING (COP)

COP is a strategic philosophy that offers direction and policy guidelines for police leaders and officers. The philosophy is an assessment of beliefs, attitudes, and values that determine police action and rational for behavior. Appropriate guidance for police behavior, citizen interaction, and cooperation, evolves from the COP philosophy.

The integration of community policing receives less emphasis as the shift to homeland security and counterterrorism responsibilities increase. Many police executives feel pressured to meet these new requirements; the amplified funding for antiterrorism planning represents a positive incentive. Community policing and shared partnerships require ILP integration, as the need for community support and dialogue increase in implementing a formidable anti-terror campaign.

However, the fundamentals of the COP philosophy, relating to community empowerment, may conflict with ILP goals and objectives. Police leaders may experience conflict with local community leaders, including Neighborhood Watch, concerning priorities. Conflicts may develop over perceptions of important community leaders, versus police executive ILP strategic goals and objectives.

ILP, closely related, in process, to problem-oriented policing, supplements CompStat leadership. The POP and SARA planning process examine underlying crime problems, from uniformed officers and crime analysts' perspectives. Officers engage in the scanning stage, problem identification, and formulate remedial actions.

ILP develops intelligence using a systematic approach, from diverse sources. Executive leadership responds to intelligence briefs, determines priorities, and tasks the organizational staff and line members. Positioning the COP philosophy at the decentralized end of the spectrum, encourages positive momentum from the street, to a highly centralized ILP operation.

Leadership targets priorities for effective intervention and prevention, once command defines key criminal elements and enterprises. The appeal to executive police leadership is command over critical thinking, and essential decision-making. The ILP leadership is a top down process and closely connected to command and control.

The COP and POP approach represents a more decentralized decision-making process, i.e., a street level, bottom-up movement. Observers readily recognize why police executives and commanders favor the ILP approach; they are ultimately responsible for everything that goes right or wrong. ILP offers increased leadership equilibrium to the COP philosophy. Refer to Figure 2-1 for the basic elements of the COP philosophy.

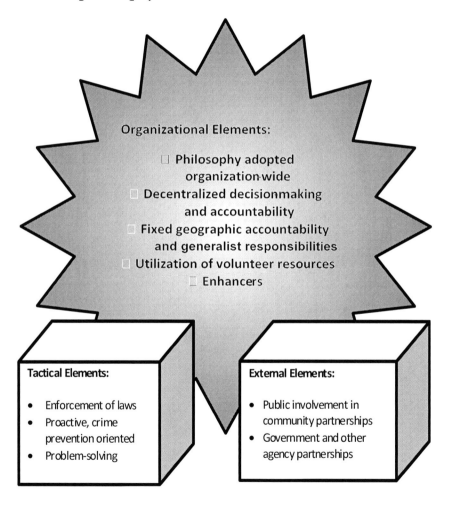

Organizational Elements:

☐ Philosophy adopted
organization-wide
☐ Decentralized decisionmaking
and accountability
☐ Fixed geographic accountability
and generalist responsibilities
☐ Utilization of volunteer resources
☐ Enhancers

Tactical Elements:

• Enforcement of laws
• Proactive, crime
prevention oriented
• Problem-solving

External Elements:

• Public involvement in
community partnerships
• Government and other
agency partnerships

Figure 2-1   The Core Elements of Community Policing,
Adapted from: http://www.cops.usdoj.gov.

COMMUNITY-ORIENTED POLICING

The COP philosophy varies among communities. Department mission and values statements represent assorted COP definitions. However, establishing trust is the essential goal of a successful community partnership; cooperative environments enhance crime intervention and prevention strategies. The COP philosophy requires ILP, POP, and SARA planning strategies to successfully implement, and achieve police goals and objectives.

PROBLEM-ORIENTED POLICING (POP)

POP is the strategic arm of COP, and without the problem-solving component; the philosophy does not have the momentum to improve community quality of life issues, including level and fear of crime.

Law enforcement agencies can address crime in targeted areas of a community, and focus on the SARA problem-solving model: *scanning, analysis, response,* and *assessment.* [2] The focus on causes, requires applying appropriate solutions to hot spots, plus targeting specific locations gleaned from crime analysis and crime prevention surveys. Intelligence-led policing principles support crime prevention initiatives through crime specific planning. For additional information, concerning POP policing, refer to Table 2-2.

Table 2-2 Concepts of Problem-Oriented Policing

Problem-Oriented Policing
❖ Adapt a proactive stance
❖ Apply SARA planning process
❖ Focus on crime analysis
❖ Focus on substantive problems
❖ Group incidents as problems
❖ Recognize the relationship between or among incidents
❖ Treat the underlying problem or problems
❖ Focus on systematic inquiry
❖ Develop tailor-made responses
❖ Evaluate newly implemented responses

(Left vertical label: Intelligence-Led Policing)

Source: Adapted from: Goldstein, H. Problem-Oriented Policing (McGraw-Hill, New York, 1990): 39-49.

COMPSTAT: LEADERSHIP AND CHANGE AGENT

The City of New York modified their police response to crime. The application of crime analysis, statistical analysis, and focused patrol responses enhanced crime prevention efforts and proved more effective than random patrol. Officers positioned at the right location, at the right time, have opportunities to intervene and prevent crime. The CompStat results are impressive. Together, ILP and CompStat leadership strategies are essential elements of homeland security interventions.

Police intelligence planning and statistics remain the most visible component of the CompStat process. Leadership is an essential ingredient of the CompStat process. Empowering commanders and delegating authority to innovate at their own discretion, is essential to successful prevention, and intervention. Empowering leaders is futile without responsibility, accountability and measured outcomes.[3] For additional information, concerning the concepts of CompStat policing, refer to Table 2-3.

Table 2-3   CompStat Leadership Strategies
TEAMWORK: Coordination of efforts from every level is essential. Precinct commanders, crime analysts, detectives and the public are vital keys: ❖ Empower precinct commanders ❖ Hold precinct commanders responsible and accountable ❖ Crime statistics, reports and staff meetings ❖ Accurate and timely intelligence ❖ Rapid Deployment ❖ Effective tactics ❖ Relentless follow-up and assessment
CRIME ANALYSIS: ❖ Speedy identification of crime patterns ❖ Speedy distribution of crime information ❖ Consistent information gathering ❖ Information analyzed quickly and accurately ❖ Information distributed to the department and public sector as needed
Adapted from: Giuliani, R. & Safir, H. "CompStat: Leadership in Action," New York City Police Department, (1997): 1.

(Sidebar: Intelligence-Led Policing)

FOCUSED POLICING

ILP, POP and CompStat are principal considerations for conducting focused policing. A focused effort concentrates on crime hot spots, and recurring offenses. CompStat and related strategies seek to remedy street crimes and disorder; CompStat is a form of focused policing. "There is solid evidence that geographically concentrated enforcement at crime and related hot spots can be effective, at least in the short run. The focused policing strategies are superior to the standard model, which offers little or no scientific evidence of effectiveness." [4] The

Focused policing acknowledges that a crime cannot occur devoid of three elements that form a crime triangle: (1) *offender*, (2) *victim*, and (3) *crime scene or location*. [5] The intelligence or crime analyst must discover as much as possible about all three sides of the triangle, while examining the interconnecting links. Focused policing operates best when leadership, intelligence analysis, and technology merge to apply diverse methods, to the crime triangle.

ILP, COMPSTAT AND HOMELAND SECURITY

CompStat can reduce crime, the terrorism threat, and assists homeland security operations with associated leadership and statistical crime analysis techniques. The CompStat forecasting potential enhances intelligence dissemination and coordination of information, critical to homeland security and a timely preventative response. The ILP philosophy/management policing style augments homeland security operations as well as worldwide law enforcement functions.

Homeland security has altered the approach police agencies conduct operations; the struggle to accommodate security requirements remains persistent and consistent. The integration of homeland security procedures, suggests a continuing priority. The COP philosophy is an essential component of our homeland security posture, and the war against terrorism. Collections of critical information, from loyal Americans, who represent every segment of society, positively enhance strategic and tactical threat assessments. There exists a continuing need to integrate homeland security procedures, and law enforcement coordination. Intelligence analysis represents a focal point for criminal information, on terrorist activities. The coordination of ILP, POP, and CompStat assists in the war against terrorism, and supports essential operational strategies.

ILP employs overlapping strategies with the CompStat approach to policing. The ILP approach, driven by criminal enterprises and terrorism, tends to address commodity flow analysis; while CompStat is incident driven and street crime oriented. ILP strategies are more global, strategic oriented, and less concerned about immediate jurisdictions. ILP involves a regional or international approach.

The goal of ILP is to disrupt the enterprise and terrorist organization, rather than encourage the immediate arrests of street criminals. ILP is more concerned with long-term threat analysis and planning. The CompStat policing style drives patrol operations, tactical units, and immediate remedial actions. CompStat is statically oriented and focused on time sensitive objectives.

CompStat focuses on immediate terrorist and homeland security risks. In addition, considerations include patrol and investigative responses, on the tactical level. Moreover, ILP supports tactical efforts with criminal intelligence, but remains focused on the "big strategic picture." The common connection of both ILP and CompStat is the need to analyze criminal information from the grass roots level, and disseminate up the chain of command, to meet police executive decision-making operational requirements. Critical and accurate criminal information flow assists in effective police leadership decision-making. The goal is consolidation of criminal information, from all sources, for analysis and dissemination.

CompStat provides the leadership component that reinforces the department's philosophy, mission and values statement. CompStat is congruent with empowerment and participatory leadership objectives. The significance of authority delegation and accountability is clearly defined. Patience, coaching, and mentoring all play a role in coordinating and encouraging team participation. The success of any approach

reflects effective police leadership that encourages the cooperation of officers and civilian staff.

EFFECTIVENESS OF POLICING STRATEGIES

Some police agencies prefer Community-Oriented Policing (COP), Problem-Oriented Policing (POP), or Neighbor-
hood-Oriented Policing (POP), while others favor CompStat.
In addition, agencies may opt to apply combinations of
existing strategies. Competition remains, including advocates
for individual policing strategies. The degree of emphasis on
a particular strategy will depend on accurate ILP collection,
of criminal information data, analysis, and the concluding
criminal intelligence product.

The National Research Council Panel (2003) reviewed
research concerning police effectiveness, and ranked police
strategies: The NRC evaluation on police strategies measured
the effectiveness of the "standard model," COP, POP, and focused policing. "The 'standard' or traditional model demonstrated little or no evidence of effectiveness. The COP strategy
demonstrated little or no evidence of effectiveness, weak to
moderate concerning community relationships. The POP
policing strategy demonstrated moderate evidence of effectiveness and strong evidence of effectiveness concerning crime
hot spots. The research produced varied results, but con-
cluded that focused policing and diverse approaches seemed
superior when combined." [6] The findings suggest that single
police strategies are not earning high grades on effectiveness.
Refer to Table 2-4 for comparisons of policing strategy effectiveness.

Table 2-4   Effectiveness of Policing Strategies

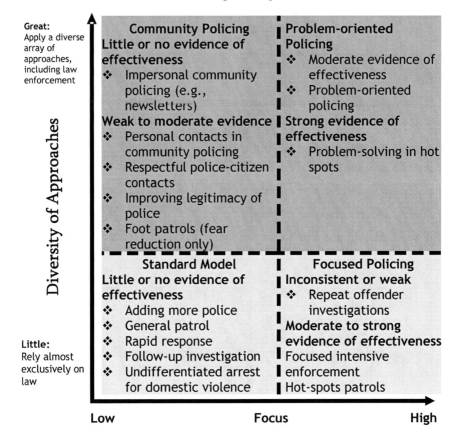

Adapted from National Research Council, Fairness and Effectiveness in Policing: The Evidence. Committee to Review Research on Police Policy and Practice. Edited by Wesley Skogan and Kathleen Frydl. (Washington, DC: 2003) The National Academies Press. Figure 6.1 and Table 6.1, pp. 248-249. SOURCE: Ronald V. Clarke & John E. Eck (2003). Crime Analysis for Problem Solvers in 60 Small Steps, U.S. Department of Justice, and the Center for Problem Oriented Policing (Washington, DC: GPO, 2003): 3.

The U.S. Department of Justice and COPS Office shed luminosity on police effectiveness extrapolated from the NAS study: "The lessons during a third of a century of research are now clear. Effective police work requires both focused attention and diverse approaches. The least effective policing uses neither element. The explanation for this is also clear. If diverse approaches are used without focus, it is difficult to apply the appropriate approach to the places and people who most require it. If police are focused on hot spots, but only enforce the law, they limit their effectiveness." [7] For additional information, concerning the effectiveness of policing strategies, refer to Table 2-4.

Two factors are keys to the thorough use of intelligence within the department. First, the support of top-level management is imperative. Second, intelligence will be better understood and accepted throughout the department, if members of the organization are provided a seminar, highlighting its benefits. Consumers must be aware of what intelligence is how it can be used, as well as its limitations if it is to be valuable. [8]

STRATEGY RESTRUCTURING

Police strategies overlap and interconnect, making classification difficult. In addition, law enforcement professionals may apply terminology interchangeably. Diverse localities and professional advocates of one paradigm may borrow ideas and concepts from another.

COP, an expansive philosophical goal, focuses on community interaction and the general public. Problem-oriented policing (POP) analyzes specific crime problems and builds external partnerships. POP focuses on community members and civic groups, to solve specific underlying crime problems.

COP provides the strategic picture for POP, to function in its crime prevention and intervention role. COP serves as the core community power generator for POP, SARA, and CompStat police strategies. Diverse strategies require blending and coordination, to achieve organizational harmony. The coordination of leadership and reorganization of managerial structure avoids conflict and achieves synchronization.

Strategic leadership assures cooperation, integration, and positive ILP intelligence objectives. "ILP is a concept in law enforcement that focuses on using intelligence products for decision-making at the strategic and tactical levels." [9] Intelligence-led policing (ILP) is a management instrument for coordinating crime analysis, for traditional street crimes.

Intelligence analysis focuses on conspiracy crimes, rather than crimes like robbery, larceny, etc. Therefore, ILP requires crime analysis augmentation to support POP, and CompStat operations. Moreover, ILP provides the coordination and sharing of intelligence. Crime analysis indirectly and directly supports POP and CompStat operations.

ILP + COPPS + Comp Stat = Excellent Strategies and Tactics. However, there are subtle differences. POP and CompStat differences may be noted in the following paragraph: "Problem-oriented policing is not the same as CompStat, though they share some common features. Both focus police attention, though CompStat as normally practiced, restricts itself to geographic hot spots, while POP can be applied to a wider array of crime concentrations. Though both use data to drive police action, the variety of data and depth of analysis used in POP, is greater than quick-paced CompStat targeting." [10]

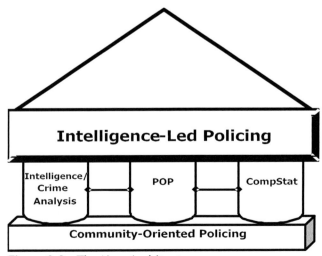

Figure 2-2   The New Architecture

"CompStat uses law enforcement tactics almost exclusively, while POP uses these along with a wider variety of responses. CompStat may have short-term impacts on geographic hot spots of crime, which wear-off and require more enforcement. A problem-oriented approach seeks long-term solutions. If CompStat is used as a "first-aid" response, while POP is applied to enact a longer-term cure, then the two approaches can work well together." [11] Crime analysis serves as the foundation for POP and CompStat, and remains the essential set of skills that drives both strategies.

CASE STUDY APPLICATION

The Chief of Police initiates a discussion at the staff meeting concerning the Intelligence-Led Policing philosophy. Chief Gordon Piland comments: "We need to change some of our organizational structure, to accommodate the ILP intelligence requirements."

Major Taryn Fanelli in charge of the Bureau of Field Services moans: "That is not going to come without resistance to change. We have highest level of intelligence requirements and need additional analysts."

The Chief recommends: "We need to establish a system to manage intelligence. Moreover, the present system needs to be revamped to develop information protocols, with the goal of identifying potential terrorists' targets and criminal enterprises. In addition, we need to expand our system, to improve coordination with the private sector, protect civil liberties, and promote external information sharing."

Major Scott Thomas replies, "We don't have to reinvent the wheel here; we could try a blended or holistic approach with our present policing strategies and assets." Lt. Shane Bruce has a presentation at the end of the meeting, which will clarify the main changes. "We are a level one police organization and have an intelligence officer; however, our

Intelligence Unit needs a manager." Refer to my handout on the levels of intelligence, for additional information.

Table 2-5   Levels of Intelligence
Source: Marilyn Peterson, U.S. Department of Justice, Bureau of Justice Assistance, Intelligence-Led Policing: The New Intelligence Architecture (Washington DC: GPO, 2005), p. 12-13.
Level 1: Highest level ❖ Agencies produce tactical and strategic intelligence products that benefit their own department as well as other law enforcement agencies. ❖ The law enforcement agency at this level employs an intelligence manager, intelligence officers, and professional intelligence analysts.
Level 2: ❖ Produce tactical and strategic intelligence for internal consumption. ❖ Intelligence supports investigations rather than to direct operations. ❖ May have a computerized database that is accessible to other departments. ❖ Typically, do not assign personnel to provide significant intelligence products to other agencies. ❖ May have intelligence units, intelligence officers, analysts, and intelligence manager
Level 3: ❖ Law enforcement agencies with anywhere from dozens to hundreds of sworn employees. ❖ May be capable of developing intelligence products, but are more likely to rely on products developed by partner agencies. ❖ May hire private intelligence analysts for complex cases. ❖ Do not normally employ analysts or intelligence managers. ❖ May have named one or more sworn "intelligence officers." ❖ May have sent them to intelligence or analytic training.
Level 4: Category that comprises most agencies in the United States ❖ Few dozen employees or less. ❖ Do not employ intelligence personnel. ❖ If assigned, generally has multiple responsibilities and is often a narcotics, gang or counter-terrorism officer. ❖ Most involved in a limited information-sharing network made up of county or regional databases. ❖ Some have received intelligence awareness training and may be able to interpret analytic products.

Major Mario Seamon, Bureau of Administrative Services, comments: "We might incorporate one senior ILP position at the Chiefs level, and attach two associate ILP staff members to the Bureau of Field Services and Bureau of Investigative Services. Moreover, the staff and line components would coordinate and improve policy, control, and intelligence services with several crime analysts attached directly to the patrol investigative operations."

Lieutenant Shane Bruce of the Training and Education Division comments: "We should consider staffing our new ILP Unit to reflect the International Association of Law Enforcement Intelligence Analysts recommendations. According to IALEIA, a police organization of our size should employ additional staff dedicated to the ILP program." IALEIA recommends:

"A typical intelligence unit might have a manager or supervisor, three to 12 intelligence officers and a similar number of analysts. This formalized intelligence unit might be found in agencies or organizations, with 75 or more sworn officers. In a smaller agency, analysts could be in a unit without designated collectors, while investigators in other units, provide data. In even smaller agencies, one or two individuals, sworn or non-sworn, could be used to perform rudimentary analysis and serve as intelligence liaison personnel. In the larger agencies, one possible ratio of analysts to investigators would be one analyst to 12 investigators or detectives. In agencies specializing in sophisticated crime, the ratio could be one analyst to five investigators." [12]

Lt. Shane Bruce adds: "We need to hire more civilian intelligence specialists, and promote our senior analysts to management positions. Moreover, we need to support our new ILP program with more analysts. In addition, we need to place the new analysts in the line operations units. Direct interaction among analysts, detectives and patrol officers will produce superiority in improving intelligence requirements. Because of our continuing organized crime, gangs, and terrorism investigations, the need for analysts continues to expand. Management needs to integrate intelligence and crime analysis operations. The excellent team effort will provide superior analysis, prevention and intervention strategies."

FOCUS POINTS: SYNCHRONIZATION

The NAS study supports diverse approaches, emphasizing POP and focused policing. The need exists for additional research that examines the ILP paradigm and investigates the integration and synchronization of police strategies. The NAS study made an excellent contribution; the next step is to implement a scientific study of the ILP paradigm, and intelligence-led policing component.

This controlled study, with the assistance of outside independent researchers, would investigate three or more similar sized cities. This paradigm shift would require a national effort and could promote innovative national and international implications concerning police strategies. Police intelligence serves as the foundation for excellent leadership, planning, decision-making, and policy implementation.

The process of sorting out diverse police strategies is a difficult task; each approach may encompass overlapping principles. For example, evaluating the COP philosophy is problematic because it focuses on the human enterprise; not rendering itself appropriate to quantitative measurements, in the same manner as measuring offenses and arrest rates. POP and CompStat methods offer additional opportunities for crime statistics and intelligence analysis.

The COP philosophy serves as the core concept for defining a police agency's relationship, with the community.

COP defines agency behaviors and provides guidance for satisfactory officer interaction with members of the department and public. The COP philosophy provides a foundation for police excellence.

POP asks the question: Where is the department going? The SARA planning process identifies related crime problems and suggests how the department will get there. CompStat provides the leadership process and addresses focused policing. In addition, ILP, POP, SARA, and CompStat, together, answer three significant questions: How will police department get there? How will the police department know when it arrives? Moreover, where does the police department go next?

ILP, COPPS, and CompStat require synchronization for maximum police effectiveness. Several practical advantages exist in the synchronization of multiple strategies: (1) the exploratory examination of the whole system, magnifies an entire constellation of successful transitions and research opportunities, (2) the holistic paradigm offers opportunities for changing the present disordered state of policing strategies, and (3) this change can eventually lead to legitimacy, organizational change, and movement toward a future state, that improves homeland security, crime intervention, and prevention strategies. For additional information, concerning a holistic police paradigm, refer to Table 2-6.

The paradigm formula provides the "strategic picture," deriving pathways to practical solutions, serving the nation, communities, and neighborhoods. Addressing homeland security, community crime problems, and disorder requires successful synchronization of all existing strategies, into a holistic paradigm formula: **ILP + COPPS + CompStat + Quality Leadership = Police Excellence**. The collective strategies depicted in a holistic police paradigm represent a larger part of the whole, providing a consolidated ILP coordination effort.

Table 2-6 Blended Holistic Paradigm

INTELLIGENCE-LED POLICING	PROBLEM-ORIENTED POLICING (POP)	COMPSTAT
<ul><li>ILP philosophy</li><li>Management oriented</li><li>Mission statements</li><li>Policy statements</li><li>A collaborative enterprise</li><li>New policies and protocols</li><li>ILP incorporated in planning process</li><li>Information sharing</li><li>Quality Analysis</li><li>Analytical techniques</li><li>Training</li><li>Technical support</li><li>Legal safeguards</li><li>Security safeguards</li></ul>	<ul><li>Adapt proactive stance</li><li>Apply SARA planning process</li><li>Focus on crime analysis</li><li>Focus on substantive problems</li><li>Group incidents as problems</li><li>Recognize relationship between or among incidents</li><li>Treat underlying problem or problems</li><li>Focus on systematic inquiry</li><li>Develop tailor-made responses</li><li>Evaluate newly implemented responses</li></ul>	**Teamwork: Precinct commanders, crime analysts, detectives and the public are vital keys:**<ul><li>Empower precinct commanders</li><li>Hold precinct commanders responsible and accountable</li><li>Crime statistics, reports and staff meetings</li><li>Accurate and timely intelligence</li><li>Rapid deployment</li><li>Effective tactics</li><li>Relentless follow-up and assessment</li></ul>**Crime Analysis:**<ul><li>Speedy identification of crime patterns</li><li>Speedy distribution of crime information</li><li>Consistent information gathering</li><li>Information analyzed quickly and accurately</li><li>Information distributed to department and public sector as needed</li></ul>
Source: Adapted from: Peterson, M. "Intelligence Policing: The New Intelligence Architecture," (US Department of Justice, BJA, GPO, 2003): vii.	**Source:** Adapted from: Goldstein, H. Problem-Oriented Policing (McGraw-Hill, New York, 1990): 39-49.	**Source:** Adapted from: Giuliani, R. & Safir, H. "CompStat: Leadership in Action," (NYC Police Department, 1997): 1.

Police strategies are important because officers serve as front-line guardians of world peace. The synchronization of police strategies is not the perfect solution; however, it offers another important dimension to proactive policing. Predicting the future is not without risk, and represents the most difficult of endeavors.

ILP reorganization requires readjustments, synchronization of Intelligence Unit assets, and hiring additional intelligence analysts. Moreover, input into the organizational configuration considers staff and line operations. The reorganization also considers staffing requirements and assignment of key investigators and patrol personnel.

CONCLUSION

Intelligence-led policing is a leadership, management and decision-making tool, separate from intelligence analysis. ILP serves to facilitate coordination and circulation, of essential criminal information. The traditional intelligence cycle is maintained and operated by intelligence analysts.

ILP is directly associated with COPPS and CompStat policing strategies. The prototype provides policy on the flow of intelligence data, and coordination of management systems. Moreover, ILP provides guidance for managing intelligence data and criminal information. This law enforcement strategy serves as a management model and remains instrumental to the implementation of a holistic paradigm.

ENDNOTES

1. Marilyn Peterson, U.S. Department of Justice, Bureau of Justice
    Assistance, Intelligence-Led Policing: The New Intelligence
    Architecture (Washington, DC: GPO, 2005): vii.

2. Herman Goldstein, Problem-Oriented Policing; A practical Guide
    for Police Officers (New York: McGraw-Hill, New York, 1990),
    39-49.

3. Robert W. Giuliani, R. and Howard Safir, "CompStat: Leadership
    in Action," New York City Police Department, (1997): 1.

4. Ronald V. Clarke, and John E. Eck, U.S. Department of Justice,
    Center for Problem Oriented Policing Crime Analysis for Problem
    Solvers in 60 Small Steps. (Washington DC: GPO, 2003): 3-4.

5. U.S. Department of Justice, Bureau of Justice Assistance,
    Neighborhood-Oriented Policing in Rural Areas: A
    Program-Planning Guide (Washington: DC: GPO, 1990): 44.

6. National Research Council, Fairness and Effectiveness in Policing:
    The Evidence: Committee to Review Research on Police Policy
    and Practice. (Eds.) Wesley Skogan and Kathleen Frydl
    (Washington, DC: The National Academies Press, 2003): 248-249.

7. Clarke and Eck, 2003: 3-4.

8. Booklet Committee, International Association of Law
    Enforcement Intelligence Analysts, Intelligence-Led Policing:
    Getting Started, January 2005, 3.

9. Deborah Osborne and Susan Wernicke, Introduction to Crime
    Analysis (New York: Haworth, 2003), 20.

10. Ronald V. Clarke, and John E. Eck, 2003, 6.

11. Ronald V. Clarke, and John E. Eck, 2003, 6.

12. Booklet Committee, IALEIA, Intelligence-Led Policing, 4.

CHAPTER 3
Crime Analysis Strategies

We approach the case, you remember, with an absolutely blank mind, which is always an advantage. We had formed no theories. We were simply there to observe and to draw inferences from our observations.
— Sir Arthur Conan Doyle

The crime analyst is objective, and maintains a neutral, skeptical, and detached point of view. Successful crime analysts generate favorable habits of the mind and scientific procedures. Analyst presentations expand constructive attitudes toward case analysis, development, and closure. Law enforcement leaders and officers need to understand the value of scientific data by: (1) focusing on the problem, (2) analyzing arguments, (3) judging analytical credibility of sources for information, and (4) judging deductions and possible courses of action.

CHAPTER FOCUS: CRIME ANALYSIS

This chapter focuses on crime analysis and its relationship to POP and CompStat responsibilities for preventing and controlling crime. The purpose of this chapter is to define and describe crime analysis and GIS crime mapping strategies. There are four basic forms of crime analysis: (1) *strategic*, (2) *tactical*, (3) *administrative*, and (4) *operations*. The chapter emphasis is on crime analysis critical thinking strategies. Refer to Table 3-1 for additional information on the chapter focus.

Table 3-1 Focus Points (Crime Analysis Concepts)

Critical Thinking Concepts	Crime Analysis Concepts
❖ Favorable mind habits ❖ Drawing inferences ❖ Noting observations ❖ Focusing on the problem ❖ Analyzing positions ❖ Judging credibility ❖ Judging decisions	❖ Crime analysis ❖ Analytical processes ❖ Strategic analysis ❖ Strategic planning ❖ Tactical analysis ❖ Administrative analysis ❖ Operations analysis ❖ Trend correlations
Tactical Strategies	**Geographic Information Systems**
❖ Tactical planning ❖ Tactical analysis ❖ Target selection ❖ Statistical analysis ❖ Geographical analysis ❖ Tactical crime linkage ❖ Patrol deployment	❖ Crime mapping ❖ Visual grammar ❖ Mapping symbols ❖ Mapping layers ❖ Geocoding ❖ Hot spots ❖ Clusters ❖ Circles

Intelligence-Led Policing

CRIME ANALYSIS DEFINED

There are many crime analysis definitions; the following offers some clarification: "Crime analysis is the systematic study of crime and disorder problems, as well as other police related issues, including socio-demographic, spatial, and temporal factors, to assist police in criminal apprehensions, crime and disorder reduction, crime prevention, and evaluation."[1]

According to the California Office of Criminal Justice Planning: (1) Crime analysis is defined as a set of systematic, analytical processes directed at providing timely and pertinent information relative to crime patterns. (2) Trend correlations assist operational and administrative personnel in planning the deployment of resources for the prevention and suppression of criminal activities. (3) Thus, crime analysis aids the investigative process, increasing apprehensions and the clearance rate of criminal cases. (4) Furthermore, within this context, crime analysis supports a number of department functions including: patrol deployment, special operations and tactical units, and investigations. (5) Strategic planning and applied research are enhanced through crime analysis and (6) Successful crime prevention strategies offer optimal opportunities when accurate data serves as the basis for action. In addition, administrative services, budgeting and program planning are often connected to successful planning and accurate criminal information. [2]

Criminal analysis is the field of study, and three areas of sub-disciplines are related: (1) Crime analysis, (2) Intelligence Analysis, and (3) Criminal Investigative Analysis. Intelligence-Led Policing is the new philosophy that manages the field of Criminal Analysis and related sub-disciplines. The goal is to produce strategic and tactical analytical reports that support operational decisions.

STRATEGIC ANALYSIS

Strategic analysis anticipates future crime trends and provides guidance to police commanders. The information helps law enforcement leaders deploy resources and predict future requirements. Strategic analysis is: (1) the analysis of a crime group, (2) overall criminal activity, or situation, which (3) results in the production of a report or that group, activity or situation and (4) includes recommendations for future actions. [3] Statistical reports may be included that reflect anticipated changes that indicate resource reallocations and up-dated acquisition requirements. The product of strategic analysis is often a strategic assessment, concerning a particular group threat.

TACTICAL ANALYSIS

Tactical crime analysis is the study of reported crime, calls for service and related information. The analyst reviews, maps, and tabulates modus operandi, offender characteristics, spatial/or temporal factors, including victim or other characteristics. Once data is collected, crime mapping becomes an essential component of tactical crime analysis; spatial characteristics assist in linking criminal activity, relationships and offender(s).

ADMINISTRATIVE ANALYSIS

Administrative analysis involves the dissemination of findings, general data information, or non-specific crime research. The presentation is a brief summary that avoids in-depth research and statistical analysis. The information conference or media release should be brief, clear and concise. In general, this information is not sensitive and appropriately presented in a public forum.

The audience may include local government, council members and citizens. The objective is to inform diverse customers and audiences, remaining mindful of privacy requirements and respecting confidentiality. Appropriate security procedures value privacy, individual rights and avoid negative media releases.

OPERATIONS ANALYSIS

Operations analysis provides information on police patrol practices. The analysis and information assists police leaders in planning patrol allocations and logistical support. Analytical information improves decision-making and the quality of police services, by examining workload responsibilities and personnel deployment.

Operations analysis is: (1) the analytical study of police delivery services, (2) provides commanders and police managers with a scientific basis for decisions, and (3) improves operations or resource deployment. Operations analysis supports leaders who implement department planning, direction and control strategies. The related objectives and tasks sustain essential functions that support police operations. [4]

CRIME ANALYSIS: TACTICAL PLANNING

ILP, COP, POP and CompStat represent incomplete police strategies without incorporating crime analyst skills. Crime analysis encourages critical thinking and successful problem solving strategies for addressing street or common crimes. Ultimately, crime analysis leads to superior crime prevention and intervention. Excellent leadership, decision-making, personnel deployment, and logistical requirements, require crime analysis support. Crime analysis, not rhetorical dialogue, reduces crime, statistical data and improves success.

TACTICAL PLANNING STRATEGIES

The following definition illustrates the role of crime analysis and tactical planning: Crime analysis is defined as a set of systematic, analytical processes directed at providing timely and pertinent information relative to crime patterns and trend correlations. The rationale for crime analysis is within the planning process and the deployment of resources for the prevention and suppression of criminal activities. [5] Target analysis defines: (1) target profile, (2) target selection, and (3) statistical analysis. Crime analysis data assists in the allocation of patrol deployment operations and determining logistical requirements.

TACTICAL ANALYSIS DEFINITION

While definitions are important, they only represent the initial step for crime analysis. "It is critical for any tactical analyst to be able not only to detect a crime series, but also to define it clearly. You cannot analyze it if you cannot define it." [6] Tactical crime analysis requires critical thinking and connecting the hot spots, crime clusters and circles, or putting the "tactical picture" together.

TARGET PROFILE ANALYSIS

Target profile analysis, occasionally defined as victim profiling, identifies persons, structures, vehicles, or other entities, as potential crime targets. The purpose is to prevent crimes or warn potential victims of possible criminal behavior. In addition, profiles might identify criminal suspects who have a particularly rewarding modus operandi, or propensity to commit certain kinds of criminal offenses. The target profile data might include time of attack, type of attack, location and target vulnerability.

According to the model presently in use in the United Kingdom, the basic tools are: linkage analysis, statistical analysis and profiling. The key tools of the "problem profile" include: (1) scale of the problem, (2) potential suspects and recommended tactics, (3) the "target profile" of suspects/ offenders that identifies weakness of their criminal activities, and (4) recommended tactical options. The purpose is to identify offender characteristics to guide investigative efforts and focusing the efforts to the most feasible suspect. [7]

TARGET SELECTION

Generally, tactical problem-solving strategies are short-term operational activities, based on data collected, which immediately precedes target selection and deployment. The analyst usually selects data from preceding days, weeks, or months, for crime detection and prevention activities. [8] The analyst's objective is to identify patterns, series and related spatial analysis, hot spots or other crime characteristics.

STATISTICAL ANALYSIS

Statistical analysis remains the foundation for the tactical deployment of officers. Leaders base assignments on geographic features, neighborhoods, blocks or addresses, and efficient, effective, rapid response times. Statistical geographical analysis defines areas that represent significant and recurring offenses. Appropriate officer allocation supports a dynamic patrol force that handles routine calls for service, targets specific offenses, and maintains a reserve force capable of responding to emergencies.

PATROL DEPLOYMENT AND OPERATIONS

Crime statistics is the foundation for tactical crime analysis; crimes committed in a series, are scrutinized for probability statistics: "From the crime analyst's point of view, descriptive and inferential statistics are inextricably linked. The number of robberies committed over a period of time, can be shown on the table or a graph (descriptive statistics). However, by observing a criminal's habits, pattern or MO, the analyst is often able to infer or predict what the criminal will do next (inferential statistics). This information supports leadership in directed patrol development, tactical action plans, and detectives in achieving successful investigations. Indeed, correlating behavior to individuals may be the most effective way we have of assisting the investigative process." [9] Refer to Tables 3-2 and 3-3 for additional information on the modus operandi (MO) concepts.

Table 3-2 Modus Operandi Criteria

1. Target	High priced condominiums
2. Geographic area	Seaside high income residential property
3. Method of operation	Professional burglar familiar with security protocols and locality
4. Type of property	Jewelry, cash, small "hot product" technology items of value
5. Time of day	1800 - 2100 hours when residents are out for evening dinner or entertainment.
6. Means of attack	Stealth: quickly enters unoccupied dwelling using burglary tools
7. How attacked	Burglar scales balconies and enters through unlocked patio sliding glass doors
8. Trademark	Unusual "monkey-like" physical attributes that allow him to scale hi-rise condominiums with ease and agility
9. Signature clues	Rearranges condo furniture before leaving

Source: Adapted from Major General L.W. Atcherly, The Atcherly M.O. System, 1913.

Table 3-3 Trademark Behaviors

1. Victim	Assault, sexual assault, rape, homicide, etc.
2. Core behaviors	Smoked, poisoned dog, vandalism, ate food, committed sexually related acts, etc.
3. Special victim oriented behaviors	Left a note, fear tactics, telephone calls, harassment, revenge behaviors, etc.
4. Vehicle description	Type of vehicle, make, model, color, license plate number, special features, etc.

GEOGRAPHICAL ANALYSIS

Statistical geographic analysis attempts to anticipate when a criminal may repeatedly commit crimes. Geographic Information System(s) or crime mapping best serve this function when combined with statistical techniques. Geography and criminal activity have a statistically significant relationship to specific crimes. For example, one researcher found a clear relationship exists between the physical and geographic characteristics of drug markets, and the types of individuals most likely to buy and sell them. [10]

"Graphical methods illustrate comparative crime data by beat, reporting district, neighborhood, and so on. Bar graphs depict percentages for particular crimes, in specific areas, during specific time periods. In addition, bar graphs provide an excellent overall picture of crimes throughout a jurisdiction. A statistical geographic analysis enhances identification of crime patterns and series in beats, reporting districts or entire jurisdictions, and is most often used to mathematically project the location of future crime occurrences." [11]

TACTICAL CRIME LINKAGE

Critical thinking facilitates consequential use of crime knowledge and intelligence. Crime analysis means not only acquiring data, but also integrating research results into meaningful tactical recommendations. In addition, end users of criminal intelligence must acknowledge its value and act on the information. The avocation of criminal information requires imagination and vision for future applications.

Velasco and Boba describe the following eight crime analysis terminology, and stress the need for standardization. Dictionary definitions initially explained patterns and trends. However, crime analysts extrapolated additional concepts from significant GIS contributions. The following definitions are not comprehensive, but general guidelines for analyzing criminal activity. [12]

A **pattern** is an arrangement or order discernable in any crime related phenomena.

A **trend** is a specific type of pattern that assumes a general direction or tendency. In practice, a trend often has a time component, and is represented as an increase or decrease over time. Patterns and trends are important to the crime analyst, since they represent a framework to begin identifying relationships.

A **series** is a run of similar crimes, committed by the same individual(s) against one or more victims or targets. For example, a suspect in a white sedan, approaches several young females at different locations as they walk home from school, and orders them to enter his vehicle. Alternatively, an elderly gentleman is repeatedly burglarized. These activities are notable because they involve crime committed by the same individual(s), against various victims or a single victim.

A **spree** characterizes a high frequency of criminal activity, to the extent that it appears almost continuous. It involves the same offender(s) and usually occurs over a short time period, although this could be a few hours, a few days or a longer period, depending upon the circumstances. For example, the driver's side window is broken and property is stolen from several vehicles, parked along the same residential street overnight. Even though there is no suspect information, this activity is categorized as a spree due to the similarities in MO, and proximity in time and location. These similarities suggest that the same individual committed the incidents.

A **hotspot** is a specific location or small area where an unusually high level of criminal activity occurs, that is committed by one or more offenders. For example, over several months, two armed robberies of pedestrians, and seven burglaries, occur at an apartment community that is usually crime-free. For tactical crime analysis, this area is a hotspot because it represents a notable amount of activity, at one location. It should be noted that hotspots could overlap with other types of activity.

A **hot dot** is an individual associated with an unusual amount of criminal activity, either as an offender or a victim. For example, over the course of two months, police arrest the same individual for assault, theft, and criminal trespass, the subject of several field contacts. This individual is categorized as a hot dot because of the notable amount of police activity.

A **hot product** is a specific type of property that is the target in similar or different types of crime. Clarke, who defines hot products as "those consumer items that are most attractive to thieves," coined this term. [13] For example, during a six-month time span, twenty tailgates are stolen from trucks of various makes and models, throughout the city. This activity is notable because similar properties have been taken.

A **hot target** refers to a particular type of frequently victimized target, not included in the previous definitions of hot spots (small areas), hot dots (persons), or hot products (goods). For example, across the city, ten incidents of church vandalism, a dozen clothing store burglaries, or a number of crimes against public transit commuters, might make any of them "hot targets," particularly if there is no indication that the crimes are committed by the same offender(s).

INTELLIGENCE-LED POLICING AND POP STRATEGIES

Intelligence-Led Policing (ILP) adds two approaches to the Problem-Oriented Leadership equation, and supplements crime analysis by initiating: (1) offender interviews, and (2) analyzing repeat victimizations. Interviews, a long established process, provide information for problem-solving. In addition, analyzing repeat victimizations is not a recent practice. Detectives occasionally or randomly practice these techniques; however, the innovation stems from systematic application of strategies to ILP intelligence gathering, crime analysis and police problem-solving.

OFFENDER INTERVIEWING

Offender interviews offers insight into the how and why offenses take place. Analyzing strategies may lead to identification of other criminals, committing similar offenses. Once motives for offenses are defined, crime prevention and Neighborhood Watch Programs benefit through enhanced security.

"Active offenders can provide a wealth of information about crimes, motives and techniques. This information extends well beyond the crimes for which offenders are under investigation or arrest. Such information can be valuable to the police in problem-solving approaches to crime. This information may have strategic or tactical value. Research with active offenders has focused on five categories of offenders: (1) drug dealers and users, (2) residential burglars, (3) armed robbers (4) gang members, and (5) gun offenders." [14]

ANALYZING REPEAT VICTIMIZATION

Analyzing repeat victimization has multiple problem-solving advantages that lead to hot spot identification, and offender travel patterns. Statistical probabilities can enhance crime specific planning that focuses directed patrol strategies to intercept offenders, while targeting suitable time intervals. Modus operandi (MO) and trademark (TM) analysis may identify a pattern and possible case linkage.

"The term 'victimization' usually refers to people, such as a person who has been victimized by domestic violence. Repeat victimization can best be understood as repeat targets since a victim may be an individual, a dwelling unit, a business at a specific address, or even a business chain with multiple locations. Even motor vehicles may be repeat victims." Refer to the federal COPS booklet entitled, Burglary of Retail establishments for an example of business victimization. [15]

"There are two primary reasons for repeat victimization: one, known as the 'boost' explanation, relates to the role of repeat offenders; the other, known as the 'flag' explanation, relates to the vulnerability or attractiveness of certain victims.

In the 'flag' explanation, some targets are unusually attractive to criminals or particularly vulnerable to crime; these characteristics tend to remain constant over time. In such cases, the victim is repeatedly victimized by different offenders.

In the boost explanation, repeat victimization reflects the successful outcome of an initial offense. Specific offenders gain important knowledge about a target from their experience, and use this information to reoffend." [16]

CONNECTING STRATEGIES

Directly related to interviewing offenders and analyzing repeat victimization, is routine activity theory, and rational choice theory. Offender interviews assist in analyzing methods of operation, travel patterns, and mental templates for

committing crimes. Rational choice describes criminal decision-making and reasoning considerations.

ROUTINE ACTIVITY THEORY

Criminals are human, therefore subject to daily routines
and travel patterns. These behaviors reoccur systematically in
a particular segment of the community. Researchers suggest
that routine activity theory specifies basic elements of a crime:
(1) **an offender**, (2) **suitable target** and (3) the **absence of
capable guardians. The formula expresses the following: crime
= (offender + target - guardian) (place + time).** [17] Thus, crime
prevention and intervention strategies may be mapped and
formulated based on crime analysis.

Routine activity suggests that criminal offenders choose
crime sites based on their daily travel paths from home,
school, work and recreation. Activity areas for criminal offenses may include crime sites near major highways, schools,
shopping centers, and recreational areas. For an example of a
recreational problem area, refer to the federal COP booklet
entitled, Assaults in and Around Bars. [18] Victimization occurs
primarily due to exposure to crime opportunity, and target
opportunity Therefore, the police should "**map, clock** and
calendar" offenses. [19]

RATIONAL CHOICE THEORY

Criminals often act on impulse; however, choices are based
on rational thinking and opportunity. Criminals are rational
about avoiding detection; however, some criminals are better
decision makers than others. Certain criminals have more
opportunities to commit specific offenses; the more complex
crimes are reserved for those who have specialized skills and
access to privileged positions. The rational criminal thinks

about their basic needs, and possible apprehension. Exceptions include mentally ill criminals and certain chronic drug offenders.

Rational choice theory explains the decision-making and reasoning of criminals. Criminals make a decision to commit a crime based on structure: (1) **where the crime occurs**, (2) **target characteristics** and (3) **available means** to complete the crime. In addition, rational choice involves the **personality**, **status**, **sex** and **age** of the criminal. Rational choice is both **offense** and **offender** specific; for example, a juvenile burglar may locate a lucrative target, but only engages in random vandalism. The juvenile offender may lack the prerequisite skills to accomplish the burglary, because the site has an alarm system. [20] Crime analysis and crime mapping may assist in deterring vandalism and potential juvenile burglaries, when criminal intelligence is applied to suppression strategies.

The decision to engage in criminal behavior is impacted by the number of structural opportunities. These opportunities have several significant factors: (1) **risk** and (2) **opportunity** influence decision-making. One becomes a criminal through the **learning process, target location** and **techniques** to execute the crime. [21] Offenders are likely to avoid or not commit crimes, in a specific area, if they reason that: (1) profits are too low, and (2) attractive and legal opportunities to generate income are available. Rational choice involves the criminal's perception of conventional or criminal opportunities. [22] Criminal opportunities are reduced when the patrol model for the allocation of officers to computerized (MAPP) software targets hot spots. [23]

GEOGRAPHIC INFORMATION SYSTEMS (GIS)

GIS crime mapping is an integral component of the crime analysis process and intelligence cycle, which leads to accurate criminal intelligence. Geographic information represents an essential leadership and planning foundation. Crime analysis and mapping information serve as the foundation for relating to ILP, community-oriented policing, problem-oriented policing, CompStat, and SARA planning methods.

EVALUATION AND ASSESSMENT

Mapping strategies provide excellent evaluation and assessment tools. "Computerized crime mapping technology enables law enforcement agencies to analyze and correlate data sources, to create detailed snapshots of crime incidents, and related factors within a community or other geographical areas." [24] Numerous applications exist for successful crime mapping strategies.

CRIME MAPPING APPLICATIONS

Research suggests departments report that crime mapping improves: (1) information dissemination, (2) evaluation and (3) administration. Specifically, police departments use mapping to: (1) inform officers and investigators of crime incident locations, (2) make resource allocation decisions, (3) evaluate interventions, (4) inform residents about crime activity, and changes in their community, and (5) identify repeat calls-for-service. [25]

Crime mapping is especially suited to strategic and tactical analysis. Typically, maps depict identified criminal offender residences and their specialties, targeting those who commit drug violations, burglaries, and sex crimes. Geographic Information System(s) (GIS) mapping represents "A powerful set of tools for storing and retrieving at will, and transforming and displaying spatial data from the real world, for a particular purpose." [26] Refer to Figure 3-1 for an illustration of GIS mapping generalizations.

Source: Adapted from Keith Harries, U.S. Department of Justice, National Institute of Justice, Mapping Crime: Principle and Practice (Washington. DC: GPO, 1999), 70.

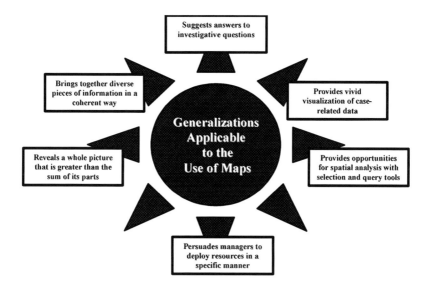

Figure 3-1   Generalizations Applicable to the Use of Maps

A map has a visual grammar or structure that must be understood and used if the best map design is desired. The selection of map type is often determined by geographic properties and data attributes. Crime-mapping data has its own language; not understanding the language may interfere with data visualization and interpretation.

CRIME MAPPING: TACTICAL ANALYSIS

Crime analysis, crime mapping and tactical interventions help eliminate the motives, opportunities, and means for individuals to commit crimes. [27] This information provides officers with exact times and kinds of offenses, offenders' methods of operation, and targets of attack, crime generators, and hot spot locations. GIS mapping tracks criminal events, and supports law enforcement officers in planning appropriate courses of action.

Crime mapping may assist in identifying overlapping criminal offenses, including burglary and narcotics violations. Crack house locations and drug distribution patterns can be mapped for planned interventions, suppression and prevention strategies. Optimistically, crime analysts and law enforcement officers may forecast future locations of potential gang conflicts.

VISUAL COMMUNICATION

As one moves from visual thinking to visual communication, from private thoughts to publication, analysis and synthesis takes place. Synthesis is the human and scientific product; at the core of this process, filtering and refining of data. [28] For example, "One layer of a map display, could represent a descriptive variable, such as the locations of crimes in the past month, while another layer could represent a possible explanatory variable, such as the unemployment rates of persons living on each city block, the location of abandoned houses, or citizen reports of drug activities." [29] When these layers "join," a synthesis and comprehensive picture of the crime hot spot, becomes a data snapshot and subject to remedial responses.

BASIC SYMBOLS: CRIME MAPPING

The crime incident is entered into GIS; a point is inserted at a corresponding location. A database table is opened, and the new offense is inserted into the table. Symbols are assigned to represent offenses. For example, robbery, burglary, or homicide, may be represented as geometric figures like squares, circles, triangles, guns, knives or tombstones; colors designate time periods. GIS data includes street names and addresses, for right and left sides of every block. [30] The symbols vary according to local policies, procedures, and the imagination of individual crime analysts.

Some opportune crime mapping applications include: (1) crime locations, (2) crime hot spots, and (3) crime patterns. In many cases, a geocoding crime location is required in the crime mapping process; otherwise, incidents are directly loaded from the Computer-Aided Dispatch (CAD) system. The basic approach in law enforcement is to collect attribute data from crime incident reports, and then create an offense incident table. GIS spatial data that is relevant to law enforcement, include: (1) point data (crime locations), (2) line data (streets), (3) area data (boundaries), and (4) many other forms of crime data. The crime analyst may define high incident areas as hot spots or crime clusters.

TARGETING HOT SPOTS

Once criminal information is gathered, officers can analyze hot spots in an effective and efficient manner. For example, officers can pinpoint hot spot locations through computer mapping and photographs. [31] Then outline the problem by numbering the offenses, plotting the times, places crimes occurred, and noting techniques used to commit the crimes. After gathering additional intelligence, and carefully analyzing the problem and causative factors, law enforcement officers implement appropriate intervention and prevention strategies. The following case study illustrates tactical analysis strategies and crime mapping applications.

CASE STUDY EXAMPLE: THE ANALYST BRIEFING

Shannon is a crime analyst for a metropolitan police department of approximately 1,000 sworn and civilian members. She is a respected civilian with approximately ten years of service. Shannon understands that her analyst briefings require an educational component to enlighten and persuade the commanders and staff/line officers.

In addition, Shannon's training and experience prepare her to present briefings, which target meaningful tactical analysis data, in a concise and illustrative manner. She always enhances her briefings with sight and sound presentations that incorporate PowerPoint and crime mapping technology illustrations. In addition, Shannon's carefully constructed Crime Bulletins, illustrating multiple burglaries in the county, reinforce and support her briefing presentation.

Officers begin to gather and find seats for the morning shift commander and sergeant briefing. Lt. Haslett, upon entering the room, calls everyone to attention for Shannon's briefing presentation. It takes several seconds to quiet "war story" conversations.

Shannon walks to the podium, confident in her crime analysis and mapping technical skills, and calmly states: "Good morning everyone. Most of you know me; therefore, I will suspend the formalities and present my tactical analysis in action briefing format."

Shannon introduces her analysis in the first slide: "The problem centers on 15 hot spot cases and serial burglaries, which form a distinct cluster in the affluent part of the county. We used the circle method and calculated travel distances among cases 1-15."

Shannon successfully explains GIS crime mapping essentials including: title block, legend, and map symbols. She then comments: "The statistical data is limited to spatiotemporal profile analysis, including time on target, and hot spot clustering. The hot spots are in the affluent sector of the county, and geographically comparable. You are all familiar with the beachside condominium development."

Shannon comments: "This guy burglarized these high-rise condos for over one year, when residents were having dinner in popular restaurants. The burglar's trademarks include monkey-like, athletic abilities; he scales balconies!" The officers break into laughter; a few grumble under their breath: "What do we call him, the 'monkey burglar'?"

Shannon, remains unflappable in spite of the comments, and continues her briefing, "He steals cash, jewelry and small valuable 'hot product' technology items. This guy is a professional class burglar, who does not leave by the front door; he scales buildings by traversing connected balconies. Moreover, he seems knowledgeable about local security operations.

"His modus operandi forms a unique pattern of offender evolution. For example, he rearranges the furniture like an interior designer, and steals treasured framed photographs of young female family members. This burglar's psychological signature clues are distinctive. Victims report that upon entering their own home, they feel they might be in the wrong apartment. They are immediately shaken and confused by the experience."

The morning sunshine reflects off the badge of a young female officer, who raises her hand and asks the question:

"How do you know that the offender is not a woman?" Laughter erupts from the male officers.

Shannon replies: "Well, it's possible, but not probable because of the upper body strength required in this burglar's MO. Jane, we know you have that kind of athletic ability. However, the statistical rate for female burglary offenses is low. In addition, one victim caught a glimpse of him escaping, as he leaped towards her neighbor's balcony. Evidence indicates he was wearing black clothing and retreated down the balcony."

Shannon triggers another PowerPoint slide, "The key tools of the 'problem profile' include: (1) scale of the problem: frightened residents are purchasing weapons and taking shooting lessons, and (2) potential suspects at this point: none. He likely travels a considerable distance to his potential targets, and is quite familiar with the area. (3) The 'target profile' of the suspect: He operates under the cover of darkness and strikes between 1800-2100 hours, wearing black clothing. In addition, he does not leave detectible prints behind, which suggests the wearing of gloves.

"The most important temporal factors occur when he enters and exits the buildings. His chief weaknesses are his style of dress, time frame, and the MO places him in public view for approximately ten minutes while scaling the balconies. Owners leave the sliding class doors to their patios unlocked, because they feel secure in the clouds." The COPPS program has formed a Neighborhood Watch and warned owners to secure all patio doors, even on upper floors.

Shannon triggers the final slide that suggests tactical options: "The Crime Analysis Section recommends that unmarked tactical team cars conduct surveillance near the cluster of hot spots identified on the crime mapping slide. Uniform patrol units should remain alert for Crime Bulletin updates. In addition, detectives should follow-up on pawnshops and professional fences, attempting to get rid of items on the list of hot products.

Lt. Haslett walks up to the podium, and concludes the briefing: "Shannon, thank you for the excellent crime analysis briefing and remarks. You have convinced everyone, even skeptics, of the value of your tactical analysis. My officers will cooperate and provide feedback information as soon as possible."

Ultimately, the field response planning will be initiated by middle leadership with designated goals, objectives and action plans in response to crime analyst data. The shift leadership will formulate objectives that have specific tasks, conditions and standards. Mission plans tell what the requirements are, but avoid destroying initiative. The how, to accomplish the mission, is left to essential shift commanders, sergeants and officers.

FOCUS POINTS: ILP AND CRIME ANALYSIS

Crime analysts address strategic, tactical, administrative, and operational requirements, while developing a series of related intelligence products. Crime analysis coordinates systematic analytical processes that provide timely criminal information for strategic and tactical planning. The applied crime research and presentations spans several related content areas: (1) strategic, (2) tactical, (3) administrative, and (4) operational analysis.

In addition, tactical analysis includes: (1) target analysis, (2) target profiles, and (3) statistical analysis, which enhance police deployment and logistical requirements.

The tactical knowledge allows police leaders to be proactive, rather than reactive, in their responses to crime. Geographical and statistical analysis formulates the decision-making process for placing officers in the precise place, and time for addressing possible criminal scenarios. Tactical linkage defines the crime knowledge base for developing meaningful tactical recommendations.

Crime mapping pinpoints hot spot locations and places where criminals commit crimes. An analytical model developed from crime mapping, defines hot spots and clusters of crime incidents, in a visual context. This crime snapshot serves a focal point for strategic and tactical planning. GIS crime mapping provides leaders the assessment tool to define who, what, where, and when of crime, with a higher statistical probability than random patrol. The visualization of crime data is worth more than a thousand words, it provides insight.

ILP, COP, POP and CompStat require crime analysis for successful crime prevention and intervention outcomes. Analysts are central to drawing inferences and conclusions, from the data evidence. They focus on the crime problem, judge the credibility of sources and deductions, provide consequential recommendations, and effective courses of action. Ultimate strategic and tactical actions comprise police commander and leader responsibilities.

CONCLUSION

Crime analysis planning assists in answering four essential leadership questions: (1) Where are the crimes occurring? (2) How are they taking place? (3) Who are the perpetrators? (4) How can police deployment operations prevent and engage intervention strategies? Finally, accurate assessment will determine successful arrival and provide guidance for the next intervention destination. The crime analyst serves as the navigational instrument for police leaders to find the way, and arrive in a judicious manner.

ENDNOTES

1. Rachel Boba, Crime Analysis and Crime Mapping (Thousand
    Oaks, California: Sage Publications, 2005), 6.

2. Career Criminal Apprehension Program: Program Guidelines
    (Sacramento, CA: Office of Criminal Justice Planning, 1992), 8.

3. Marilyn B. Peterson, Applications in Criminal Analysis: A
    Sourcebook, 275.

4. Philip E. Taylor and Stephen J. Huxley, "A Break from Tradition
    for the San Francisco Police: Patrol Officer Scheduling Using an
    Optimization-Based Decision Support System", Interfaces, Volume
    19, No. 1, January-February 1989, 4.

5. Career Criminal Apprehension Program: Program Guidelines
    (Sacramento, CA: Office of Criminal Justice Planning, 1992):
    Steven Gottlieb, Sheldon Arenberg, and Raj Singh, Crime
    Analysis: From First Report to Final Arrest (California: Alpha
    Publishing Company, 1998), 13.

6. Dan Helms, "Trendspotting: Serial Crime Detection with GIS,"
    Crime Mapping News, Spring 2000, 1-4.

7. United Kingdom Home Office, "Operational Policing: National
    Intelligence Model, Internet URL, 2006.

8. Velasco and Boba, "Tactical Crime Analysis and Geographic
    Information Systems," Police Foundation, Crime Mapping News,
    Spring 2000, 1-2.

9. Gottlieb, Arenberg and Singh, 1998, 301.

10. John E. Eck, A General Model of the Geography of Illicit Retail
    Market Places. In John E. Eck and David Weisburd, ed. Crime and
    Place: Crime Prevention Studies, Vol. 4. (Monsey, NY: Willow
    Tree Press, 1995).

11. Gottlieb, Arenberg and Singh, 1998, 440.

12. Velasco and Boba, Spring 2000, 1-2.

13. Ronald V. Clarke, Policing and Reducing Crime Unit, Police Research Series, Paper 112, "Hot Products: Understanding, anticipating, and Reducing Demand for Stolen Goods," (London: Home Office, 1999).

14. Scott H. Decker, U. S. Department of Justice, Office of Community Oriented Policing Services, Using Offender Interviews to Inform Police Problem-Solving (Washington, DC: GPO, 2005): 2-3.

15. Ronald V. Clarke, U. S. Department of Justice, Office of Community Oriented Policing Services, Burglary of Retail Establishments (Washington, DC: GPO, 2002): 1-15.

16. Deborah Lamm Weisel, U. S. Department of Justice, Office of Community Oriented Policing Services, Analyzing Repeat Victimization (Washington, DC: GPO, 2005): 4-12.

17. Marcus Felson, "Routine Activities and Crime Prevention in The Developing Metropolis," In Criminology Theory Reader, Stewart Henry and Werner Einstadter, ed. (New York: New York University Press, 1998.)

18. Michael S. Scott, U. S. Department of Justice, Office of Community Oriented Policing Services, Assaults in and Around Bars (Washington, DC: GPO, 2001): 1-26.

19. Marcus Felson, "Linking Criminal Choices, Routine Activities, Informal Control and Criminal outcomes," In D.B. Cornish and R.V. Clark, eds. The Reasoning Criminal: Rational Choice Perspectives on Offending, (New York: Springer-Verlag, 1986), 128.

20. Lloyd Phillips and Harold Votey, "The Influence of Police Interventions and Alternative Income Sources on the Dynamic Process of Choosing Crime as a Career," The Journal of Quantitative Criminology, Volume 3, 1987, 251-274.

21. Ronald Akers, "Rational Choice, Deterrence and Social Learning Theory in Criminology: The Path Not Taken," Journal of Criminal Law and Criminology, Volume 81, 1990, 653-676.

22. Liliana Pezzin, "Earning Prospects, Matching Effects, and the Decision to Terminate a Criminal Career," Journal of Quantitative Criminology, Volume 11, 1995: 29-50.

23. Erick J. Fritsch, John Liederbach, and Taylor Robert, Police Patrol allocation and Deployment (New Jersey: Pearson/Prentice-Hall, 2009), 40.

24. Cynthia Mamalian and Nancy La Vigne, U.S. Department of Justice, National Institute Of Justice, The Use of Computerized Mapping by Law Enforcement: Survey Results, Research Review (Washington, DC: GPO, 1999): 1.

25. Mamalian and La Vigne, 1999, 2.

26. Peter A. Burrough, Principles of Geographical Information Systems (Oxford: Oxford University Press, 1998), 6.

27. Ronald V. Clarke, Opportunity-Reducing Crime Prevention Strategies and the Role of Motivation, In P.O. Wilkstrom, R. V. Clarke, and J. McCord, eds. Integrating Crime Prevention Strategies: Propensity and Opportunity (Stockholm: National Council for Crime Prevention, 1995).

28. Keith Harries, U.S. Department of Justice, National Institute Of Justice, Mapping Crime: Principle and Practice (Washington, DC: GPO, 1999): 38.

29. Thomas F. Rich, U.S. Department of Justice, National Institute of Justice, Research in Action, The Use of Computerized in Crime Control and Prevention Programs (Washington, DC: GPO, July 1995): 1-3.

30. Harries, 1995, 42-49.

31. Rich, 1995, 1-11.

CHAPTER 4
Compstat Integration

There is nothing as deceptive as an obvious fact.
— Sir Arthur Conan Doyle

Why would anyone avoid an obvious fact or facts? Simply stated, rationalizations of the mind, seeing what we want to see, and believe. Rationalizations that support the status quo evolve from fear of change, and the unknown. It takes considerable leadership to move others towards social change. However, the mission is possible.

The classic leadership dilemma is emergency thinking, rather than long-term planning and strategic innovations. Police leaders with strategic purpose and vision, will initiate strategies that integrate the architecture of Intelligence-Led Policing (ILP). Strategic leaders will demonstrate diplomacy and courage, when implementing future policing requirements.

CHAPTER FOCUS: POP INTEGRATION

Intelligence-Led Policing: Leadership, Strategies and Tactics bridges the gap between strategic leadership, intelligence, and crime analysis operations. ILP represents an intelligence management system that coordinates criminal information sharing. ILP and COP philosophy concepts support effective police practices.

Problem-oriented Policing (POP) and SARA provide the long to midrange strategic planning model. Intelligence analysis supports long-term strategies, and threat assessment preparation. The CompStat leadership model offers short-

term planning for street and emergency tactical operations.
CompStat strategies encourage crime-fighting tactics that
utilize: (1) crime analysis, (2) leadership, and emphasize (3)
tactical strategies. Refer to Table 4-1 for additional information on the chapter focus and concepts.

Table 4-1   Focus and Concepts

	ILP Intelligence Integration	ILP SARA Planning Strategies
Intelligence-Led Policing	❖ Community-oriented policing ❖ Intelligence-led policing ❖ Intelligence analysis ❖ Intelligence cycle ❖ Crime analysis ❖ Problem-solving policing ❖ CompStat tactics	❖ Define the problem ❖ Scanning ❖ Analysis ❖ Response ❖ Focus on the causes of crime(s) ❖ Focus on systematic inquiry ❖ Assessment
	ILP Problem-Solving Policing	**ILP CompStat Leadership**
	❖ Problem-solving policing ❖ Proactive responses ❖ Develop partnerships ❖ Focus on underlying causes ❖ Group incidents as a problem ❖ React to underlying problems ❖ Develop tailor-made responses	❖ Crime-fighting strategies ❖ Accurate and timely intelligence ❖ Teamwork ❖ Staff coordination ❖ Rapid deployment ❖ Effective tactics ❖ Relentless follow-up and assessment

INTEGRATING ILP REQUIREMENTS

The integration and coordination of ILP, POP and Comp-
Stat are essential to the successful execution of crime prevention and intervention efforts. The synchronization of policing
strategies avoids competing and counter-productive outcomes.

Therefore, the policing paradigm is illustrated by the following formula: ILP + COP + POP + CompStat = **Consolidated Intelligence and Coordinated Decision-Making.**

A unified command, occupying the same location and centralized control, is the essence of ILP management philosophy. In addition, the central office would supervise decentralized intelligence/crime analysts attached to police operation and investigative functions. The consolidation of intelligence and crime analysis is a basic organizational requirement for achieving information sharing, and integrated analysis. The next logical step requires the synchronization of POP and CompStat policing strategies. Refer to Figure 4-1 for the integration, and conceptualization of ILP strategies.

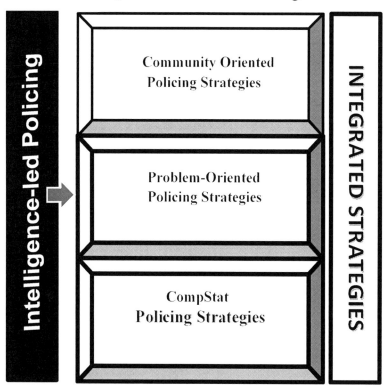

Figure 4-1   ILP Integration Strategies

The philosophy of community-oriented policing is firmly entwined in the fabric of American policing. However, the planning process incorporates POP and SARA strategies to realize COP philosophy goals and objectives. These problem-solving strategies focus on crime generators and hot spots, which distress communities. CompStat enhances the COP and POP models, and when properly coordinated, the tripod can improve police effectiveness.

PROBLEM-SOLVING POLICING

The positive nomenclature might be defined as problem-solving rather than problem-oriented policing. However, Herman Goldstein coined the term and expressed a general theory for the POP theory, and SARA planning strategies. His theory of policing suggests that problems would best be recognized not as incidents, but symptoms of underlying problems. [1]

A problem is described as a cluster of similarly related or recurring incidents, which have root causes. Moreover, this related cluster of activities or problems represent significant community concerns, and require a substantial police response to address the problems. Once the problem(s) are identified, police agencies can focus on addressing possible causes and remedial actions. [2] The focus is on the underlying causes, rather than disconnected individual responses. Citizen and community partnerships play a role in policing itself. The premise is that the police cannot fight crime alone without citizen support. [3]

Moreover, armed with basic crime and intelligence analysis information on the underlying problem(s), effective leadership decision-making solutions are possible. The essential part of the equation, is enlisting citizen cooperation and community support. The emphasis is not reacting to a series of events. The basic tactics include incorporating a holistic approach to identifying appropriate and timely solutions. [4]

The emphasis is on prevention and improving police effectiveness. ILP centralization of criminal intelligence and communication facilitates information enhancement for positive remedial actions and solutions. ILP criminal information management systems, intelligence and crime analysis, POP, SARA and CompStat require communication and feedback. Refer to Figure 4-2 for an analysis of the ILP channels of communication and feedback.

Figure 4-2   ILP, POP and CompStat Communication Strategies

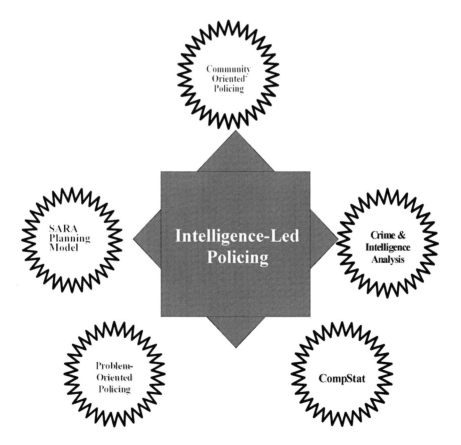

SARA PLANNING MODEL

SARA planning roots can be traced to an early study conducted in Newport News, Virginia. The police department successfully experimented with the SARA Planning model: Scanning, Analysis, Response, and Assessment. SARA is similar to the crime analysis process, or intelligence cycle.

While appearing compartmentalized and unbending, the SARA processes, in practice, is overlapping and interconnected. The SARA initial planning stages are often revisited as new information and intelligence becomes available. Refer to Figure 4-3 for an illustration of the acronym SARA, initiated by William Spelman and John Eck. [5]

Figure 4-3 SARA Planning Process

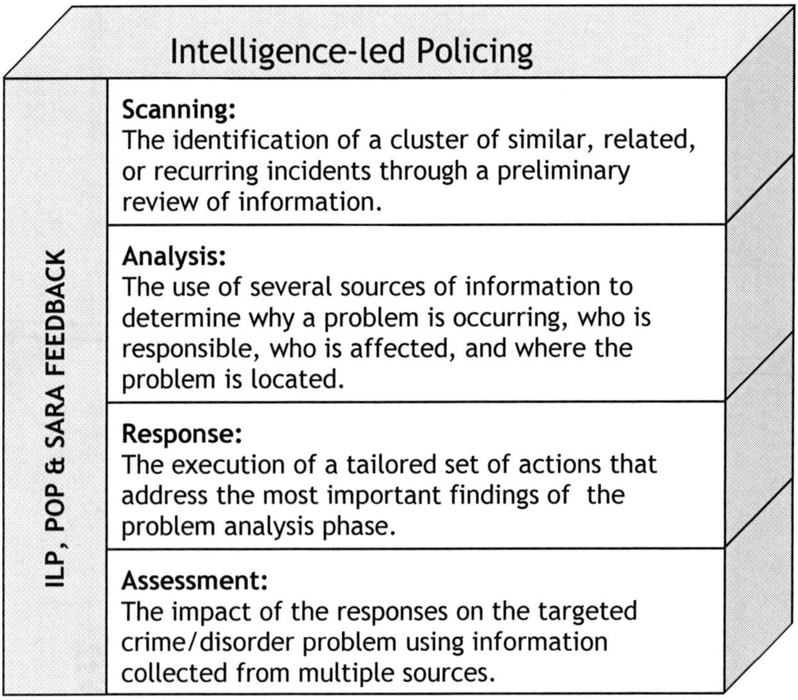

Intelligence-led Policing

Scanning:
The identification of a cluster of similar, related, or recurring incidents through a preliminary review of information.

Analysis:
The use of several sources of information to determine why a problem is occurring, who is responsible, who is affected, and where the problem is located.

Response:
The execution of a tailored set of actions that address the most important findings of the problem analysis phase.

Assessment:
The impact of the responses on the targeted crime/disorder problem using information collected from multiple sources.

ILP, POP & SARA FEEDBACK

Problem-oriented policing requires applied research, strategic and tactical planning. SARA planning mandates logic and reasoning: (1) carefully define specific problem(s), (2) conduct in-depth analysis to understand their causes, (3) accomplish expansive searches for solutions, (4) eliminate the causes, (5) achieve predetermined solutions, and (6) evaluate and assess outcomes. The following paragraphs illustrate the SARA planning stages.

SARA PLANNING STAGES

Scanning: The identification of a cluster of similar, related, or recurring incidents through a preliminary review of information, and the selection of this crime/disorder problem among competing priorities for future examination.

Analysis: the use of several sources of information to determine why a problem is occurring, who is responsible, who is affected, where the problem is located, when it occurs, and what form the problem takes. Analysis requires identifying patterns that explain the conditions that facilitate the crime or disorder problem. Sources of information may include police data (CAD, arrest incident data, etc.); victim and offender interviews; crime prevention surveys; officer, business, and resident surveys; social service and other government agency data; and insurance information.

Response: The execution of a tailored set of actions that address the most important findings of the problem analysis phase, and focus on at least two of the following: (1) preventing future occurrences by deflecting offenders; (2) protecting likely victims; or (3) making crime locations less conducive to problem behaviors. Responses are designed to have a long-term influence on the problem, and do not require a commitment of police time and resources, that is not sustainable over the long term.

Assessment: The impacts of responses, on the targeted crime/disorder problem, using information collected from multiple courses, both before and after the responses have been implemented.

Special Note: The POP and SARA planning strategies are essential components of CompStat. The over-all coordination of ILP assists in providing the intelligence and crime analysis, necessary for effective leadership. CompStat provides the leadership and knowledge base for field operations. Therefore, commanders, leaders, and supervisors are provided the best opportunities for excellent decision-making.

COMPSTAT INTEGRATION

CompStat has similar information requirements. Therefore, ILP, POP and SARA planning procedures represent excellent contributions to the CompStat leadership process. The following paragraphs were adapted from the excellent observations of the CompStat strategies, by Rudolph W. Giuliani and Howard Safir. [6]

The four steps to Crime Reduction have been critical to the Department's crime-fighting success. The four steps are: (1) accurate and timely intelligence, (2) rapid deployment, (3) effective tactics, and (4) relentless follow-up and assessment. The steps are carefully scrutinized, because each step is needed for large-scale, ongoing, crime reduction.

INTELLIGENCE REQUIREMENTS

Accurate and timely intelligence is essential for crime reduction; innovative departments understand the strategic and tactical crime picture. Incorporating ILP, crime and intelligence analysis, POP and SARA strategies enhance that endeavor.

Routinely debriefing prisoners is an important way to glean criminal information. Suspects often understand essential street crime information, and may be motivated to disclose this information to police officers. Suspects are interviewed about the specific crime(s) for which they are arrested, but they can also be asked about other crimes, specifically, and in general. Officers in the field, need timely and accurate crime information so they can patrol, investigate crimes, and apprehend suspects as safely as possible.

COMPSTAT COORDINATION

The Precinct Crime Information Center, features up-to-date pin-ups of crimes, information on crime patterns, and wanted suspects, etc. The basic sources include: (1) messages and announcements on the sergeant's clipboard, which supervisors read and discuss with officers at each roll call; (2) roll call statements by the Precinct Commanding Officer, Executive Officer, and precinct detectives, and (3) Anti-Crime personnel concerning crime conditions and wanted suspects, support the flow of criminal information.

Patrol officers, anti-crime officers, and detectives communicate with each other. Plainclothes and uniformed officers exchange information. If plainclothes units take information, but never divulge; uniformed officers, in return, will stop supplying information. In most cases, patrol officers should know if detectives are looking for a suspect. Patrol officers can often find suspects (and witnesses), if they know where to look.

CRIME PATTERN INFORMATION

The public needs to know about crime patterns and conditions, for their own safety. In return, they can provide information to the police. Pattern robbers and other repeat offenders are frequently arrested because of citizen-shared information. Giving information, sketches of suspects, etc. to the newspapers, radio and television offers an important venue to supply crime information to the general public.

High-quality, accurate, and speedy crime analysis is vital to crime reduction. Excellent crime analysis includes: (1) swift identification of crime patterns, (2) rapid distribution of crime pattern information, suspect and vehicle descriptions and, (3) the general public (when and where appropriate). Crime pattern information is swiftly and widely distributed, because repeat offenders commit heinous crimes. There are relatively few violent criminals in society; however, they pose a significant threat by repeatedly committing the same types of serious crimes.

Commanding officers ensure that crime information is: (1) gathered constantly, (2) analyzed rapidly and accurately, (3) distributed within the police department, and to the public, as needed. Analyzing crime trends and patterns is important because: **"If you can predict it, you can prevent it."**

Precinct commanders, crime analysts, detectives, supervisors and police officers, all working together, make intelligence gathering and distribution effective; teamwork requires partnerships.

EFFECTIVE TACTICS AND DEPLOYMENT

Once crime intelligence is gathered, commanders ensure they deploy their own resources as swiftly as possible to address the crime conditions. Resources include: (1) uniformed patrol personnel, (2) plainclothes patrol personnel, and (3) precinct detective squad personnel.

Effective tactics require planning: **"Failure to plan is planning to fail."** Commanders must develop clear, effective, flexible, tactics to address crime conditions. Commanders stand ready to modify their plans when crime requirements change.

The key to effective tactics is focusing appropriate resources and logistics on specific problems. Random patrols often produce random results. CompStat provides information that enables leaders to envision tactical development, and track plan implementation. Effective follow-up procedures are necessary for successful planning and tactical outcomes.

RELENTLESS FOLLOW-UP AND ASSESSMENT

High-quality intelligence, rapid resource deployment to address crime, and effective strategies to combat crimes, are not sufficient. Commanders constantly follow-up on activities, and assess results. If results are not positive, something needs to change. The CompStat process is a vital tool for relentless follow-up and assessment. It informs department executives and commanders at all levels, and sets the foundation for essential changes in tactics and deployment. Refer to Table 4-2 for a summary of the CompStat leadership strategies.

Table 4-2 CompStat Integration

Leadership Accountability	Leadership Coordination
■ Two vital keys to CompStat's effectiveness are empowering precinct commanders, and holding precinct commanders responsible for reducing crime within their commands. ■ Coordination of effort between different parts of the organization is critical. **Teamwork is essential to crime reduction and prevention.**	■ Commanders review crime reduction strategies, and change them as needed. ■ Tactics planning addresses crime problems, and changes plans when necessary. ■ Accurate and timely intelligence: What crimes are happening? When? Where? Why? ■ **Rapid Deployment:** applying resources to identified crime problems.
Crime Analysis Reporting	**Follow-Up & Assessment**
■ Crime statistics are complied and analyzed in CompStat reports, and commander profiles. ■ Crime issues, problems and solutions are discussed at crime strategy meetings held twice each week. ■ CompStat Reports and crime strategy meetings keep everyone informed.	■ Crime reduction is a continuing process, not just a one-time event. ■ Consistently applying the 4 Steps help keeps that process going. ■ **Relentless Follow-up and Assessment** (looking at results to make sure that plans are working).

The CompStat Paradigm: Management Accountability in Policing, Business and the Public Sector, by Vincent E. Henry, is a definitive resource on CompStat. The author is a former NYPD sergeant and presently serves as an associate professor. He stresses the importance of Staff Crime Control Strategy Meetings as a forum for CompStat planning, analysis and statistical assessment. Staff meetings emphasize strategies, tactical and statistical results.

Henry defines CompStat as follows: "The CompStat paradigm is a hybrid management style that combines the best and most effective elements of several organizational models as well as the best elements of the philosophies that support them. CompStat retains the best practice of traditional policing, for example, but also incorporates insights and practices from the Community Policing and Problem solving policing styles. It also utilizes the kind of strategic management approaches used by successful corporate entities that thrive in highly competitive industries. Because the CompStat paradigm is so flexile and because it emphasizes the rapid identification and creative solution of problems, it can be applied in virtually any goal-driven human organization." [7]

He recommends that staff meetings allow open exchanges among Precinct Commanders and executives. At times, debates may engage strong emotions as commanders seek to justify positions. The CompStat paradigm places accountability with commanders/middle managers, rather than headquarters executives and street officers. [8]

Henry suggests that judicious executives acknowledge and praise superior performance. Moreover, accountability is the key to excellent performance, and everyone should be held to reasonable performance standards. Middle leaders, detectives and street police officers have recent street knowledge, when compared to headquarters staff and executives. Precinct Commanders are strategically positioned to make CompStat tactical, logistical and human resource decisions. Staff strategy meetings help achieve direction and accountability. [9] The following hypothetical case study serves an example of staff meeting interaction.

CASE STUDY: STAFF STRATEGY MEETING

The "brass," police executives and commanders, start to gather for their bi-weekly meeting. The smell of strong coffee and tension is in the air. The stakes are high when com-

manders seek their share of crime fighting resource allocations. Such gatherings are often personal and competitive;
information sharing is part of the meeting, but results are the
primary agenda.

The program is often determined by high profile cases,
ILP management, POP, and CompStat strategies. These meetings highlight the best and inventive leadership attributes;
candid dialogue demonstrates weaknesses and strengths.
Commanders must perform aggressively and achieve accountability, and then they will have the proverbial spotlight on
their leadership abilities.

Command meetings stress interaction, communication,
and statistical results concerning crime reduction strategies.
Commanders respond to CompStat's clearly defined goals and
objectives. The standards are for the most part, reasonable
and attainable. However, interpersonal conflict climbs, with
few limits on personal expression or opinions. These meetings
might present career benchmarks for commanders who
demonstrate improvements on crime reduction and statistical
objectives.

The morning exchange starts with remarks from one of
the elite commanders, who became a legend for his coolness
under fire, as a street officer. Thomas steps to the podium and
initiates his report. "Good morning everyone, I have a matter
of grave concern; it concerns an indigenous terrorist group."
The Deputy Chief of Operations breaks the silence, "What
group and what is the level of threat involved?"

Captain Thomas responds, "They are calling themselves
the American Al Qaeda Front (AAF) and are claiming Islamic
Revolution as their cause. They consider themselves to be an
independent franchise of the Osama Bin Laden terrorist
group. They recently organized a Mosque in an old aban-

doned warehouse, and are preaching hatred instead of religion. The foundation for their conversion occurred while serving prison sentences for felony convictions."

"The first bits of incipient and fragmentary information were relayed by the COP Neighborhood Watch Program. Residents complained about panhandling and other 'broken window theory,' i.e., graffiti and abandoned buildings issues. Mosque members have attempted to force residents to make financial contributions through intimidation techniques."

A grumpy Deputy Inspector and former Intelligence and Organized Unit commander, remarks, "What does Intel have to say?" Captain Thomas deflects the question to the intelligence analyst: "This is the perfect opportunity to introduce our intelligence analyst commander. Lt. Conway will give his portion of the briefing."

Lt. Conway presents the first slide of his briefing: "Good morning. According to our intelligence files, including state and federal sources of information, this group is in the developmental stages. Our reliable informant suggests that the group consists of former correctional inmates who have an extensive criminal background in robbery, extortion and drug trafficking. The content validity was confirmed by debriefing recent arrestees and deep undercover officers."

The Lieutenant comments, as another slide pops-up: "The following information is sensitive concerning threat analysis, and should not leave his room in any format. AAF is planning a terrorist action that is directed at soft targets, i.e., religious buildings, shopping malls and transit systems. This terrorist group is attempting to purchase automatic weapons, from any available source. Surveillance Teams have tracked one of the suspects to a commercial source that sells ammonium nitrate, which as everyone knows is used in fertilized bombs."

"The good news is that they have not succeeded in advancing their terrorist conspiracy, because of their failure to acquire terrorist tools. In addition, a verifiable connection to the Osama Bin Laden terrorist group is not clear. Group members are not interested in sacrificing themselves as suicide bombers. The cell is poorly organized and under-developed. In addition, the terrorist leadership does not follow proper security and counter-intelligence procedures."

"At this point I would like to introduce our civilian crime analyst, James Bailey; he will document street crimes and related analysis." Bailey comments: "Good morning everyone! Here is my estimate of the criminal aspects, AAF, and terrorist organization. The religious motivation of this group is questionable, the criminal component undeniable."

"The first GIS crime mapping slides replicate the geo-graphical and statistical factors of the criminal activities. The hot spots for robbery (marked by the red dots) indicate the proximity of the wealthy neighborhood that is adjacent to one of the poorest in the city. We have identified some pos-sible suspects. Some are similar matches to individual patterns in our records system."

"The circle method identifies a pattern that is overlapping for both neighborhoods. Many of the members of AAF are on parole for robbery offenses. The main suspects should be targeted for surveillance and decoy team assignments. Some of the CompStat team members are presently working on the strategies and tactics."

The second crime-mapping slide portrays vivid coverage of further drug offenses. Bailey points out various locations in proximity to the group's Mosque and apartments that are involved in crack cocaine distribution. The drug street distri-bution hot spots are identified by the green triangles on various city blocks. "The AAF group members claim they are against drugs; however, the rationale is they need the money to finance the revolution." Bailey adds to his closing slide, "Thank you for your time and attention."

Captain Thomas ends the briefing with staff police problem-solving strategies recommendations: "This AAF terrorist/criminal group needs to be taken down and dismantled. Intelligence needs to be analyzed and coordinated under the new Intelligence-led policing management system." Four intelligence and investigative objectives need to be accomplished:

(1) "We need to coordinate with parole authorities and seek parole revocation violations and get these people behind bars."

(2) "The CompStat teams should start rapidly deploying some emergency responses directed at the robberies and drug offenses as soon as the link and association analysis identifies the criminal pattern."

(3) "The terrorist investigation requires follow-up and continued surveillance of this group's activities."

(4) "The continuing strategic and tactical intelligence needs to move the investigation into a full-blown terrorist conspiracy case."

Deputy Chief Adams approaches the podium, "We need to close this case quickly. Everyone will be putting in a lot of overtime. The meeting is adjourned."

FOCUS POINTS: INTEGRATION STRATEGIES

POP policing attempts to formalize what astute police officers were applying for years. Police officers could think critically, analyze the problem and apply problem-solving skills.

POP is an extension of traditional or professional policing. It is on that premise that both will work cooperatively.

Crime analysis was not alien to everyday policing problems before the formalized research era of POP, SARA and CompStat. The problem-solving approach was not a counter-revolution to the traditional reactive style of policing. The POP strategies are evolutionary, not revolutionary.

Police officers are problem-solvers who address everyday community problems to appalling crimes. Some interventions must be decided in seconds and constitute life-threatening scenarios. Police intelligence and crime analysis support the police problem-solving process.

Police officer job descriptions should include the concept of "problem-solving." The role of the police officer requires excellent judgment, especially in street encounters. POP and CompStat offer opportunities to control some non-emergency long to mid-range and short-range decision-making protocols.

POP requires non-traditional and traditional proactive responses. The systematic inquiry includes focusing on underlying causes for the crime pattern. The goal is to group incidents for remedial non-tactical and tactical remedies. Once the tailor-made solutions are implemented, assessment of the results follows.

Integration of police strategies may require organizational realignments and revision of the division of labor. POP requires the expertise of applied researchers, police officers, detectives, and crime and intelligence analysts. POP is best deployed as a staff function to support line operations, COP Neighborhood Watch programs and CompStat tactical missions.

CompStat changed the way the police perform concerning organization, administration and operations. The application of crime analysis, statistical analysis and tactical patrol responses proved very effective. Officers placed at the right location at the right time can intervene and prevent crime.

CompStat crime-fighting strategies necessitate timely and accurate intelligence. ILP, intelligence and crime analysis support the street tactical efforts and remedial outcomes. Teamwork and staff coordination enhance rapid deployment. Effective tactics and relentless follow-up assist the evaluation and promote excellent outcomes.

The CompStat tactical results did not go unnoticed across the nation. One cannot argue with successful crime statistics and sound results. However, ILP, and the consolidation of intelligence and analysis will require some accommodation and coordination. The integration of COP and POP will require restructuring to facilitate integration.

Most police agencies in the Unites States do not have financial and human resources to assemble or reorganize intelligence and crime analysis functions. Some agencies are fortunate to have one specialist, but not both and some analysts serve both capacities. The absence of both analysis functions makes it extremely difficult to receive or share intelligence.

Large to mid-sized police departments will struggle with integration and reorganization issues. Police agencies with fewer personnel will have to task one individual to intelligence and establish linkage to information-sharing technology.

Some officers may be assigned additional duties that support functional areas of ILP, COP, POP and CompStat on a temporary basis. According to Federal Bureau of Investigation statistics, the average city in the United States has approximately 41 sworn officers. [10] Regardless of the size of the police agency, coordination with local, regional and federal intelligence sharing resources are of paramount importance.

CONCLUSION

Terrorist and criminal threats require innovative policing strategies and tactics to combat the ever-present challenge to western civilization and the American way of life. The technology revolution and related software has altered the leadership equation in support of intelligence, and crime analysis strategies. In this era of rapid social and technological change, the transition will be accomplished through careful planning and successful innovations.

The integration of ILP intelligence requirements and crime analysis strategies provides real-time intelligence sharing. The integration and synchronization of COP, POP and CompStat can impact life and death decision-making and enhance the possibility for positive outcomes. Positive proactive leadership remains the most essential part of the equation.

ENDNOTES

1. Herman Goldstein, Problem Oriented Policing: A Practical Guide for Police Officers (New York: McGraw-Hill Publishing Co., 1990).

2. Goldstein, 20.

3. Goldstein, 66.

4. Goldstein, 20.

5. John E. Eck and William Spelman, Problem-Oriented Policing in Newport News (Washington, DC: Police Executive Research Forum, 1987).

6. Rudolph W. Giuliani and Howard Safir, Compstat: Leadership in Action (New York: New York City Police Department, 1997), 1.

7. Vincent E. Henry, The Compstat Paradigm: Management Accountability in Policing, Business and the Public Sector (New York: Looseleaf Law Publications, 2003), 24.

8. Henry, 260-272.

9. Henry, 260-272.

10. Federal Bureau of Investigation, Crime in the United States (Washington, DC: GPO, 2002): 319.

PART II
STRATEGIC LEADERSHIP

Role model the leadership and define the mission.

Develop intelligence analytical products.

Engage others in the information sharing process.

Develop the target-centered planning process.

Centralize and consolidate the planning process.

Synchronize the planning process and gain access to decision makers.

PART II: STRATEGIC LEADERSHIP

LEADERSHIP FOUNDATIONS	GUIDEPOST BEHAVIORS
❖ Role model the leadership and define the mission.	❖ Inspire, share the vision, build trust, and foster collaboration.
❖ Engage others in the information sharing process.	❖ Maximize the Johari Window and establish the feedback process to the blind spot and unknown.
❖ Centralize and consolidate the planning process.	❖ Intelligence-led policing, intelligence analysis and crime analysis support the planning process.
❖ Synchronize the planning process and gain access to decision makers.	❖ Centralized planning improves staff coordination and planning articulation.
❖ Develop the target-centered planning process.	❖ Identify the crime triangle, and coordinate with the fusion center.
❖ Develop intelligence analytical products.	❖ Intelligence-led policing provides police decision makers with written and verbal presentations that support police operations.

CHAPTER 5
Strategic Leadership and Communication

You see, but you do not observe.
— Sir Arthur Conan Doyle

Police officers rely on effective communication and feedback from the department police chief and commanders. Leaders may not choose the right course of action in the decision-making process, not because of existing *knowledge*, but from the *unknown*. The unknown is what one cannot see or observe. That which one cannot observe and receive feedback acts as the principal deterrent to effective leadership and decision-making. Enhanced communication allows leaders to see and observe by achieving a proper feedback loop.

CHAPTER FOCUS

Intelligence-Led Policing (ILP) helps reduce the unknown or information gaps, provides feedback, and enhances effective decision-making. The process of receiving and sharing criminal information provides reciprocal feedback opportunities. Police leaders cannot achieve successful prevention and intervention strategies without critical information, intelligence sharing, and collaboration. Unwillingness to share intelligence is a major obstacle to receiving appropriate and timely feedback.

This chapter focuses on strategic leadership, and communication feedback. Leadership vision requires feedback from diverse sources of human and technical information. Excellent communication is the primary means of organizing feedback, for developing vision and forecasting the future.

ILP offers opportunities to improve leadership communication, among police leaders, analysts, and agency members. When leaders share information, doors to the *unknown* become accessible through the feedback process. Excellent feedback may assist with sharing information, community partnerships and building bridges to external law enforcement agencies. Table 5-1 provides additional information on the chapter focus, and related concepts.

Table 5-1   Focus Points

	Vision and Direction	**Leadership and Goals**
Intelligence–Led Policing	❖ Envision the future ❖ Past is starting point ❖ Apply analytical skills ❖ Modify and share feedback ❖ Define vision statement ❖ Define ILP ❖ Lead up front	❖ Change, grow, and innovate ❖ Inspire a shared vision ❖ Enable others to act ❖ Role model, so others may follow ❖ Plan small wins that build commitment ❖ Encourage the heart ❖ Celebrate team accomplishments
	Johari Window Strategies	**Decision-Making Opportunities**
	❖ Leaders are candid ❖ Willingness to disclose self ❖ Avoid façade or hidden area ❖ Personal power in public area ❖ Gain access to blind area ❖ Gain access to unknown area ❖ Obtain behavior feedback	❖ Johari Window analysis ❖ Leadership applications ❖ Training applications ❖ Internal applications ❖ External applications ❖ Sharing intelligence ❖ Expand communication base

LEADERSHIP AND VISION

James Kouzes and Barry Posner offer a six-part challenge process for leaders: (1) Leaders search for challenging opportunities to change, grow, innovate, and improve; (2) They encourage risk taking and learning from mistakes; (3) They inspire and enlist others to support a shared vision for the future; (4) They enable others to act, fostering collaboration by promoting cooperative goals, building trust, and strengthening resolution; (5) They role-model, demonstrate alignment with values, and set positive examples for others to follow; and (6) They plan small initial wins that promote consistent progress, and build commitment. In addition, they encourage the heart by recognizing contributions to the success of every project, and celebrate team accomplishments. [1]

SENIOR LEADERSHIP VISION

Police senior leaders look to the future, more than middle managers and sergeants. ILP fosters the potential to estimate future trends, and implement appropriate remedial responses. Mission success depends on leadership's ability to communicate and forecast the future.

Vision is the thoughtful future analysis and planning that enables law enforcement agencies to develop a system, which forecasts the future with reasonable certainty. Vision originates from department officers, civilians, and local communities. The past is important as a starting point; however, ILP management philosophy, intelligence, and crime analysis lead the way to successful crime control strategies.

Vision derives from ILP analytical skills and an intuitive sense of the future. The successful execution of vision suggests that police leaders need to lead from the front lines, where the action is, not from a seated desk position. Once in the field, successful leaders accurately revise the vision to suit emerging developments. The leader's presence allows them to see, observe, modify, and share feedback from officers.

Policy written statements prepare leaders to move forward, with a vision for direction and sharing criminal intelligence, with officers and civilians. The mission statement is important as a guiding methodology; when leaders communicate and share information, it increases access to the unknown.

MISSION COMMUNICATION STATEMENT

One method of sharing vision is the mission definition statement. The statement forms the basis for the primary directorate to implement policy and direction. Law enforcement executives acknowledge the value of a well-defined mission definition, integrated into decisions, at every level of the department. The ILP mission definition and policy statements define shared acceptable attitudes, conduct, and performance standards. The mission statement provides feedback to every member of the police department.

For example, The Royal Canadian Mounted Police outlines their Intelligence-Led Policing definition: "Intelligence-Led Policing is a term that has only begun to gain currency in the last few years. For this reason, it lacks a single, overarching definition. Most would agree, however, that at its most fundamental, intelligence-led policing involves the collection and analysis of information to produce an intelligence end product designed to inform police decision-making at both the strategic and tactical levels. Intelligence serves as a guide to policing operations, rather than the reverse.

ILP is innovative and, by some standards, even radical, but predicated on the notion that a principal police task is to prevent and detect crime rather than simply react to it.

Intelligence-Led Policing may hold the key to our survival. Whatever form it takes, intelligence-led policing requires commitment" [2]

Larger police agencies in the United States may find the best way to communicate and receive adequate feedback is to formulate an intelligence mission statement. Below is an example of an intelligence mission statement for police departments that have an intelligence unit.

The _____ Department's Criminal Intelligence Unit will collect and analyze information on individuals and groups who are suspected of being involved in _____ and will provide this information to the chief executive officer for crime prevention and decision-making purposes. [3]

For agencies that do not have an intelligence unit but want to adopt an intelligence mission to support intelligence-led policing, the mission statement could be that given below:

The _____ Department's intelligence mission is to actively participate in intelligence sharing initiatives by providing information and receiving intelligence products that will be used to enhance the department's ability to prevent and deter crime while abiding by legal constraints and being sensitive to the public's rights and privacy. [4]

While there are many dimensions and mission definitions for ILP, each jurisdiction will eventually find its own path. Some may incorporate ILP as a management style or prefer the sub-discipline of intelligence analysis, which targets criminal organizations and criminals. Some jurisdictions may choose to have a crime analysis focus. Regardless of department or jurisdiction size, the need to address intelligence, crime analysis, and information sharing remains.

JOHARI WINDOW: FEEDBACK AND SHARING

The Johari Window Model offers opportunities to examine leadership, training, and ILP from communication and feedback perspectives. Two psychologists, Joseph Luft and Harry Ingham, conceived the "Window Model" as means of giving and receiving information feedback. [5] This Model offers police applications in leadership, training, and intelligence operations. Refer to Table 5-2 for examples and Johari Window concepts.

Table 5-2   Overview of Johari Window

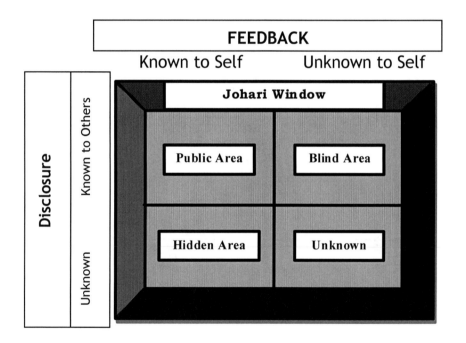

Source: Adapted from: Joseph Luft, Group Process: An Introduction to Group Dynamics (California: National Press Books, 2ed., 1984).

STRATEGIC LEADERSHIP STRATEGIES

The "Johari Window" encourages the expansion of shared intelligence and achieving accurate feedback, but requires personal risks for leaders. The ILP management/leadership style requires candid leaders who establish trust and mutual respect. Excellent leadership suggests information exchanges, rather than one-way dialogues, not involving feedback.

Feedback provides information concerning how organization members feel about and perceive leadership behaviors. Open leaders who are willing to disclose, encourage opportunities to understand how others feel about their leadership. Stone-faced leaders deny followers opportunities to disclose feelings because of poor approachability, the façade, and the absence of leader feedback.

The Johari Window offers leaders the possibility of expanding personal power. Feedback is the reaction of officers and civilians (feelings and perceptions), thereby informing leaders about how his/her behaviors affect them. Leaders equipped with crucial feedback are in the best position to be effective decision-makers. Candid leaders amplify communication and feedback, enhancing follower information and support.

The lack of feedback is a statement in itself; it is a silent announcement about the leader's effectiveness. Poor reciprocal communication isolates and places the leader outside the informal communication loop. Leaders, who hide behind their façade, or remain silent and do not take risks, fail to communicate and remain isolated. Open leaders who ask for feedback and disclose information about self, position themselves to influence others.

The willingness to self-disclose affects multiple relationships in police organizations. Disclosure and openness works in a variety of organizations, group situations, or with individuals. Communication techniques do not require disclosing the intimate details of one's life. The leader should avoid over-disclosure, damaging respect or status. Sharing essential information is target specific; however, opportunities may unfold for expressing personal feelings.

The goal is to obtain information not known to self, but known to others. The opportunity to gain information from the *blind spot*, and *unknown* portions of the four Johari quadrants, proves essential to successful decision-making. Sharing information from the *hidden area* (sometimes referred to as the façade) of the leader provides greater understanding for subordinates to follow and share feedback. Leadership self-disclosure encourages rapport and trust relationships with individual officers, civilians, informal groups and the police organization.

Peering into the Johari Window allows police leaders to expose the façade or the *hidden area* (the issues others do not know about the leader). The purpose is to gain sufficient knowledge about the *blind spot and unknown* (the issues the leaders do not know about). Refer to table 5-3 for examples of Johari Window hidden and open concepts.

Thus, shrinking the windowpanes or quadrants around the *blind spot* ultimately offers insight into the *unknown area* and related issues. Insight provides opportunities to communicate, seize initiatives, and problem-solve with appropriate strategic and tactical remedies. Refer to Table 5-4 for an example of the blind spot area and "unknown" Johari Window quadrants.

Table 5-3   Johari Window - Hidden and Open Areas

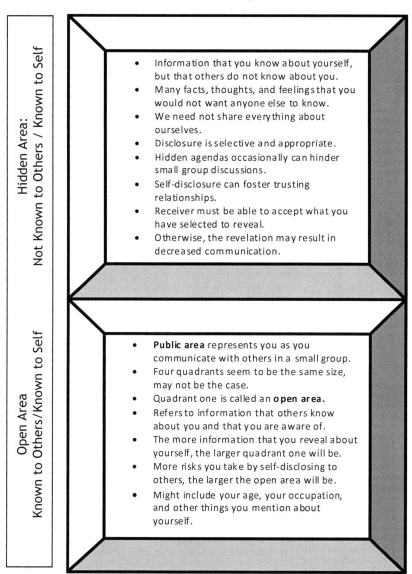

Hidden Area:
Not Known to Others / Known to Self

- Information that you know about yourself, but that others do not know about you.
- Many facts, thoughts, and feelings that you would not want anyone else to know.
- We need not share everything about ourselves.
- Disclosure is selective and appropriate.
- Hidden agendas occasionally can hinder small group discussions.
- Self-disclosure can foster trusting relationships.
- Receiver must be able to accept what you have selected to reveal.
- Otherwise, the revelation may result in decreased communication.

Open Area
Known to Others/Known to Self

- **Public area** represents you as you communicate with others in a small group.
- Four quadrants seem to be the same size, may not be the case.
- Quadrant one is called an **open area.**
- Refers to information that others know about you and that you are aware of.
- The more information that you reveal about yourself, the larger quadrant one will be.
- More risks you take by self-disclosing to others, the larger the open area will be.
- Might include your age, your occupation, and other things you mention about yourself.

Source: Adapted from: Joseph Luft, Group Process: An Introduction to Group Dynamics (California: National Press Books, 1970).

Table 5-4   Johari Window – Blind and Unknown Areas

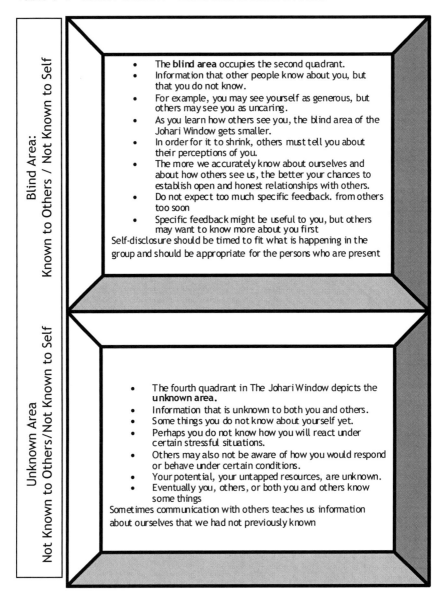

- The **blind area** occupies the second quadrant.
- Information that other people know about you, but that you do not know.
- For example, you may see yourself as generous, but others may see you as uncaring.
- As you learn how others see you, the blind area of the Johari Window gets smaller.
- In order for it to shrink, others must tell you about their perceptions of you.
- The more we accurately know about ourselves and about how others see us, the better your chances to establish open and honest relationships with others.
- Do not expect too much specific feedback. from others too soon
- Specific feedback might be useful to you, but others may want to know more about you first

Self-disclosure should be timed to fit what is happening in the group and should be appropriate for the persons who are present

- The fourth quadrant in The Johari Window depicts the **unknown area.**
- Information that is unknown to both you and others.
- Some things you do not know about yourself yet.
- Perhaps you do not know how you will react under certain stressful situations.
- Others may also not be aware of how you would respond or behave under certain conditions.
- Your potential, your untapped resources, are unknown.
- Eventually you, others, or both you and others know some things

Sometimes communication with others teaches us information about ourselves that we had not previously known

Blind Area: Known to Others / Not Known to Self

Unknown Area Not Known to Others/Not Known to Self

Source: Adapted from: Joseph Luft, Group Process: An Introduction to Group Dynamics (California: National Press Books, 1970).

The *open space* is the key to personal power, the quadrant, or windowpane where leaders have opportunities to be authentic and open. Openness allows for the exchange of what one knows about self and what others know. This form of personal leadership interaction and risk taking invites the necessary feedback for effective decision-making.

Leaders unwilling to share the *hidden* or *façade* window-pane and keep secrets do not receive proper feedback. The returning flow of information or feedback data helps shrink the blind area and unknown. Refer to table 5-5 for feedback and Johari Window concepts.

Table 5-5   Johari Window Feedback Opportunities

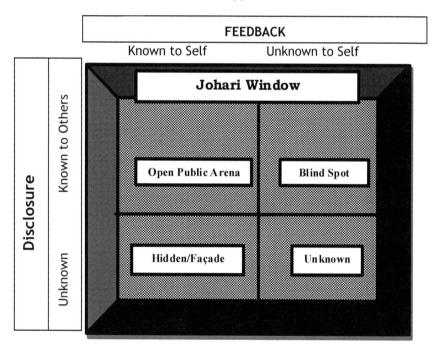

Source: Adapted from: Joseph Luft, Group Process: An Introduction to Group Dynamics (California: National Press Books, 1970).

INTELLIGENCE LEADERSHIP OPPORTUNITIES

Johari opportunities for effective communication and feedback improve criminal information management. Strategic and tactical opportunities result when the *blind spot* and *unknown* panes shrink, creating new vision requirements. Vision requirements are particularly important in counter terrorism, global enterprise crime and organized drug trafficking operations.

Why is the Johari Window an excellent intelligence strategic and tactical approach to critical thinking? The answer: communication is the very substance of ILP management. The Johari solution enhances intelligence information strategies and eliminates major communication impediments. Information sharing and feedback provide intelligence concerning the *blind spot* for leaders, and opens the door to the *unknown*.

TRAINING APPLICATIONS

Training concerning ILP strategies is of paramount importance to communicating the new management model. Excellent leadership requires superior training. ILP success depends on excellent training, open communication, and feedback. The Johari Window is a superior training medium for introducing ILP concepts.

Communication may involve verbal or nonverbal cues and learner perceptions. There is no way of verifying whether the learning has taken place, without adequate feedback concerning the ILP learning modality. Leadership determines how the learners perceive them, through the feedback process. Personal disclosure assists in modifying the learning process. Learners have opportunities to express how they feel about the learning process.

Instructor/leader evaluations at the end of the training, are behind schedule to influence the currently affected audience. Therefore, ILP feedback (reaction from the learners) needs to occur during the learning process. In addition, the impact is substantial, once instructors receive input about self-disclosing behaviors from learners.

The Johari Window is an excellent theoretical model that enhances intelligence-training opportunities. When instructors/leaders establish real-time feedback and communication, learning takes place in an efficient and effective manner. The applications are endless if the instructor/leader's mind is open to the opportunities, and insight of sharing information.

INTELLIGENCE FIELD OPERATIONS APPLICATIONS

Leadership training concerning intelligence, crime analysis, and technology functions are prerequisites to understanding ILP requirements. Peering through the four quadrants or windowpanes of the Johari Window provides a telescope for ILP intelligence management systems. Leadership participation in intelligence operations is the deciding factor in the equation of communication, and intelligence operations.

The logical extension to critical and analytical thinking opens Johari Window applications to field intelligence staff and field operations. ILP and the Johari Window are consistent with excellent communication, theory, and practice. The basic four quadrants frame the need for police executives, commanders, and supervisors to have consistent and persistent communication with analysts. Police leaders need to reveal (avoid the façade or hidden area) and encourage feedback to access the blind and unknown areas, from an intelligence perspective. Refer to Table 5-6 for an example of Johari Window intelligence applications.

Table 5-6   Johari Window and Intelligence Opportunities

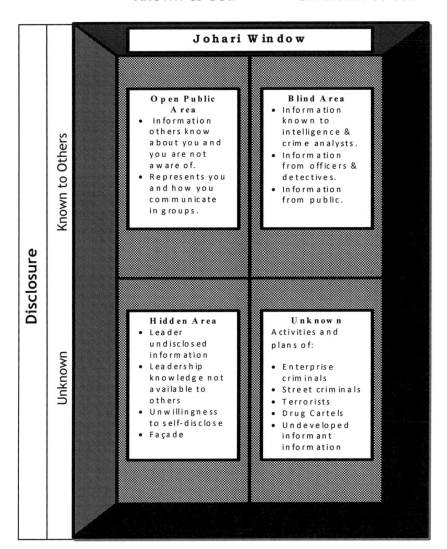

Source: Adapted from: Joseph Luft, Group Process: An Introduction to Group Dynamics (California: National Press Books, 1970).

JOHARI INTELLIGENCE APPLICATIONS

The Johari Window turned externally can assist in obtaining accurate information and criminal intelligence. The feedback may prove essential to police strategic and tactical applications, focused on criminal environments. Information or raw data may lead to effective analysis, and confirmable criminal information. There are distinct differences between information and intelligence. Refer to Figure 5-1 for differences concerning information and intelligence.

Figure 5-1   Illustrative Differences: Information and Intelligence

Intelligence			
Analyst report: conclusions about criminal behavior based on integrated analysis	Analysis of enterprise crime or terrorism trends	Forecast about potential criminal events: analysts use past experience	Estimate of person's income from criminal enterprise based on a market & trafficking analysis

Information			
Observations by: investigators, surveillance teams, citizens	Details: banking, investments, credit reports, financial	Travel: mode, names, itinerary, date, time, locations, etc.	Licensing: vehicle operators and professional, of all forms
Criminal history and driving records	Offense reporting records	Statements by: informants, witnesses, suspects	Registration information: vehicles, watercraft, aircraft

Adapted from: Global Intelligence Working Group. Criminal Intelligence for the Chief Executive. A Training Program for the Chief Executive, 2004.

The Johari Window and the intelligence cycle are overlapping intelligence requirements in the pursuit of information and feedback. The overlapping intelligence cycle and Johari qualities offer a unique method for verifying information content. Basic information provides the raw data for collection, planning, and direction. The transformation requires analyst expertise coupled with the intelligence cycle.

COMMUNICATION SOURCES: FEEDBACK

The centralization and coordination of criminal information and computer technology offer improved real-time feedback communication. Time is the critical element in unfolding tactical situations and criminal investigations. Criminal intelligence that is real-time or near-term, offers rapid solutions.

Police leaders, detectives, and police street officers are significant elements of successful law enforcement. Computer technology only supports their efforts, and obtains the necessary technical feedback and criminal information. The following NYPD program is an example of how real-time intelligence improves communication, feedback, strategic, and tactical intelligence, thereby, giving leaders the decisive advantage.

CASE EXAMPLE: NYPD's REAL TIME CRIME CENTER

The New York City Police Department (NYPD) Real Time Crime Center demonstrates the classic example of computer technology and improved feedback communication. The NYPD "Fast Synthesis" approach supports short time or immediate police investigative tactical operations and current intelligence requirements. Deputy Chief Joseph D'Amico, authored segments of the following case example. The article originally appeared in the Chief of Police.

REAL TIME CENTER APPLICATIONS

NYPD's Real Time Crime Center (RTCC) staff makes sense of the massive amount of raw information available to them, from the details of the million emergency calls received each year to the millions of parole files maintained by the state of New York. For its part, IBM Global Services built out the RTCC's data warehousing capability using IBM's DB2 Universal database software.

The RTCC includes three key elements: the data warehouse, the data-analysis capabilities, and the "data wall," part of the nerve center of the RTCC. In a room lined with 18 Mitsubishi screens projecting images from around the city, dozens of analysts and detectives tap away at workstations to try to glean clues from vast stores of data. Network redundancy protects our communications capabilities in the event of a natural or man-made disaster.

RTCC's data-analysis capabilities are truly staggering. The new system can comb through 120 million New York City criminal complaints, arrests and 911 call records dating back a decade, five million criminal records and parole files maintained by the state of New York, and more than 31 million records of crimes committed nationwide. Refer to Figure 6-3 RTCC Software Arsenal for additional information.

IMMEDIATE RETURNS

The ability to search multiple data sources at once, a feature known as federated searching, can reveal clues that in the past, even the NYPD's most diligent detectives would not pursue, simply due to the amount of documentation they struggle to examine or the connections they would have to make via extensive cross-referencing of records.

Figure 5-2   RTCC Software Arsenal to Analyze Information

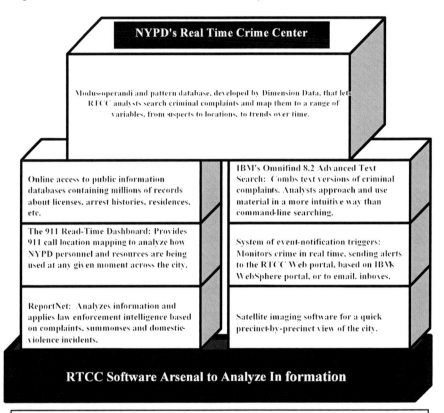

Source Adapted From: Joseph D. D'Amico, "NYPD's Real Time Center," The Chief of Police (July/August 2006), 23-27.

Using a federated search, a detective can enter a query, which then "crawls" through the 311 and 911 records, case management records, public databases, and so on, collecting related information as it goes. In addition, the RTCC recently rolled out new search capacities that let users search on multiple keywords as well as a feature that utilizes graphical clues (a red Honda, a suspect who's bald, etc.) to help police officers and detectives make quick visual connections among various elements of a crime.

NYPD GOAL: STOP CRIME TRENDS

These search capabilities would help one of NYPD's main goals; stopping crimes before they become trends. For example, not long ago there was a rash of thefts of expensive halogen lights on cars. Search features in the RTCC would help the NYPD detective not only notice a crime pattern, but observe certain locations or times of day in which halogen lights were most likely to be stolen. In addition, which suspects were most likely to do the stealing?

The collective clues gathered from four or five seemingly disparate crimes may yield the final piece of information that cracks the case and leads police officers to a criminal. RTCC's data mining abilities facilitate these collective clue connections easily. Technology in the RTCC helps law enforcement personnel understand the patterns that indicate trends are forming and strategize on how to best attack these problems.

> Source: Joseph D. D'Amico, "NYPD's Real Time Center," The Chief of Police (July/August 2006), 23-27.

The feedback from technology opens the door to improved communication. The NYPD's Real Time Center permits rapid access to pertinent raw data that opens the realm of the blind spot and unknown. The software recovers information that was formally stored in the minds of detectives. The vast data of the present form of ILP is beyond the human memory capacity.

FOCUS POINTS: STRATEGIC LEADERSHIP

Police senior leaders excel when prepared with the best estimate of possible criminal and natural disaster situations. The ILP and strategic planning process, along with informed leadership, spotlights future strategic requirements. Timely leadership preparedness is important; however, accurate future assessment is even more imperative.

Accurate data provides opportunities to prepare for future events, and intervene in a timely manner. Vision helps establish direction for others to follow. The vision statement serves as the origination point for defining the ILP mission statement, and provides direction and leadership strategies for reaching a desired destination. Defining both originates from police officers, civilians and community needs.

Successful leaders share inspired vision so others may follow. Excellent police leadership requires changing and adapting to community needs and the criminal environment. This means acknowledging successful strategies and making necessary adjustments to initiate innovative strategies and tactics, to accommodate rapidly changing events. Recent realities include homeland security, terrorism, and natural disasters.

Superior leaders role model and demonstrate successful behaviors. They provide resources in a timely mode, enabling officers to respond appropriately. Leadership praises officer and civilian victories, and successful team efforts. Rewarding accomplishments builds morale, and enlists others to join the mission commitment.

The blending of the Johari Window and ILP analytical skills offers a systematic structure to communicate and receive essential feedback. Candid leaders, willing to disclose information, are in the best position to receive adequate feedback. Successful ILP and new leadership requirements include a willingness to: (1) self-disclose, (2) avoid the façade, (3) build trust, (4) accept feedback from others, and (4) learn about themselves.

Johari opportunities are many and offer an excellent telescope for obtaining maximum information: (1) The leadership applications are obvious and abundant for improved communication and feedback, (2) The related area of training is essential to sell and explain the ILP management philosophy, and (3) Training provides opportunities for learner clarification, communication, and feedback. The twin process of leadership and training opportunities are vital components for understanding and acceptance of strategic innovations.

Internal applications of the Johari Window run parallel to the intelligence cycle and sharing of criminal and related information. The value of the model focuses on collaboration, collation, and dissemination of intelligence information. External applications in the area of verification, targeting analysis, and timely strategic and tactical interventions, unfold with the proper feedback.

The intelligence cycle is the primary means of validating intelligence, the Johari window is only a source of obtaining feedback. Analysts have the ability to verify that communication because the mid-cycle adjustments overlap other related data collection processes, and multiple analysis cycles provide the best opportunity for actionable criminal intelligence.

CONCLUSION

Successful leaders access the public area, and use it to launch admittance to the blind and unknown areas. The current sphere of criminal activities, terrorist conspiracies, and natural disasters mandate innovative intelligence requirements. The new ILP strategic leadership formula employs information sharing and benefits from technology to achieve excellence in fighting crime, terrorism, and natural disasters.

ENDNOTES

1. James Kouzes and Barry Posner, The Leadership Challenge: How to Keep Getting Extraordinary Things Done (California, San Francisco: Josey-Bass, 1996).

2. Royal Canadian Mounted Police, Criminal Intelligence Program: (http://www.Rcmp.ca/crim/intelligence_e.htm).

3. Godfrey, E. Drexel, and Don R. Harris, U.S. Department of Justice, Office of Criminal Justice Assistance, Basic Elements of Intelligence, LEAA (Washington, DC: GPO, 1971): 21.

4. Marilyn Peterson, U.S. Department of Justice, Bureau of Justice Administration., Intelligence-Led Policing: The New Intelligence Architecture, (Washington DC: GPO, 2005): 16.

5. Joseph Lufts, Group Process: An Introduction to Group Dynamics (California: National Press Books, 1970).

CHAPTER 6
Leadership and Planning

It has long been an axiom of mine that the little things are infinitely the more important.

— Sir Arthur Conan Doyle

When it comes to crime prevention and intervention, little things are important. Little crimes lead to big crimes. When communities fail to address the little things, criminals feel they own the neighborhood or territory. Small crimes like "broken windows" and graffiti, when ignored, create appearances that the police and community do not care about their neighborhoods. [1] If those beliefs remain unchallenged, frightened citizens permit criminals to prevail.

When the police do not address little things, it gives criminals permission to rape, pillage, and commit a whole host of crimes. Police agencies publicly address the little things, and follow-up on the big things, with Intelligence-Led Policing (ILP), intelligence, and crime analysis strategies. Excellent planning supports the police mission and related police operations.

CHAPTER FOCUS

The chapter focus is on police planning, leadership, and its relationship to strategic and tactical field tactics. In addition, the chapter will discuss police planning, timing or temporal factors, and police fusion centers. The leadership connection will receive specific attention, along with targeting street criminals, current intelligence, and tactical strategies.

The chapter focus will center on planning synchronization and centralized planning reform. Specific planning topics include: (1) synoptic planning process, (2) emergency operations planning (EOP), (3) incident action planning (IAP), and (4) planning articulation. The consolidation and coordination of ILP, intelligence analysis, and crime analysis planning is essential to successful policing outcomes. This chapter builds on the preceding chapters and related readings, figures, and tables.

Table 6-1   Chapter focus

	Planning Synchronization	Centralized
Intelligence-Led Policing	❖ Police decision makers ❖ Intelligence coordination ❖ Intelligence analysis ❖ Crime analysis ❖ Community oriented policing ❖ Problem oriented policing ❖ CompStat operations	❖ ILP management ❖ Defining planning ❖ Planning articulation ❖ Staff coordination ❖ Synoptic planning ❖ Emergency operations planning ❖ Incident action planning
	Johari Window Strategies	**Decision-Making Opportunities**
	❖ Define the problem ❖ Suspense date ❖ Location ❖ Officer allocations ❖ Mission responsibilities ❖ Operational requirements ❖ Staff coordination	❖ Target-centered planning ❖ Crime triangle ❖ Fusion centers ❖ Current intelligence ❖ Short-term intelligence ❖ Immediate intelligence ❖ Real time intelligence

POLICE PLANNING

Planning offers the best pathway to effective decision making. The failure to plan increases opportunities for future problems, which could be avoided. "Planning is thinking about the future, thinking about what we want the future to be and thinking about what we need to do now to achieve it." [2] Effective planning can accomplish the following: (1) improve problem analysis, (2) provide better information for decision making, (3) help clarify goals, objectives and priorities, (4) result in more effective allocation of resources, (5) improve department coordination and cooperation, (6) improve program performance, (7) give the police department a clear sense of direction, (8) provide the opportunity for greater public support, and (9) increase the commitment of police and civilian personnel. [3]

Strategic long-term planning is global in nature, and offers a quality research point of view. There is ample opportunity to collect, analyze and verify the accuracy of strategic data. Strategic intelligence primarily identifies the strengths, weaknesses, opportunities, and threat analysis of selected targets. This form of strategic planning examines capabilities, plans, intentions, and potential criminal opportunities.

Strategic goals consist of scanning for criminals, and their organization(s). The basic qualities of strategic planning include: (1) global considerations, systems oriented, and (2) criminal/terrorists capabilities. Strategic planning includes advanced statistical analysis, and large scope problems. Multiple long-term targets are expansive and set the stage for qualitative and quantitative intelligence analysis. Strategic or long-term research analysis applies to international drug smuggling trends, financial systems, and product diversification.

The term *operational intelligence planning* has mixed connotations and applications. In the general sense, it focuses on capabilities and intentions, and identifies threats, planning, and execution of specific operations. A predictive component supports long-term or strategic investigations concerning multiple similar targets. The primary focus is on identifying, targeting, detecting, and intervening in criminal offenses. [4] Therefore, operational intelligence is a specific form of strategic intelligence planning.

PLANNING STRATEGIES: SYNCHRONIZATION

The little things or details in the planning process can make a significant difference in successful tactical outcomes. Skilled execution of tactical operations depends on carefully planned details coming together. Police leaders generate opportunities for superior crime fighting when staff planning is centralized. Moreover, the synchronization of the planning process, promotes opportunities for successful tactical outcomes.

An overlapping planning relationship supports strategic intelligence analysis, and problem-oriented policing (POP). Problem-oriented policing has a long-term view that focuses on community oriented policing (COP) strategies. The long-term considerations are similar to strategic intelligence analysis: (1) capabilities of criminals and organizations, and (2) related community problems.

COP and POP apply statistically incident-based reporting, in the search for broadly based targets. Strategic intelligence involves scanning for broadly based targets. The POP and SARA models are similar to the strategic intelligence model. POP differs in the use of citizen strategies: (1) community feedback, (2) partnerships, and (3) Neighborhood Watch participation. Refer to Table 6-2 for a comparison of strategic long-term research, problem-oriented policing, crime analysis, and CompStat requirements.

Table 6-2   Intelligence-led Policing Planning Synchronization

Intelligence-led Policing	Synchronization of Strategic Intelligence, POP, Crime Analysis and CompStat	
	Strategic Intelligence Rigors research analysis Strategic view Temporal considerations: • Global • Capabilities Scanning criminals and criminal organization(s) Strategic planning Systems oriented Advanced statistical methods Long term multiple targets Broadly defined targets Large scope problems	**Problem-Oriented Policing (POP)** Long term view Community oriented policing strategies Temporal considerations • Capabilities • Community problems SARA planning model: scanning, analysis, response, and assessment Partnership oriented • Neighborhood Watch • Community feedback • Statistical and incident-based Informal and formal community patrons Broadly defined targets
	Crime Analysis Current tactical research Fusion center-oriented Applied research Temporal considerations: • Short-term • Immediate Based on crime data Investigative objectives Tactical and field oriented Short-term and immediate target(s) Tactical Applications	**COMPSTAT Planning** Current tactical research Fusion center-oriented Applied research Temporal consideration: • Short-term • Immediate Based on crime data Investigative objectives Tactical and field oriented Short-term and immediate target(s) Tactical applications

CENTRALIZED PLANNING

Planning bridges the gap between where the agency is presently, and where officials want police ILP services to go. The planning process helps identify and select successful methods to achieve positive goals and objectives. Defining how the police agency will reach their desired destination involves an excellent analytical planning process.

Planning involves determining target needs and a basic definition of the problem. The following criteria are essential to the planning process: (1) suspense date for accomplishment, (2) location, (3) officer allocations, (4) those held responsible for the mission, and (5) mission operational requirements.

PLANNING ARTICULATION

Planning and ILP management have mutual goals and objectives; therefore, both are not mutually exclusive. Strategic planning cannot exist in a vacuum, without ILP management of criminal information and mutual feedback. ILP intelligence analysis and feedback permits strategic planning to function effectively. Moreover, quality coordination with tactical planners avoids counter-productive outcomes in high profile strategic cases.

Large metropolitan law enforcement agencies require seven points of planning linkage: (1) police decision makers and central strategic planning, (2) intelligence-led policing, (3) intelligence analysis, (4) crime analysis, (5) community-oriented policing, (6) problem-oriented policing and (7) CompStat operations. Police leaders serve as central points of coordination and key decision makers.

The essence of the traditional synoptic planning model, is future decision-making. Centralized planning forms the foundation for critical thinking, and strategic intelligence analysis. ILP and intelligence analysis can support: (1) problem-oriented policing and SARA planning, (2) CompStat and operations analysis, (3) emergency operations planning, (4) incident action planning, and (5) evaluation. The synoptic planning model forms a natural conduit for the consolidation of these mutual planning foundations.

Figure 6-1   Six Points of Planning Linkage

**Intelligence-Led
Policing**

**Strategic
Planning**

**Intelligence
Analysis**

**Crime
Analysis**

**Problem-
Oriented
Policing**

Decision Makers

**Compstat
Operations**

**Community-
Oriented
Policing**

Synoptic Strategic Planning

The Department of Justice recommends the following eleven-step planning sequence as described in the traditional synoptic planning model:

(1) prepare for planning;

(2) describe the present situation;

(3) develop projections;

(4) consider alternative future states;

(5) identify the problems;

(6) set goals;

(7) identify alternative courses of action;

(8) select preferred alternatives;

(9) plan for implementation;

(10) implement plans; and

(11) monitor and evaluate progress. [5]

The cycle repeats and other planning and evaluation strategies are incorporated.

The connection and coordination points between strategic intelligence analysis and the synoptic planning model merits consolidation and centralization. This centralized planning operation would take the long-view strategic picture. Moreover, a centralized strategic planning process interfaces with crime analysis, intelligence analysis, CompStat, and tactical planning. In addition, a valuable spin-off contribution to tactical, emergency, and operational planning becomes plausible.

EMERGENCY OPERATIONS PLANNING (EOP)

EOP planning focuses on developing an operational document, which incorporates a written response plan for emergency operations. The threat assessment process identifies vulnerable targets and potential terrorists or other emergency responses. Strategic plans list interagency responsibilities, the chain of command, and logistical support. Basic planning concepts have application to many communities. However, individual community adaptations are the individualizations of the basic model.

Occasionally, some agencies may refer to the EOP as a comprehensive emergency management plan. The coordination of police, fire, and emergency services receive special emphasis; however, military coordination is a component of the planning process. The emphasis is on agency liaison coordination, front-end planning, and logistics.

The terrorist incident action and tactical response plan is an essential element of EOP operations. The plan incorporates a model approach and unified command similar to military operations. The basic organization includes: (1) planning, (2) management and administration, (3) personnel and operations, and (4) logistics.

INCIDENT ACTION PLANNING (IAP)

The incident action plan is a standard course of action, relevant to a real-time possible scenario. Written tactical plans address serious incidents; less significant incidents do not require written documentation. IAP applies to a specific operational time, and in some instances, the incident planning process may unfold informally as the changing emergency scenario continues. An impromptu briefing may take place in the field that includes a brief outline of protocols, and mission objectives. Extended missions, over time, may require formal briefings on a prearranged schedule format.

Tactical or terrorist scenarios require an immediate response; operations and tactics may be spontaneous. Advanced planning and rehearsals set the foundation for forceful tactics, and swift execution. Planning support incorporates back-step planning procedures for personnel requirements, and logistical supplies. Planning, training, and field training set the foundation for successful operations.

EVALUATION AND ASSESSMENT

Evaluation is necessary to redirect the leadership process, and help reorient the planning process. It answers three crucial questions: (1) Has the agency arrived? (2) Where is the agency now? (3) Where does the agency go from here? It provides the map for developing strategic goals and objectives;

furthermore, it provides plans for directing officers to new specific tasks.

The evaluator gleans information that guides the leadership in a decision-making process. The process reduces uncertainty and assists police officers in emergency responses. Lessons learned in the after-action briefing, form the basis for revising the planning process, and changing goals, objectives, and procedures.

TIMING IS EVERYTHING

Current planning focuses on law enforcement activities, which mandate immediate actions and responses. Police tactical situations may be crucial; therefore, intelligence must unfold in a timely and reactive manner. Current intelligence positively connects to crime analysis and CompStat operations. Police operations tend to require current intelligence analyses, since tactical and emergency frameworks serve as dominant modes of operation. Timing is essential; intelligence requirements that support the tactical mode necessitate fluency.

CompStat and tactical scenarios require current tactical intelligence and applied strategies. Crime data requirements and time considerations include: (1) short-term intelligence for plan execution, and (2) immediate tactical scenarios. Police target(s) are generally short-term, immediate, tactical, and current intelligence analysis oriented. The analysis is database and crime data oriented with investigative and enforcement objectives. Current intelligence addresses tactical indications/criminal intentions, and warnings.

CompStat analytical support has current intelligence and real-time requirements that parallel the need for crime analysis. Police agencies have an excellent opportunity to coordinate, and plan current intelligence requirements with fusion centers. Crime analysis and CompStat are ideally suited for fusion center support.

FUSION CENTERS

Police fusion centers may offset fast responses through planned coordination and liaison activities. Fusion centers correlate and analyze intelligence data to assist police commanders, officers, and detectives in the tactical planning process. The service provides coordination points for local, regional, state, tribal, and federal law enforcement agencies.

Fusion centers search and gather information from multiple databases; analysis-generated products support law enforcement planning, and on-going field scenarios. Criminal information supports anti-terrorism activities and other crime related issues.

FAST SYNTHESIS

Incoming data requires a fast synthesis when supporting short-time or in-progress police tactical operations. This short-fuse synthesis or fusion refers to tactical scenarios, where a swift estimate of the situation becomes necessary. Hasty data analysis requires developing an accurate tactical picture, analytical documentation and field support.

The fusion center and watch coordination of participating agencies, permits a collective response to crime and terrorism. A total team effort is superior to unconnected law enforcement agencies, which stand alone. The collation of generated tactical criminal intelligence, identifies specific threats, potential offenders, criminal and terrorist organizations.

FUSION CENTER ADVANTAGES

Fusion center articulation provides an enhanced way to react and allocate resources. Associated law enforcement agencies may develop: (1) real-time intelligence requirements, (2) finished analytical products, (3) preeminent methods of response(s), and (4) influence leadership decision-making. Enhanced situational awareness improves coordination with enforcement agencies.

INTELLIGENCE CYCLE TARGETING

The Criminal Intelligence Cycle prepares leaders to move forward, with a vision for direction, and sharing criminal intelligence with officers and civilians. The intelligence cycle is important as a guiding methodology; when leaders communicate and share information, access to the unknown increases.

The intelligence cycle is the primary means for obtaining and confirming feedback from the criminal world. Three basic steps include: (1) *define the intelligence problem*, (2) *identify the target*, and (3) *define the collection plan*. Refer to Figure 6-2 for an example of the intelligence cycle, which incorporates many feedback loops.

The intelligence cycle reinforces the *targeting, communication*, and *feedback* process. The cycle is not a complete cycle, but provides many feedback cycles of information for targeting. The loop runs continuously and subject to change and revision, because the criminal threat is dynamic. The intelligence cycle requires adjustments over time.

Figure 6-2   Intelligence Cycle

The intelligence cycle does fully meet the basic requirements of the linear process. The loop is not complete after
running through basic steps. The cycle is a social communications and information sharing process. Teamwork requires
the collaboration and cooperation of analysts, police decision-
makers, investigators, and police officers.

TARGETING COORDINATION

Defining the target and related intelligence process requires coordination and team effort. Defining the strategic and tactical picture is a pinpointing strategy. The process begins with a statement of the problem, and defines the analytical purpose. ILP provides the centralized guidance and management coordination for the targeting process.

TARGETING PROCESS

Targeting criminals and their organizations provides direction for police responses. Career criminals have the highest priority for the allocation of police personnel, and logistical resources. A target-rich criminal environment exists. Therefore, targeting the most dangerous criminals first and focusing on cases that offer quick solutions, becomes a priority.

Criminals who commit minor crimes are important because they degrade the quality of life for neighborhood residents. Police targeting operations must deal with high profile crimes, and citizen fear of crime. High quality targets are important; however, citizens continue to define routine quality of life crimes as significant. Refer to Figure 6-3 for an example of targeting information, selection, and evaluation.

TARGET-CENTRIC APPROACH

ILP and intelligence analysis provide products for target planning, and identification. Intelligence analysis and crime analysis present ideal opportunities for police leaders to conduct successful police CompStat, or other tactical operations. Senior leaders and middle managers approve plans for timely deployment and execution. Targets may include person(s), place(s), organization(s) or other criminal targets.

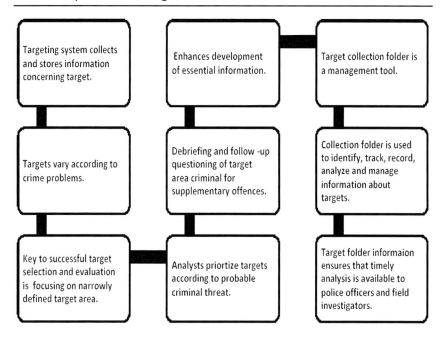

Figure 6-3   Targeting Information: Selection and Evaluation

A target-centric approach or objective-oriented intelligence process provides a model for targeting. The goal is to define a collective image of the target, which describes its components. The target offers participants information to perform their area of responsibility. Then, participants are in the best position to contribute and allocate resources. In addition, contributors define and create an accurate target representation or picture. [6]

Once the target is in place and the problem defined and assessed, the planning process moves forward. The centralized planning process is ideally suited to coordination and synchronization procedures. The target-centered approach allows others to join the planning process. The crime triangle is a means to focus on the target planning process. Centralized planning and coordination avoids conflict and maximizes the bringing together of strategic and tactical planning operations. The case study is a hypothetical example that illustrates the advantage of centralized planning.

CRIME TRIANGLE

A crime cannot occur without three elements that form the crime triangle: offender, victim and location. Identifying the basic elements of investigation: who, what, when, where, how, and why remain essential tasks when examining the crime triangle. The more crime analysts and detectives examine these variables, the more likely successful intervention and prevention will prevail. [7]

Crime occurs when a likely offender and suitable target come together in time and place. This is especially the case when capable guardians are not present. This model makes no distinction between a human victim and an inanimate target. Both opportunities can meet the offender's purpose or objective. Moreover, the model defines a capable guardian in terms of both human actors and security devices. This human formula led to the original problem analysis triangle with the three sides representing the offender, the target, and the location. Identifying partners and guardians opens the door to problem-oriented policing partnerships. [8]

ANALYSIS RESPONSES

Officers must understand the actions and interactions between offenders, victims, and the crime scene, before developing appropriate responses. Criminal intelligence information gathered in crime prevention surveys, serves as the foundation for this analysis. However, the intelligence process also includes analysis and dissemination of criminal information.

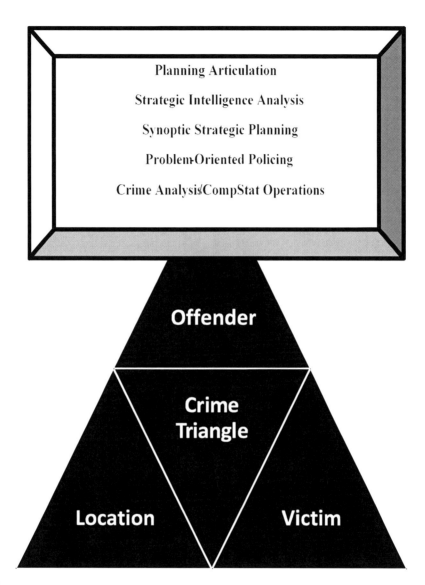

Figure 6-4   Crime Triangle

SPATIAL ANALYSIS

Spatial analysis generally focuses on a small geographical area, and includes physical, demographic, and crime history characteristics. Blocking out neighborhood areas on a map, that have a frequency of crime occurrences, shows where most illegal acts occur, and subsequently, targets the locations and levels of crime intensity. The crime analyst then applies the techniques of spatial analysis and crime templating.

Criminals do not move randomly through neighborhoods– a predictable pattern usually exists. A criminal who is motivated to commit crimes uses cues to locate, identify, and target sites and hot spots. Experience provides offenders with serial cues associated with environmental opportunities and risks. For example, familiarity with a neighborhood reinforces criminal patterns, a process often referred to as cognitive mapping or mental imaging. Consequently, offenders plan potential crimes and make decisions based on template information. [9]

Designated hot spots provide criminals with mental images for safe havens, places where criminals feel they can commit crimes with less chance of detection. Microanalysis of criminal behavior links criminal conduct to geography. This type of analysis represents the processing and selection of mental cues and images, selected by the offender. Therefore, police leaders use templates to understand offender patterns, and predict likely courses of action.

CRIME TEMPLATES

Crime prevention surveys can assist in identifying the criminal mindset or template. Templates provide a means for continuous identification of offenders, and their vulnerabilities. The templates can help reveal travel patterns and methods of operation, and help officers predict how and where offenders may select activities and crime sites. Hot spots serve as focus points for analysis and crime prevention responses.

Templates have several advantages. They help (1) estimate locations where critical events and activities might occur, (2) identify victims and crime scenes, (3) project time-related events within crime sites or hot spots, (4) present mapping techniques, and (5) determine a guide for tactical decisions and proactive patrol allocations. While a template may be unable to predict exactly when and where a criminal will strike next, it provides information that can help police choose appropriate courses of action. For example, in many instances, police officers have determined that templates indicate crime often occurs only short distances from an offender's residence. [10]

TRAVEL DISTANCE

Offenders gain template knowledge from familiar environmental experiences (e.g., living in a certain geographical area). Most property crimes, such as burglary and vandalism, are committed within two miles' travel distance of the offender's residence. Yet, offenders may avoid targets closer to home because of the risk of apprehension. Opportunity, reward, and fear of arrest determine the difference between "good" and "poor" crime hot spots. [11] An area that provides cover and concealment represents a favorable hot spot, whereas a well-lit, heavily patrolled area would prove a poor choice for criminal activity.

After the scanning, analysis and pre-assessment planning phases, the response phase and crime prevention strategies are implemented. Responses are determined based on community needs, and collaboration with community guardians and partners. The strategies may be traditional proactive patrol techniques; more often, the strategies are nontraditional and involve community cooperation. [12] After the response phase, the evaluation and the post-assessment phases follow.

CRIME DISPLACEMENT

Crime displacement is a concern, but not the primary concern during the planning and targeting process. Police leaders, planners and analysts should anticipate the possibility of displacing crime. There are five main ways in which the theory of crime displacement suggests crime is moved around. Refer to Table 6-3 for a list of the five basic forms of crime displacement.

There is no perfect solution, only opportunities to make a difference. Negative outcomes or unintended consequences are factored into the problem-solving process. There are a few documented cases where crime displacement offset the crime prevention improvements in the near-term. The long-term strategic picture is the goal, and there is a learning curve factor in the short-run. [13]

Table 6-3   Crime Displacement Table

Territorial Displacement
Crime moves to a new location.
The movement may result in increasing crime in a contiguous area.
Example: Crime is moved to a new jurisdiction
Temporal Displacement
Crime offending moves to another time while remaining in the same area.
Example: Some offenses may move to daylight, darkness or weekends.

Tactical Displacement
Offender utilizes a new means to commit the same offense.
Example: A shift in burglary from unlocked doors to breaking windows.
Target Displacement
This displacement includes the choice of a different type of victim within the same area.
Example: Increase in the use of weapons by store owners may force robbers to choose elderly pedestrians as victims.
Functional Displacement
Offenders change to a new type of offense.
Example: Shifting from larceny to burglary.
Example: Shifting from burglary to robbery.

CASE STUDY: CENTRALIZED PLANNING

The Hometown City Central Planning Committee is commencing for its bimonthly meeting concerning an open-air drug market, which is plaguing the inner city. Various members of the planning committee, are present: (1) The Commander of Field Operations, (2) ILP Manager, (3) The Intelligence Analysis Section Supervisor, (4) Crime Analysis Section Supervisor, (5) Lieutenant, COPPS Unit (6) Commanders, (7) Planning Supervisor and (8) meeting facilitator.

Many police and civilian members of the Hometown City Police Department attend the central planning meeting. The civilian Planning Supervisor, Edward Jenks, opens the meeting by defining the problem and targets for the agenda.

"Welcome everyone and thank you for coming to our central planning meeting. I am Edward Jenks. Hometown City has an open-air drug market problem; street dealers operate in an insulated environment. This section of the city is a depressed neighborhood, with the highest crime rate. The main target is Mulberry and Vine Streets in central city. The inner-city drug market problem has several suburban county interconnected drug distribution centers.

"I would like to introduce our Crime Analyst Supervisor, Shannon. She will inform you about the updated crime analysis assessment."

"Greetings, I am Shannon Briggs, and I have prepared the crime analysis briefing. Here is the current situation on the first PowerPoint slide. Street gangs are in control of the neighborhood, and have organized a crack cocaine street pusher network."

Another PowerPoint slide pops-up, and Shannon responds: "Supply and demand are excellent and the price of crack has decreased in the neighborhood. This market presents a risk to customers, and community members. Occasionally, customers are ripped-off in robberies that are bogus drug transactions. Moreover, the drug market increases the potential for drive-by shootings, burglaries and related drug prostitution."

A third PowerPoint slide commences and Shannon continues: "These younger street dealers meet their customers in the early evening hours. The target times are primarily between 1800 to 2300 hours to consummate the crack transactions. They operate on corners of busy intersections, with poor lighting conditions. The pushers coordinate with specific customers via cell phones. The local candy store serves as a central point of coordination. Customer spotters operate from the top floor window. The owner acts as an enabler and receives financial compensation, according to one of our informants, and field intelligence reports."

Shannon advanced the fourth slide: "The modus operandi allows maximum access to customers with the advantage of lower visibility. The crime triangle consists of: (1) *offenders* (including street pushers and their gang leaders), (2) *victims/customers*, and (3) the *location*, a mobile open-air drug market, situated at two hot spot intersections."

Captain Jack Warner comments, "We have launched a number of CompStat operations over the past year, with limited results for our efforts. The arrest of runners and street pushers has little impact on the open-air market operation, because the juveniles are soon released and back on the street. Moreover, the juveniles receive light sentences and are easily replaced as business attritions."

Lieutenant Stewart Martens, comments, "From a COPPS perspective we have made a few informal friendly contacts. The dealers have a support system and community enablers. Community members are afraid to voice opposition because of the fear of crime, and street violence. We have not been able to get a Neighborhood Watch Program started because of the poverty and fear of crime factors."

The fifth PowerPoint slide is a GIS mapping analysis that is full of hot spots and clusters, across the geographical area of three related jurisdictions. Shannon comments: "Notice the pattern in central city, and the disbursement to the bedroom counties. This open-air market runs parallel to a closed market, to local suburban communities. When confronted with high enforcement crackdowns, supergangs will close down the open air market, or displace the operation. The displacement of the basic street distribution points is a temporary dislocation. Cell phone text messages relocate the pushers and new distribution locations; business continues as usual.

"I would like to introduce Jeb Turner, the Intelligence Analyst Supervisor. We have collaborated and shared our related analytical areas. Jeb has some interesting observations to contribute to our discussion, from an intelligence analysis perspective."

"Good morning everyone," the PowerPoint slide appears on the wall size screen. Jeb comments, "Supergangs are principle sellers of crack cocaine, and their market is well organized. The organization includes turf-based youth gangs, who have a new mission, including open-air drug markets. Supergangs are connected to adult criminal organizations and drug wholesalers. These criminal associations include national and international drug trafficking connections. The supervision of younger members and low level distribution remains under the control of organized supergang senior members.

"For example, participants in the drug network tend to be older Original Gangsters (OG) and career criminals. Major traffickers are in direct contact with drug dealers, the backbone of the crack cocaine trade. At the center of the drug trafficking, the crew boss who received his supply of cocaine from a drug dealer. These adults hire adolescent street drug sellers and gang members to perform as runners and lookouts."

Jeb comments on the next slide: "The crack distribution ring is loosely organized from three to twelve members, handling small amounts of crack. The crew may be a street or youth gang committing criminal activities, like drug trafficking. Armed guards often protect drug-dealing crew members. Occasionally, the crew boss serves this protective function to avoid robberies and rip-offs. The drug-selling crews would receive credit for two or three rocks of crack cocaine, on a loan basis. [14]

"I would like to introduce my new ILP manager, Roger Stewart; we are currently undergoing reorganization to accommodate the new Intelligence-Led Policing Program."

"Good morning, thank you for the introduction; it appears that we have underestimated the open-air drug market. This is not a local flea market, but a form of organized crime. The combination of crime and intelligence analysts, working together on this project, is producing a better strategic and tactical intelligence picture.

"In addition, these supergangs are evolving into a form of organized crime, and the shift is toward commodity crime. They are providing illegal goods and services like a business enterprise. What is more disturbing is the investment of these illegal profits, in legitimate businesses. The presence of enforcers and corrupters continue to play a role in the drug market trade.

"I would like to diversify the approach to this investigation, and take a systems approach. We need to coordinate with other local police agencies, state authorities, and federal agencies. The main points of contact are the Drug Enforcement Administration and the State Attorney's Office of Drug Investigation."

Stewart further comments: "Moreover, we need to coordinate with our local and state fusion centers, High-Intensity Drug Trafficking Areas (HIDTA) Regional Intelligence Centers, National Drug Intelligence Center, and El Paso Intelligence Center, just to name a few of the available inter-agency intelligence resources. This case is not simply a local crisis; it is a regional, state and national problem. Therefore, the target requires centralized planning and considerable intelligence coordination and intelligence sharing."

The Commander of Field Operations, Col. Jane Peterson, closes the meeting with the following remarks: "After listening to the staff briefings, it seems that we need to meet concerning this open-air drug market, to pinpoint the proper course of action in the near future."

"My estimate of the situation is to back-off heavy enforcement operations, and lull these crack criminals into a sense of security. We strike after all ILP crime analysis and intelligence requirements are in place.

"The immediate steps include developing informants and debriefing all drug-related arrestees. In addition, gear-up the undercover operations so we can gather the human intelligence. Moreover, this criminal information may lead to probable cause for ex parte, and wiretapping.

"We need to calculate if our operations are in conflict with state and federal authorities. We also need to dissect this operation to understand how it works, and destroy this open-air drug market's total operation from the ground-up, so that it does not reemerge."

"We must take this community back; the people own it, not the criminals. We need to target these criminals and get them off our streets." A standing applause follows after the Colonel's remarks.

FOCUS POINTS

Long-term strategic predictions may support short-term tactical considerations and opportunities for CompStat tactical operations. The most critical law enforcement mission is tactical operations. One small omission can jeopardize the entire CompStat or tactical mission. The synchronization of strategic and tactical planning offers opportunities to incorporate details into a comprehensive planning process.

Strategic long-term research focuses on high quality intelligence, capabilities, plans, and intentions. POP has long-term applications and similar strategic requirements. Both planning methods may apply in mutual directions, strategic and tactical. The interrelationships of connecting and overlapping strategic and tactical qualities make an excellent case for centralized planning strategies.

ILP and strategic planning staff are partners offering essential intelligence and critical information for decision makers. Intelligence and crime analysis provides the means to assist in developing the best service available to the community. Coordination and centralization of the strategic planning process, sets the foundation for effective police decision-making.

The intelligence cycle and strategic planning require merging to obtain maximum effectiveness. In addition, excellent communication facilitates the necessary flow of information and feedback, for the strategic planning process. In addition, problem-oriented policing is a form of long-term planning; requiring integration with the strategic planning process.

Police intelligence tends to be current, near-term or real time; providing planning for precise operations. Police tactical scenarios require a rapid response and accurate intelligence support for the execution of incident action plans. Current tactical situations thrive on criminal or terrorist indications/intentions. Early warnings, cautiously distributed, meet current intelligence requirements.

Target-centric approach is a network process that offers participants opportunities to focus on goals and objectives, when performing their roles and areas of responsibility. A collaborative approach provides opportunities for direction and unified participation. Identifying the target and crime triangle is directly related to defining the problem.

The central planning process provides reliable and valid sources of information for improved planning. Strategic and tactical analysis requires critical thinking. The team or staff approach identifies strategic, tactical, and operational planning strategies. The final process defines the problem, acquires the target(s) and defines the goals, objectives and action plans.

CONCLUSION

There is always the risk that current intelligence, tactical planning, and operations may conflict with strategic objectives. Strategic and tactical planning requires up-to-date coordination and articulation. Police agencies may interrupt larger scale operations because of the preferred tactical operations taking precedence. Therefore, centralized planning that incorporates the key decision maker maximizes coordination requirements.

ENDNOTES

1. James Q. Wilson and George L. Kelling, "Broken Windows," Atlantic Monthly, March, (1982), 29-38.

2. John Hudzik and Gary Cordner, Planning in Criminal Justice Organizations and Systems (New York: Macmillan, 1983), 1.

3. Robert C. Cushman, Criminal Justice Planning for Local Governments, Washington, DC: GPO, 1980); Charles R. Swanson, Leonard Territo and Taylor, Robert W., Police Administration: Structures, Processes, and Behavior (New Jersey: Pearson-Prentice Hall, 2005), 631.

4. Don McDowell, Strategic Intelligence: A Handbook for Practitioners, Managers and Users (Australia, Cooma: Istana Enterprise, Pty, Ltd.), 12-13.

5. Robert C. Cushman, and Charles R. Swanson, Leonard Territo, 631.

6. Robert M. Clark, Intelligence Analysis: A Target- Centric Approach (Washington, DC: CQ Press, 2007): 13.

7. Timothy S. Bynum, Using Analysis for Problem-solving: A Guidebook for Law Enforcement, U.S. Department of Justice, Office of Community Oriented Policing Services (Washington, DC: GPO, 2001): 10; W Spelman and John E. Eck, Sitting Ducks, Ravenous Wolves, and Helping Hands: New Approaches to Urban Policing, Austin School of Public Affairs, University of Texas, 1989.

8. Marcus Felson and Clark, Ronald, "Opportunity Makes the Thief," Police Research Series, Paper 98, (London Home Office, 1998).

9. Paul Brantingham and Patricia Brantingham, Patterns in Crime (New York: Macmillan Publishing Company, 1984), 338-342.

10. Brantingham and Brantingham, 340-344.

11. Brantingham and Brantingham, 341.

12. Goldstein, Problem-Oriented Policing, 32.

13. Ronald V. Clarke, and John E. Eck, Problem-Oriented Policing Crime Analysis for Problem Solvers in 60 Small Steps, Department of Justice, COPS (Washington, DC: GPO, 2005): 12, 48, 49.

14. James C. Howell, Office of Juvenile Justice and Delinquency Prevention, "Gang Fact Sheet #12" (Washington, DC: GPO, April 1994): 1.

CHAPTER 7
Analytical Products

I never guess. It is a shocking habit destructive to the logical faculty.
— Sir Arthur Conan Doyle

Analytical products assist in taking the guesswork out of decision-making for police executives, commanders, and police supervisors. Intelligence reports and supporting analytical documents provide evidence for superior decision-making. Decision-makers need analytical products that assist in visualizing strategic and tactical crime operations. Quality analytical intelligence products foster logical conclusions and observations, avoiding counter-productive outcomes.

CHAPTER FOCUS

Law enforcement intelligence is an integrated perspective, eventually producing products for strategic and tactical application decision-making. This chapter defines the role of intelligence reporting in law enforcement agencies and intelligence products. The purpose is to explore the intelligence reporting system and analytical products that provide an accurate portrayal of the strategic or tactical picture. The discussion sets the foundation for supporting analytical methods in conspiracy and street crime investigations.

The International Association of Law Enforcement Intelligence Analysts (IALEIA) emphasizes that intelligence is an analytical product: "It is taking information collected in the course of an investigation, or from internal or external files, and arriving at something more than was evident before. This could be leads in a case, a more accurate view of a crime problem, forecasting future crime levels, and a hypothesis of who may have committed a crime or a strategy to prevent crime." [1]

Intelligence-Led Policing (ILP) is an analytical management process that produces reliable reports for intelligence purposes concerning crime trends, crimes, and community security threats. Skillful intelligence analysis, expertise, and training produce superior intelligence finished products. Analytical reporting serves as the foundation for the ILP philosophy and management system.

This chapter focuses on intelligence analytical products and briefings. Intelligence products illustrate many types of analytical frames of reference. Finished products vary according to the needs of customers and criminal case situations. The basic products include: (1) written reports, (2) verbal presentations, and (3) background papers or estimates. Intelligence products unfold at three main levels of intelligence analysis: (1) *strategic*, (2) *tactical*, and (3) *operational.* Refer to Table 7-1 for an example of the Chapter Focus and related concepts.

INTELLIGENCE PRODUCTS

Strategic products are broadly based focused papers or estimates, which involve intelligence research. The strategic product is generally expansive; details may include other graphic related support documents. Projections envision future events and include conceptual models capable of prediction or estimating present and future outcomes. Useful product applications include global enterprise crime, terrorism, and other complicated conspiracy crimes. For example, systems analysis products may involve international drug cartel structures, systems functionality, systems maintenance, and financial profits.

Table 7-1   Chapter Focus

	Introduction: Intelligence Products	Intelligence Product Levels
Intelligence-Led Policing	❖ Definition: intelligence product ❖ Developing criminal information ❖ Integrated perspective ❖ Strategic products ❖ Tactical products ❖ Operational products ❖ Assessment products	❖ Written report products ❖ Verbal presentations ❖ Background products ❖ Estimate products ❖ Near-term products ❖ Projection products ❖ Prediction products
	Product Standards	**Types of Analytical Products**
	❖ Basic IALEIA standards ❖ Procedures ❖ Central collection point ❖ Rapid retrieval ❖ Record systems ❖ Identified data sources ❖ Dissemination requirements	❖ Field information report ❖ Briefing ❖ Spot report ❖ Quarterly trend report ❖ Threat assessment report ❖ After-action report ❖ Graphic analytical products

TACTICAL REPORTING

Tactical target products may include profiles, biographies, and confirmation of criminal networks. Finished intelligence products for street gangs may include: (1) organizational structure, (2) association analysis, (3) criminal activities, and (4) geographical factors affecting law enforcement operations. Tactical analytical products may prove essential in burglary rings, drug operations, street gangs and other on-going tactical or local operations.

OPERATIONAL REPORTING

Operational intelligence reporting is primarily internal to law enforcement organizational structure and logistical necessities. The planning process centers on strategic and tactical requirements for law enforcement operations, which may include personnel, supplies and communications, etc. Police operational intelligence is closer to near term operations, involving considerable planning and support of specific operations. Final products clarify support operations and deployment information for officers.

The depth of analysis and length of reporting strategies vary according to the situation, topic, or criminal activity. The same products may fit both strategic and tactical strategies and include analytical graphic support. In addition, shared intelligence that informs may have multiple applications at various levels of criminal activities.

POLICY, PROCEDURES AND GUIDANCE

Providing guidance and policies assists in initiating sharing strategies that ensure effectiveness. Standards provide uniformity concerning procedures and direction for police officers and civilians. Standards enhance uniform procedures and offer guidelines for law enforcement agencies to follow.

The Commission on Accreditation of Law Enforcement Agencies (CALEA) defines and recommends the following standards: "Certain essential activities should be accomplished by an intelligence function: (1) include a procedure that permits the continuous flow of raw data into a central point from all sources; (2) secure records system in which evaluated data are properly cross-referenced to reflect relationships and to ensure complete and rapid retrieval; (3) develop a system of analysis capable of developing intelligence from both the records system and other data sources; and (4) provide a system for dissemination of information to appropriate components." [2]

DISSEMINATION REQUIREMENTS

Police leaders, investigators, and police officers represent essential customers. Dissemination should be timely, but sometimes there are intelligence delays and omissions for customers. When timetables, priorities, and suspense dates are part of the intelligence scheduling, mistakes seldom occur. Therefore, temporal considerations are of paramount importance in meeting the intelligence product needs of diverse customers.

INTELLIGENCE PRODUCTS SELECTION

There is an extensive selection of intelligence products essential to the ILP management strategies. The collection and presentation of information leads to useful intelligence products for leaders and decision-makers. These intelligence products may influence a whole spectrum of operational requirements and enforcement functions. Refer to Figure 7-1 for a brief summary of the four basic categories of finished intelligence and temporal framework or time suspense products.

Figure 7-1   Analytical Timeframe Products

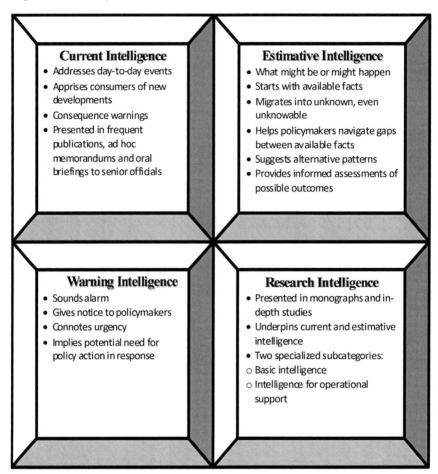

Current Intelligence
- Addresses day-to-day events
- Apprises consumers of new developments
- Consequence warnings
- Presented in frequent publications, ad hoc memorandums and oral briefings to senior officials

Estimative Intelligence
- What might be or might happen
- Starts with available facts
- Migrates into unknown, even unknowable
- Helps policymakers navigate gaps between available facts
- Suggests alternative patterns
- Provides informed assessments of possible outcomes

Warning Intelligence
- Sounds alarm
- Gives notice to policymakers
- Connotes urgency
- Implies potential need for policy action in response

Research Intelligence
- Presented in monographs and in-depth studies
- Underpins current and estimative intelligence
- Two specialized subcategories:
  o Basic intelligence
  o Intelligence for operational support

Sources: Central Intelligence Agency, Office of Public Affairs, US Marine Corps, Intelligence Production and Analysis and New Jersey State Police, Practical Guide to Intelligence-Led Policing

TYPES OF ANALYTICAL PRODUCTS

The acceptance and basic usage of these analytical products are personalized from the New Jersey State Police, Practical Guide for Intelligence-Led Policing. The following content was adapted from that source with modification and revision by the author. Finished analytical intelligence products include: (1)

briefings, (2) spot reports, (3) quarterly trends reports, (4) threat assessments, (5) warnings, (6) crime bulletins, and (7) after-action reports. [3] Individual law enforcement agencies may have their own reporting procedures; the following paragraphs represent a general overview.

BRIEFING FORMATS

Briefings represent an effective way to quickly disseminate intelligence. They permit direct interaction with the intended audience, and the audience can provide immediate feedback to the briefer concerning content conclusions. Briefings convey specific intelligence and intelligence operations details to a select audience, in a concise format.

Depending on available preparation time, briefing styles can range from formal presentations with detailed handouts and graphics, to simple oral updates. Even in the absence of formal tasking to prepare an intelligence briefing, intelligence personnel informally disseminate intelligence at every opportunity, through coordination with staff counterparts, customers and police decision makers.

Analyst oral briefings provide supplemental data (in electronic or 'hard-copy' formats) that cover essential points. In an emergency or short notice, it may preclude supplemental materials. Moreover, briefings usually reach a limited audience, i.e., the commander's staff. Analytical personnel are encouraged to prepare concise intelligence summaries to disseminate, and record critical intelligence presented at the time of briefing. Refer to Figure 7-2 for an overview of the types of briefings.

Figure 7-2   Types of Briefings

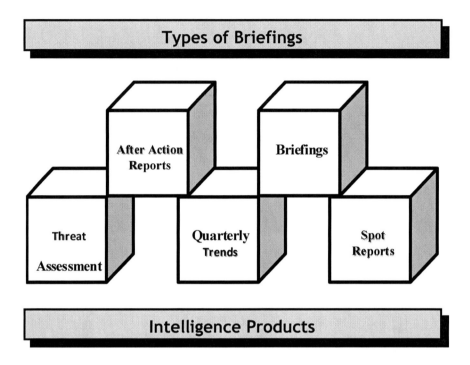

Information Briefing: The primary purpose of the information briefing is to provide a "situation orientation" for initial
planning. Moreover, a primary consideration is to enhance
situational awareness and understanding of the emerging
criminal activities. Common examples would be a briefing
about new trends in criminal activity, or criminal organization
illegal activities worthy of target investigations.

Decision Briefing: The decision briefing's purpose is to
secure a decision from the Chief of Police or senior leaders.
One example would be a briefing describing the conclusions
of an analytical project, requesting a decision from command.
Generally, the briefer presents three courses of action; leaders
choose one of the three solution options.

Confirmation Briefing: A confirmation briefing is a final
review of a planned action to ensure participants are confident

in their understanding of the objectives. Planning with participants ensures the allocation of resources and common understanding of the operation. Any significant project or event should generate a confirmation briefing, before initiation, to avoid confusion early in the process. Ideally, additional confirmation briefings should occur periodically to ensure all parties involved remain "on the pathway to success."

SPOT REPORTS

A spot report's most common rationale is to disseminate important, time-critical intelligence, without regard to a specific schedule. Spot report preparation is timely and disseminated as rapidly as possible. Generally, spot reports concern a single item. A spot report is generally required whenever an event occurs that is likely to result in a change in the disposition of resources. In addition, a spot report follow-up occurs when requiring a change to the current or future analytical assessment.

A spot report may highlight the facts influencing threat capabilities, including when a change in threat capabilities expands, or when changes in threat capabilities occur unexpectedly. Spot reports focus on priority topics defined by the police executive's intent. The spot report should include an estimate of likely outcomes, as well as a source reliability and accuracy assessment.

WRITTEN REPORTS

Intelligence written reports represent the primary means for recording criminal intelligence and information. Written reports allow intelligence analysts and law enforcement officers to participate in the most primary component of intelligence-led policing. Analysts understand the means to configure the criminal environment, develop finished intelligence products, and influence decision-makers. The analytical interpretation of the criminal world, unfolds when analysts and collectors pull information from the criminal milieu to enhance understanding.

Investigative reports are different in their perspective and presentation; they provide information. Investigative reports seek a criminal arrest and conviction, or possible exoneration of the innocent. Intelligence reports provide investigators with lead push information for interpreting the criminal environment: (1) preventing crime, (2) identifying criminal targets, (3) interdicting targets, (4) guiding resource allocation, and (5) influencing future operations and policy. Refer to table 7-2 for an illustration of the differences between investigation and intelligence.

Table 7-2   Differences in Investigative and Intelligence Reporting Styles

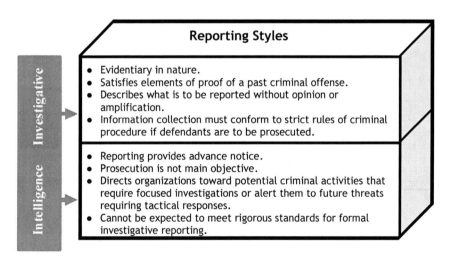

Reporting Styles

Investigative
- Evidentiary in nature.
- Satisfies elements of proof of a past criminal offense.
- Describes what is to be reported without opinion or amplification.
- Information collection must conform to strict rules of criminal procedure if defendants are to be prosecuted.

Intelligence
- Reporting provides advance notice.
- Prosecution is not main objective.
- Directs organizations toward potential criminal activities that require focused investigations or alert them to future threats requiring tactical responses.
- Cannot be expected to meet rigorous standards for formal investigative reporting.

Source: Adapted from C. Frost and Morris J., Police Intelligence Reports (California: Palmer Enterprises, 1983).

FIELD CRIMINAL INFORMATION REPORT

The primary means of collecting information from the field remains field intelligence reporting. Detectives and police officers submit basic intelligence report entries into the database. This data serves as the crucial digital collection point for the advanced reporting system. The combined knowledge of contributors at every level, serves as an expansive base for criminal information.

Police agencies may classify and label preliminary information as "Law Enforcement Sensitive" for security reasons. Moreover, the information must conform to legal mandates and Title 28, Code of Federal Regulations, part 23, "Operators shall collect, and maintain criminal intelligence information concerning an individual only if there is reasonable suspicion that the individual is involved in criminal conduct or activity…" Collection and dissemination remain sensitive areas for civil rights violations.

The bullet format delivers concise information that allows straightforward formatting, collection and collation. The format provides easy reading and communicates in a brief, timely, and concise mode. Submissions avoid compromising sources, collection methods, and strategies.

Field intelligence reports may contain several related sequence and identification numbers including: (1) intelligence report number, (2) criminal investigation number, and (3) police report number. In addition, additional identification items may include, but not limited to the following: (1) agency, (2) report date, (3) event date, (4) primary and secondary sources, and (5) topic. The evaluation section emphasizes credibility, veracity, and reliability. Refer to Table 7-3 for an example of the field intelligence report.

Table 7-3   Field Intelligence Report

Hometown Police Department
Field Intelligence Report

Case # :
Date :

Subject(s) or Location:

Information Source Identification:
- ☐ Private Citizen (Name/Number) _____
- ☐ Criminal Source
- ☐ Govt. Agency
- ☐ Law Officer
- ☐ Personal Knowledge
- ☐ Documents
- ☐ Hearsay/Rumor
- ☐ Hypothesis
- ☐ Other:

Evaluation of Source or Sources:
- ☐ Highly Reliable
- ☐ Usually Reliable
- ☐ Reliability Questionable
- ☐ Not Evaluated

Officer: **Analyst:**

Intelligence Information:

Information Content: **Information Files/Queries:**

☐ Partially Verified	☐ State Criminal Record	
☐ Unverified	☐ State Drivers License	
☐ Verified	☐ NCIC	

Recommended Follow-up:
- ☐ Investigator to Verify
- ☐ Source to Verify
- ☐ Analyst to Research
- ☐ File Only

DISSEMINATION:

The synopsis informs analysts and decision-makers in an effective and efficient manner. The event synopsis describes names of reporter(s), and summarizes essential details. The text includes a narrative of specific information concerning the activity. The basic field intelligence report deals with one subject or incident, unless unusual circumstances apply. The narrative format contains the following basic intelligence information: (1) who or whom, (2) what, (3) why, (4) when, and (4) how of the incident and collection process.

The following example describes the synopsis and basic elements of the field entry text:

(1) **Synopsis:** This entry concerns a possible organized crime prostitution ring housed in a luxury high-rise apartment complex. The call-girl operation operates from apartment 806 of the Classic Towers Condominium. Detective Jay Stanly is responsible for this submission and the intelligence information.

(2) **Narrative:** The initial complaint arrived telephonic from John and Mary Smith. Their observations revealed that male clientele frequented apartment 806 of the Classic Towers at all hours of the day and night. A few lavishly and provocatively dressed women were seen entering the apartment on a frequent basis. In addition, casually dressed women, generally carry shopping bags, also frequented the apartment.

One evening, visitors created a huge alcohol related disturbance in the hallway. Someone pulled out a gun and pounded the apartment door, leaving a distinguishable dent. The residents viewed this scenario from the peephole in their apartment door. Mr. and Mrs. Smith, both high school teachers, felt that these activities are worthy of an investigation. They made their complaint, after enduring several months of other related disturbing behavior patterns.

After conducting surveillance from the complainant's apartment, it appears they are correct about the activities directly across from their apartment located in 810 Classic Towers. The information in this complaint is completely reliable. This investigator confirmed the information through personal observations. Surveillance concerning modus operandi includes clients parking their cars, and entering the apartment during the business lunch time frame. Clients gain access to the building, after buzzing the apartment from the entrance. They generally leave the apartment within forty-five minutes.

This information is eligible for release to selective outside law enforcement agencies. However, due to the high profile nature of patrons with probable political connections, this report is "Law Enforcement Sensitive." A significant follow-up by intelligence analysts and detectives would prove appropriate and prudent.

FIELD ACTIVITY SNAPSHOT

Each report substantiates the reliability of the source, and preferably contains one source. Field report contributions provide a small intelligence snapshot; analysis will eventually focus the expansive strategic camera picture. Investigators and police officers take one basic step as field contributors, providing opportunities for strategic and tactical analysis.

QUARTERLY TRENDS REPORT

The purpose of the QTR is to describe significant changes to the operating environment. This leads to identifying and describing events and trends, which correlate to specific group or principle criminal target(s). Discussions should include group diversification and escalation of criminal activities. The QTR summarizes the identification of individual criminal targets, their role, and status in the hierarchy. The report collects data from diverse information sources, and prepares in-depth analysis.

Quarterly Trends Reports (QTR) emphasize the Police Chief's intent concerning selected offenses, i.e., official corruption, violent street gangs, wholesale narcotics trafficking, or counter-terrorism. In addition, the QTR considers intent and direction information from the various levels of command. Intelligence and crime analysis units coordinate and share intelligence at regional, state, federal level and international levels.

QTR includes predictions of future criminal activity, identification of intelligence gaps and recommendations, or prioritization of collection assets. QTR emphasizes new information collected since the last report and updates threat assessments. The focus is not on investigative activities; but rather to answer previously unidentified intelligence gaps.

The QTR defines the characteristics of the criminal organization, capabilities, modus operandi, and goals of the organization. The emphasis is on change: (1) the ability to engage in the criminal enterprise, (2) shifting strategies or priorities, and (3) internal power struggles or conflicts with other criminal organizations. The analysis focus is on next quarter's criminal activities. The conclusion targets the disruption of the criminal organization, and future collection strategies.

STRATEGIC THREAT ASSESSMENT

General strategic assessments are an overview of all known information on a criminal enterprise, or criminal activity. Strategic assessments allow an analyst to draw on past and present criminal information, which may forecast future events.

The strategic assessment may contain recommendations concerning possible enforcement measures against the criminal organization, criminal information from the enterprise network, or criminal activity. [4]

Threat assessments analyze what enterprise crime groups and operations are costing the state, and nation and what groups and operations are most threatening to the peace and economic stability, of a particular community. This type of analysis can also be proactive when it attempts to predict the vulnerability of a community to enterprise crime. However, threat assessments can become rapidly outdated and require continuous validation.

Threat assessment reports contain information about a potential human threat, criminal organization, or terrorist threat. In addition, the threat can be the consequence of a natural disaster, or hazard. The purpose of threat assessment is to collect data from multiple sources, which identify a specific threat to governments, infrastructure, property, and citizens.

Threat assessment is a collection of known information about the threat. Generally, a considerable information void exists concerning the unknown. The threat may come from criminals, specific criminal groups, or types of crime. A significant momentous threat can undermine social, economic institutions and jeopardize the nation.

Threat assessment analysis identifies the intent and capabilities of criminal group activities. The activities segment of the report includes: (1) new criminal activities, (2) changes in criminal modus operandi, (3) changes in intent, and (4) changes in capabilities. Potential targets are a separate area of discussion as well as crime context, intelligence gaps, and future developments.

The case example cited below illustrates an example of a threat assessment summary. The format consists of the (1) originator(s) of the document, (2) scope of the assessment, (3) key findings, (4) group's intent, and (5) threat capabilities. This format could also take the form of an information briefing. The source of this case example is the Pennsylvania Crime Commission, Organized Crime in Pennsylvania: A Decade of Change.

CASE EXAMPLE: THREAT ASSESSMENT

Two La Cosa Nostra (LCN) organized crime families in Western Pennsylvania have a strong and continuing dominance of illegal enterprise in that area of the state. This dominance has been heightened by two primary occurrences: the ascension of (name deleted) to boss of the organization and the fall of (name deleted)'s gambling empire.

As boss, the replacement is more aggressive and demonstrates a willingness to support LCN's involvement in the drug trade. This stance has caused the Family to demand and receive more tribute and "respect," enriching the Family's coffers through the narcotics trade. Ironically, one of the reasons for the LCN's former reluctance to distribute narcotics was the seriousness of the crime, and the likelihood of those facing drug charges, to turn government informant. The number of convictions and informants, in Pittsburgh, has demonstrated the accuracy of this predicted consequence.

However, the conviction of the boss, and the assumption of his formerly independent gambling organization by LCN, associates has been beneficial to the Family, and provided financial tribute to the LCN. The boss's conviction has created a monopolistic hold by the LCN gambling operations in Western Pennsylvania, where the previous leader of the operation, had been outside LCN control. This is an example of how some enforcement actions can benefit organized crime, by removing its competition.

In spite of convictions and indictments against Pittsburgh LCN members and associates, the organization appears to be strong and capable of continued growth through another decade. It has asserted itself as the primary crime group in the area, and by becoming more active in narcotics, has demonstrated its ability to be a full-service criminal organization. Barring exceptional law enforcement successes, the Pittsburgh LCN is likely to continue to prosper, as long as the market for illegal gambling, vice-activities, and narcotics endure. [5]

WARNING REPORTS

The warning report generally flows from the threat or vulnerability assessment. Warning reports alert authorities to an eminent or potential criminal or terrorist threat. Ideally, the warning contains a forecast or recommendations to counter or minimize the threat. Warnings may take two basic forms: (1) strategic or (2) tactical crime analysis perspective. The former would receive emphasis on conclusions calculated in the threat, or vulnerability assessment. The latter would take the format of the crime bulletin.

CRIME BULLETINS

Crime bulletins contain brief analytical statements and often warn about a specific criminal or particular criminal activity. Crime bulletins inform officers of crime patterns, trends, or series crimes occurring in their beats. Bulletins describe important criminal information on continuing events. They familiarize law enforcement officers with offenses committed, including information on days, times of offenses, locations and possible suspects. Bulletins may identify potential victims, modus operandi information, and suspect vehicles.

Bulletins reveal current information based on probabilities of where potential offenders may target victims, homes, businesses or other potential crime sites. This information enables police commanders and their officers to develop tactical plans and specialized patrol operations. Specific crime information presents law enforcement officers with the opportunity to prevent crimes, or intervene successfully.

Some crime bulletins may serve as deterrents. Information alerts Neighborhood Watch group members to crimes occurring in their communities. Crime mapping and hot spot designations contribute to understanding possible crime patterns, with citizens now placed in the best position, to report suspicious or criminal behavior. Feedback information from citizens may provide additional intelligence that allows officers to interrupt a series of crimes.

Crime bulletins referred to as "Be on the Look Out!" (BLO) inform law enforcement officers that a particular offender is wanted for interview or arrest. This bulletin is most effective when it includes specific information regarding the suspect's vehicle, personal description, and address. The offender bulletin is useful in cases of hot pursuit of known criminal offenders, especially if there is the possibility of injury to the offender, police officers or others.

The offender bulletin proves useful when tracking career criminals and repeat offenders. Friends, family members, and photographs are the most useful forms of offender information. Known offender bulletins indicate caution because of: (1) privacy, (2) civil liberty issues, and (3) the potential claim of police harassment.

Figure 7-3   Crime Bulletin Example

	MOST ACTIVE CRIMINALS Criminal Intelligence Unit Hometown Police Department	MAC Vol. 01 4/11/2008 Page 1 of 1

Name: Judy Jones

Alias: Hooker

Race: Caucasian   Sex: Female

Height: 5 feet

Weight: 120 lbs.

Hair: Brown

Eyes: Hazel

Last Known Address: 806 Classic Towers, Hometown, USA

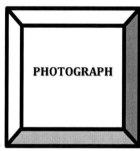

NARRATIVE:

The above-mentioned subject is wanted for pandering/felony prostitution. Judy Jones is a madam for a high-rise prostitution ring. She was arrested on 3/1/2008 for felony prostitution and failed to appear for court. She is in violation of $100,000 bond.

Ms. Jones operated her call-girl service for approximately one year before being arrested. She was operating an exclusive call-girl service for elite clients. In addition, Ms. Jones has the financial resources to leave the country and travel internationally. Her parents and former husband live locally in Hometown USA.

Confidential

For Law Enforcement Use Only

Shred When No longer Needed.

AFTER-ACTION REPORT

After-action reports identify lessons learned about specific events and police actions. They result after intelligence, tactical or other operations and highlight information that might assist in the future, including successful aspects and errors of the mission. Mission participants brainstorm, present diverse points of view, and examine ways of improving the next mission.

Another method of identifying strengths and weaknesses is to compile comments separately, and forward the information to a point of contact, for systematic analysis. The concept accepts information from observers and participants in a threat-free environment. Freedom of expression encourages the facts to come forward in the interest of truthfulness. The after-action report should not place blame, the emphasis is on lessons learned.

REVIEW AND ASSESSMENT

Finished intelligence products require review procedures to ensure accuracy and proficiency in analysis criteria. The review process allows for analytical process improvement, and assists in meeting high standards. The assessment review includes, but is not limited to the following general issues: (1) sources, (2) body of evidence, (3) alternate explanations, and (4) assertions. Moreover, additional significant review areas include: (1) assumptions that underpin the foundations of the analysis, (2) consistency with other analysis, and (3) identification of key facts and assumptions, i.e., changes which would alter the assessment.

Focus Points

The centerpiece of ILP management is analytical reporting. Police executives realize improved success when they collaborate with senior leaders, staff/line commanders, and analysts to achieve strategic and tactical objectives. Analytical products facilitate coordination, priorities and target analysis. The exchange of criminal intelligence provides guidance for identifying the mission, goals and objectives.

Strategic, tactical, and operational intelligence products are the foundation for effective police leadership. Analytical products provide verification for accurately forecasting future crime levels, crime control remedial actions, and prevention strategies. Finished products provide the basis for actionable criminal intelligence.

Field intelligence reports represent basic components of a successful intelligence reporting system. This report encourages participation and maximizes the flow of information, from police operations and investigative services. The basic field intelligence report serves as a primary information collection point, which facilitates central collation.

Four basic categories of finished analytical time framework products include:

(1) *Research Intelligence* formatted in monographs and in-depth studies, underpins current and estimative intelligence. Research intelligence has two specialized subcategories: (1) basic intelligence, and (2) intelligence for operational support.

(2) *Estimative Intelligence* defines what might be or might happen. The estimate starts with available facts, migrates into unknown, even unknowable, and suggests alternative patterns. In addition, estimative intelligence helps policymakers

navigate gaps between available facts, and provides informed assessments of possible outcomes.

(3) *Current Intelligence* addresses daily events, apprises consumers of new developments, and provides consequence warnings. Current intelligence products consist of frequent publications, ad hoc memorandums, and oral briefings to senior officials.

(4) *Warning Intelligence* sounds the alarm: (1) connotes urgency (2), gives notice to policymakers, and (3) implies the potential need for policy and action response.

Finished analytical intelligence products include: (1) briefings, (2) spot reports, (3) quarterly trends reports, (4) threat assessments, (5) crime bulletins, (6) warnings, and (7) after-action reports. There are other local analytical reports and combinations to these basic themes. Essential incident information includes the following intelligence basics: (1) who or whom, (2) what, (3) why, (4) when, and (5) how of the incident and collection process. Finished intelligence products require a review process to ensure accuracy and proficiency.

CONCLUSION

Crime and intelligence analysts update police executives, commanders and every member of the law enforcement agency, concerning criminal activity and the criminal environment. The finished criminal intelligence products that analysts provide are crucial to effective leadership, and decision-making. Oral briefings and written reports offer the latest information and finished criminal intelligence products. These analytical products and professional efforts represent the intellect of an ILP management system.

ENDNOTES

1. International Association of Law Enforcement Intelligence
    Analysts, Successful Law Enforcement Using Analytical Methods:
    (Internet Published Document, undated), 2.

2. The Commission on Accreditation of Law Enforcement Agencies,
    Standards for Law Enforcement Accreditation, Standard 51.1.1,
    Criminal Intelligence, Washington, DC. (CALEA), 2002.

3. New Jersey State Police, Practical Guide to Intelligence-Led
    Policing, 2006.

4. Marilyn B. Peterson (Sommer), "Strategic Intelligence for Law
    Enforcement," Law Enforcement Intelligence Analysis Digest,
    volume 6, no. 2 (1991-92), 19.

5. Pennsylvania Crime Commission, Organized Crime in
    Pennsylvania: A decade of Change (Commonwealth of
    Pennsylvanian Printing, 1990): 133.

PART III
TACTICAL APPLICATIONS

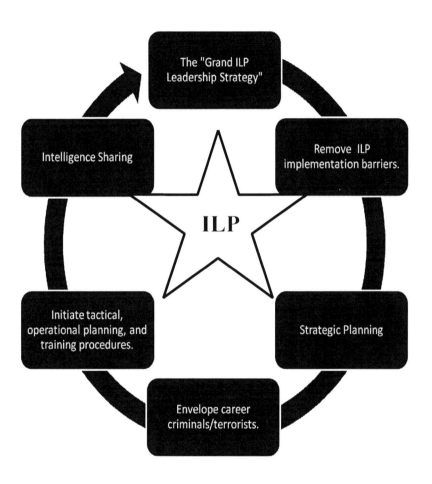

198

LEADERSHIP FOUNDATIONS	GUIDEPOST BEHAVIORS
❖ Strategic leadership: the "Grand ILP Leadership Strategy"	❖ The thin blue line and ILP represent the first line of defense and offense.
❖ Remove barriers to the implementation of ILP management strategies.	❖ Excellent leadership requires superior communication and feedback.
❖ Strategic Planning: intelligence, crime and investigative analysis.	❖ Apply the seven basic tenets of ILP, especially targeting career criminals, informants, and offender interviews.
❖ Envelope career criminals/terrorists and their organizations at their center of gravity.	❖ Effective police leadership applies the principles of criminal and terrorist conspiracy investigations.
❖ Initiate tactical, operational planning, and training procedures.	❖ The training schedule provides opportunities for field and case study simulations.
❖ Intelligence Sharing: local, regional, state, tribal and federal agencies	❖ Law enforcement agencies coordinate the strategic formula: ILP Management +Intelligence Analysis (IA) + Crime Analysis (CA) + Collection (C) + Storage (S) + Computer Analysis (CA) + Dissemination (D) = Criminal Intelligence (CI).

CHAPTER 8
Analytical Models and Charting

There comes a time when for every addition of knowl-
edge you forget something that you knew before. It is
of the highest importance, therefore, not to have use-
less facts elbowing out the useful ones.

— Sir Arthur Conan Doyle

Senior leaders and supervisors delve through mountainous facts to arrive at important decisions. Ultimately, the chief executive is responsible for effective decisions that influence officer and civilian lives. Therefore, it is important to diminish useless facts that elbow out valuable information.

Some decisions are critical and time urgent, while others require thoughtful reflection. Intelligence reports, models, and analytical charting provide the means to filter and retain useful facts. A well-executed model or analytical chart can capture the essence of multiple reports, and provide a strategic or tactical picture for decision makers. Problem visualization facilitates understanding and focused decisions.

CHAPTER FOCUS

This chapter focuses on analytical models and charting techniques that inform police decision makers. Analytical support documents provide police and civilian analysts massive details in a visual portrait of crime. One analytical graphic may be worth a thousand words.

Police commanders require analysts' critical thinking, analytical models and charting products, for successful decision-making. In most instances, effective decisions are not intuitive in the moment; superior decisions follow evidence and analytical thinking.

This chapter reviews modeling and analytical charting strategies accessible to analysts and police decision makers. Emphasis will center on the value and application of visual products, which support intelligence reporting. Refer to Table 8-1 for the Chapter Focus and related concepts.

Table 8-1 Chapter Focus

Intelligence-Led Policing	ILP Analytical Formats	ILP Analytical Standards
	❖ Descriptive analytical reporting ❖ Explanatory analytical reporting ❖ Visualization ❖ Future forecasting ❖ Reporting brevity ❖ Supporting research ❖ Decision-making	❖ Planning standard ❖ Direction standard ❖ Collection standard ❖ Collation standard ❖ Legal standard ❖ Evaluation standard ❖ Follow-up standard
	ILP Analytical Standards	**ILP Visual Reporting**
	❖ Analytical accuracy ❖ Computerized standard ❖ Content standard ❖ Outcomes standard ❖ Report standard ❖ Product format standard ❖ Dissemination standard	❖ Analytical models ❖ Analytical charting ❖ Event flow analysis ❖ Association analysis ❖ Commodity flow analysis ❖ Telephone analysis ❖ VIA charting

ANALYTICAL OVERVIEW: REPORTING

The analysis of enterprise or organized crimes requires considerable expertise and knowledge of organizational structures. The criminal structure and hierarchy insulates leadership from prosecution. Intelligence analysts produce graphs, charts, and reports that support complex investigations of a conspiratorial nature. Basic analytical models and charting strategies assist investigator understanding of complex criminal networks and their human relationships.

Reporting systems identify criminal targets; however, they may obscure important concepts that could conclude the investigation. Analytical charting provides a visual snapshot and investigative insight into criminal organizations and their participants. Analytical charting presentations identify an analytical overview of conceptual relationships. The strategic picture may present tactical applications and recommendations that might not have materialized because of copious facts, details and multiple sources of data.

Analytical reports for police decision makers are concise, clearly written, and preferably under ten pages. A report synopsis at the top of the page serves the police decision maker's time management requirement. Intelligence research tends to be lengthy, scholarly, and extensively documented. The supporting research is available on request, and cites the availability of in-depth resources.

Analytical documents, models and charts must meet the highest standards for planning, objectivity, and accuracy. Support documents, i.e., models and analytical charts, may exist separately, or part of an intelligence topic report. The International Association of Law Enforcement Intelligence Analysts recommends the following Standards for Analytical Products/Processes as the criteria.

IALEIA Standards/Processes

Table 8-2A   Standards for Analytical Products/Processes

Planning Standard: Analysts shall understand the objective of their assignment, define the problem, and plan for the necessary resources. This shall be done through the use of a collection or investigative plan or through intelligence requirements. Specific steps to be taken to complete the assignment, including potential sources of information and a projected timeline, shall be included. The needs of the client (requirements) shall be reflected in the plan.
Direction Standard: Analysts shall be involved in planning and direction. Law enforcement agencies shall use analytic expertise to develop both short-term and long-term investigative priorities and plans. Analytic expertise may also be used to develop intelligence requirements as a driving force to determine investigative priorities and for incorporation into investigative plans to drive operations.
Collection Standard: Analytic research shall be thorough and use all available sources. An analytic product shall contain all relevant data available through sources and means available to the analyst.
Collection Follow-up Standard: In the course of collection by investigators and others, analysts shall evaluate the progress of the collection to determine if the collection plan/requirements are being met and shall identify additional sources of information, as well as identify information that may be useful to other cases or activities. Where possible, analysts shall relay that information to an appropriate body for follow-up.

Source: U.S. Justice Department, Bureau of Justice Administration BJA, Global Justice Information Sharing Initiative, IALEIA, Law Enforcement Analytic Standards (Washington DC, GPO, 2004): 23-25.

Table 8-2B   Standards for Analytical Products/Processes

Legal Constraints Standard: Raw data that has been obtained in violation of any applicable local, state, or federal law or ordinance shall not be incorporated into an analytic product.
Evaluation Standard: Information collected from all sources shall be evaluated and designated for source reliability, content validity, and relevancy. Effective evaluation is important not only to the validity of the intelligence product but also to officer safety, investigative effectiveness, and solidity of evidence in prosecutions.
Collation Standard: Raw data shall be organized and formatted so the analyst can retrieve; sort; identify patterns, anomalies, and information gaps; and store the data. When possible, this shall be done in a computerized format using the most appropriate software available to the analyst.
Analytic Accuracy Standard: An analytic product shall be an accurate representation of the data. In cases where exculpatory data has been found along with proofs, both should be included.
Computerized Analysis Standard: Analyses shall utilize the best and most current computerized visualization and analytic tools available to the analyst.

Source: U.S. Justice Department, Bureau of Justice Administration BJA, Global Justice Information Sharing Initiative, IALEIA, Law Enforcement Analytic Standards (Washington DC, GPO, 2004): 23-25.

Table 8-2C   Standards for Analytical Products/Processes

Analytic Product Content Standard: Analytic products shall always include analysis, assessments, integrated data, judgments, conclusions, and recommendations. Forecasts, estimates, and models shall be developed, where appropriate.

Analytic Outcomes Standard: Analyses shall include alternative scenarios and avoid single-solution outcomes where appropriate, especially when the outcomes could have significant consequences. Analyses shall indicate the most likely hypothesis, but this hypothesis shall be arrived at through the analysis of competing hypotheses. Those hypotheses not chosen shall also be noted.

Dissemination Plan Standard: Analysts shall develop a dissemination plan to encourage sharing of the product with applicable agencies. This plan shall indicate the security level of the document. It shall be reviewed and approved by supervisory personnel.

Analytic Report Standard: Reports shall be written clearly and facts documented thoroughly. A precise, analytic bottom line should be provided. A tight, logical organization of facts shall show how the analyst arrived at conclusions. Objective and dispassionate language shall be used, emphasizing brevity and clarity of expression.

Source: U.S. Justice Department, Bureau of Justice Administration BJA, Global Justice Information Sharing Initiative, IALEIA, Law Enforcement Analytic Standards (Washington DC, GPO, 2004): 23-25.

MODELS AND CHARTING

Models are directly associated with targeting criminal behavior and support the investigative process. The creation of a model provides opportunities to test a preliminary assumption or hypothesis. The model may prove useful in proving or disproving the hypothesis. Generally, multiple models may apply in the criminal environment, assisting indirectly and directly in criminal investigations. Models may apply to internal investigative strategies or external criminal activities.

Chapter Seven describes the above-mentioned intelligence analytical products. The Intelligence Cycle serves as the foundation for intelligence products, i.e., models and charts. Models and charting strategies support the related reports. Refer to Figure 8-1 for an example of the Intelligence Cycle and related intelligence analytical products.

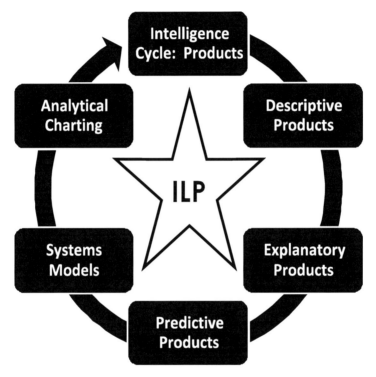

Figure 8-1   Intelligence Cycle and Products

Models and analytical charting documents support investigative teams as they approach complex conspiracy crimes. Models deal with abstractions and concepts in a concise manner. The model visualizes graphically and involves synthesis, which means incorporating the essentials to configure the whole. The following paragraphs and analytical charting techniques illustrate how they improve investigative capacity and support the above-mentioned analytical documents.

INTELLIGENCE MODELS

A model is a symbolic representation of an actual system; it is a substitute for the real system. Models describe the manner in which the system interacts; it represents an idea or actual system and the replica is a system of reasoning and logic. The representation has two basic forms: (1) physical and (2) conceptual, or abstract. The conceptual model description is an analytical process that is capable of prediction or estimating present and future outcomes.

Mathematical models are conceptual and descriptive. This chapter's discussion will be restricted to qualitative models and analytical charting, rather than quantitative statistical models.

An excellent reference for quantitative statistical models is entitled "Crime Analysis: From First Report to Final Arrest," by Steven Gottlieb, Sheldon Arenberg, and Raj Singh.

For example, Steven Gottlieb advocates, "From the crime analyst's point of view, descriptive and inferential statistics are inextricably linked. The number of robberies committed in a time interval can be illustrated on a table or graph (descriptive statistics). However, by observing a criminal's habit pattern or MO, the analyst is often able to infer or predict what the criminal will do next (inferential statistics). Indeed, correlating behavior to an individual(s) often may be the most effective way we have of assisting the investigative process."

INTERNAL ENFORCEMENT MODELS

The Federal Bureau of Investigation describes several elements of enterprise theory and related implications for law enforcement. Enterprise Theory of Investigation (ETI) has become the standard investigative model for investigating major criminal organizations. ETI encourages a proactive attack on the structure of the criminal enterprise. Effective long-range planning is the successful prosecution of the leadership, those who control the monetary element of the enterprise. [1]

Theories and visual models are applicable to internal investigative practices, like enterprise investigations. In addition, theories and models apply to the investigation of external criminal organizations, and targeting career criminals. Theories and abstractions in model formats that test theories, provide excellent visual portraits. Refer to Figure 8-2 for an illustration of enterprise theory converted to an internal model template.

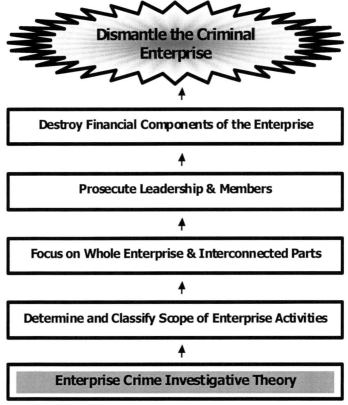

Figure 8-2   Enterprise Crime Investigative Theory/Model

EXTERNAL MODELS

External modeling strategies start with defining the criminal system and setting parameters of criminal behavior(s). Defining subsystems is essential when defining the whole problem, i.e., drug trafficking, and gang violence travel patterns. Community design may include neighborhood factors conducive to drive-by shootings. Once the system is in place, it is possible to select a related model template, or create a new model. For example, the environmental design model incorporates an engineering approach to crime prevention.

ENVIRONMENT DESIGN MODEL

Oscar Newman developed the Crime Prevention Through Environmental Design (CPTED) Model. This crime prevention approach applies principles of architectural design, that enhance the social aspects of territorial possession and principles of target hardening. There are four basic elements of defensible space: (1) *territoriality*, (2) *natural surveillance*, (3) *image*, and (4) *milieu*. Newman's model of *defensible space* or basic definition is "A model which inhibits crime by creating a physical expression of a social fabric which defends itself." The four criminological factors of this model are interconnected and have tremendous impact on the fear and level of crime. [2]

Newman defines each of these factors as important variables in creating social environments conducive to crime, or, on the other hand, aid in crime prevention:

(1) The concept term *territoriality* refers to the ability and desire of legitimate users to claim the area. Area control is based on: (a) the legitimate residents' establishment of real and perceived boundaries, (b) the general

communal climate, and (c) the recognition of strangers and inhabitants.

(2) The second concept, *natural surveillance*, refers to designing an area that allows legitimate users to observe: (a) the daily routines of neighbors, and (b) have the ability to take action when they observe the activities of strangers engaged in criminal activities.

(3) The model concept involves *image:* (a) the perception of safety within the living environment, (b) building a community, or neighborhood that does not seem vulnerable to crime, and (c) avoids isolation from the larger society.

(4) The model concept, *milieu*, suggests that the placement of the community in a larger context is important: (a) low crime and high surveillance, and, (b) will deter criminal activity. [3]

CASE STUDY: ENVIRONMENTAL DESIGN

Newman's (CPTED) Model and hypothesis was tested in one of Los Angeles crime ridden and gang oriented neighborhoods. The gang dominated neighborhoods and the contested streets produced many opportunities for street assaults and drive-by shootings. The increasing cycle of street violence was an unfolding tragedy for the gang members and innocent citizens. Repeated counterattacks produced a feeling of alarm and apprehension for the community, and Los Angeles Police Department (LAPD).

The LAPD built a buffer zone among gangs with Operation Cul-de-Sac (OCDS), and applied the Newman **designing-out** model. Traffic barriers assisted as an engineering factor in neighborhoods where gang violence peaked, according to crime analysis and police records. The approach illustrates Newman's

CPTED, and the goal was to reduce or control opportunities, for drive-by shootings. The barrier plan would reduce opportunities for violence through the elimination of major roadways. The reduced right of entry to vehicle traffic, would control access to high-crime neighborhood gang conflict violence.

James Lasley conducted a research study of Operation Cul de Sac (OCDS), testing CPTED and the related hypothesis in a field study of the project. His results indicated that: "OCDS focused on the proximate cause rather than a root cause, with the goal of using traffic barriers to decrease the mobility of rival neighborhood gangs traveling to and from gang hot spots. In this way, the barriers change situations in which gangs perceive opportunities to carry out hit-and-run crimes, such as drive-by shootings." [4] Refer to Table 8-3 and 8-4 for examples of the CPTED Model and the application of OCDS.

Studying gang social patterns and modus operandi (MO) or method of operation, provides the foundation for CPTED model interventions. Understanding the social fabric of gang criminal behaviors allows analysts to consider engineering out opportunities for criminal behavior. Newman's designing out model depends on pattern analysis and reinforcing the tenet of his basic concepts.

Table 8-3   CPTED Model and OCDS Study

DEFENSIBLE SPACE	DESIGNING-OUT GANG VIOLENCE
• **Territoriality:** The ability and desire of legitimate users to claim the area. • **Natural surveillance:** Residents' ability to take action, to view legal and illegal activities. • **Image:** Perception of safety within the living environment. • **Milieu:** Placement of community in a larger context. • Low crime and high surveillance will deter crime.	• Operation Cul de Sac (OCDS) • 10 block area • Highest number of shootings • Hard core street gangs: 25-30 • Turf-based gangs • Narcotics trafficking and other related criminal activities • Drive-by shootings=38 • Homicides=7 • Aggravated assaults=174 • Data before research design.
RESEARCH EVALUATION	**RESEARCH FINDINGS**
• **Methods:** quasi-experimental study • **Comparison:** two sites • **Measurements:** before, during and after • Comparisons to similar area without barrier implementation • Analyzing data from control and experimental OCDS sites • OCDS sites compared with experimental data from surrounding areas • Crime displacement measured in controlled surrounding areas • Researches compared crime levels before and after the program.	• LAPD data and analysis concerned part one of the Uniform FBI Crime Reporting System • Three principle areas were measured: homicides, aggravated assaults and property crimes (burglary, auto theft, automobile burglaries if locked, grand theft, bicycle theft, theft from unlocked automobiles and theft from individuals) • Crime data from annual and quarterly reports showed improvement indicating that the chances are less than 5 in 100 that the results occurred by statistical chance.

Source: James Lasley, U.S. Department of Justice, National Institute of Justice, Research in Brief, Designing Out Gang Homicides and Street Assaults (Washington, DC: GPO, 1998): 2.

Table 8-4 OCDS Study Results

LAPD OCDS GANG STUDY	**Property crime** decreased substantially during the first year of the program, but it also decreased in the comparison area where there was no OCDS, indicating that some factor or factors other than the traffic barriers were responsible for the reduction in the OCDS site.
	In the second year of the program, property crime rose, suggesting the street closures affected only violent crime.
	Crime was not displaced to other areas. Violent crime fell, not only in the OCDS area but also in contiguous areas. This may be because the areas of potential displacement are the turf of rival gangs. As such, they would be off-limits to gangs that might want to enter new territory when the traffic barriers reduced their opportunities to commit crime on their own turf.
	Traffic barriers can be used as part of an approach to maximize neighborhood residents' defensible space by increasing their span of control. Zones configured with the barriers heighten the visibility of suspect activities. They can be particularly effective when combined with "natural guardians," people who serve as informal sources of surveillance and social control.
	Although these findings indicate traffic barriers may work to reduce violent crime, it should be kept in mind that the experiment was conducted at only one site. Replications of OCDS and further evaluations are needed to fully test the effectiveness of the tactic.

Source: James Lasley, U.S. Department of Justice, National Institute of Justice, Research in Brief, Designing Out Gang Homicides and Street Assaults (Washington, DC: GPO, 1998): 2.

PATTERN ANALYSIS

Pattern analysis has a rich history, but the modern effort started with Major General L. W. Atcherly and the Modus Operandi System. This system began in London, England, formally systematizing criminal behavior patterns, at the turn of the twentieth century. The basic premise noted that criminals are creatures of habit; therefore, tend to repeat successful behaviors.

The analysis and classification of crimes are important considerations. For example, type of crime, person attacked, how attacked, means of attack, time of attack, object of attack, and trademarks are important variables in crime analysis. In addition, vehicle or methods of transportation and suspect description are essential to eventual capture and arrest. Moreover, pattern analysis would eventually lead to case linkage and closing other related cases.

ANALYST'S NOTEBOOK OVERVIEW

Modern systems provide computer software applications that fine-tune data and charting analysis. Tracing patterns and developing charting analysis before products like the Analyst Notebook software, meant reviewing spreadsheets and considerable data. The following paragraphs are citations from Analysts Notebook literature:

"Modern investigations involve vast amounts of raw, multi-format data, gathered from a wide variety of sources. Somewhere in this data lies the key to your investigation but it remains obscured by the sheer volume and apparent randomness of individual facts. Analyst's Notebook software brings clarity to complex investigations and intelligence analysis. It enables analysts and investigators to turn large volumes of disparate data into actionable intelligence.

Using Analyst's Notebook, analysts can uncover and interpret the relationships and patterns hidden within their data, displaying them in intuitive charts. These analytical charts are not merely visual aids; all entities and links retain the information they represent on embedded data cards or through direct links to databases. Organized source information substantiates and supports charts during verbal briefings or legal court cases.

Analyst's Notebook's design accommodates the information sharing needs of cross-agency operations. The result is an information-sharing environment where each agency has access to the complete intelligence picture.

Apply an array of sophisticated analytical techniques including: network, commodity flow, telephone record, financial and much more.

Identify hidden patterns and connections within data to focus on investigations. Create and update charts manually or automatically from structured data.

Combine analysis with cooperating agencies, and matching entities are automatically merged, data cards updated and new links established.

Communicate complex cases with intuitive briefing charts that capture and organize supporting data. Refer to Figures 8-3, 8-4, and 8-6 for examples of event flow analysis, association analysis, and visual investigative analysis. Analytical charting and pattern analysis provide criminal intelligence and new methods of sharing information with other law enforcement agencies.

ANALYTICAL CHARTING PRODUCTS

The analysis of enterprise crime requires considerable knowledge of organizational structure and criminal personalities. The criminal hierarchy insulates and conceals the upper echelons of leadership. Intelligence analysts produce charts, graphs, and computer-generated information that support enterprise investigations.

Excellent criminal intelligence spotlights leadership and targets them for future prosecution. Lost in a maze of facts and details, investigators might miss the essence of timing ideal investigative opportunities. Event flow analysis, association analysis, commodity analysis, and Visual Investigative

Analysis (VIA) charting techniques provide pertinent intelligence. Charting allows investigators to view the strategic picture, and all subcomponents of the criminal enterprise.

EVENT FLOW ANALYSIS

Event flow analysis generally precedes association and commodity flow analysis early in the investigation. When applied properly, the data provides a sequence of events over time, leading up to the criminal event and related post event behaviors. The series of events applies to a specific criminal violation of the law and demonstrates a modus operandi pattern of the crime. For an example of event flow analysis, not specifically stated as such, refer to a federal COPS publication entitled, Dealing Drugs in Privately Owned Apartment Complexes. [5]

Intelligence analysts organize the data into meaningful information, and provide criminal information to investigators. The event flow chart depicts the occurrences in a drawing format or chronological table. [6] The analysts and police commanders draw conclusions, after completing the chart. Complex drug investigations require event flow, and commodity flow-charting. Review Figure 8-3 for an example of an event flow chart.

ASSOCIATION ANALYSIS

Association analysis remains the cornerstone of enterprise intelligence; it can describe the criminal organization and its relative strength. Moreover, it develops indications of power and influence, the relationship to legitimate business by association matrices and link charts. "Association and network analysis is the 'bread and butter' of criminal intelligence units." [7] Association analysis provides the foundation for applications in commodity flow analysis.

Figure 8-3   Event Flow Analysis: Refer to i2 Drug Cartel Investigation

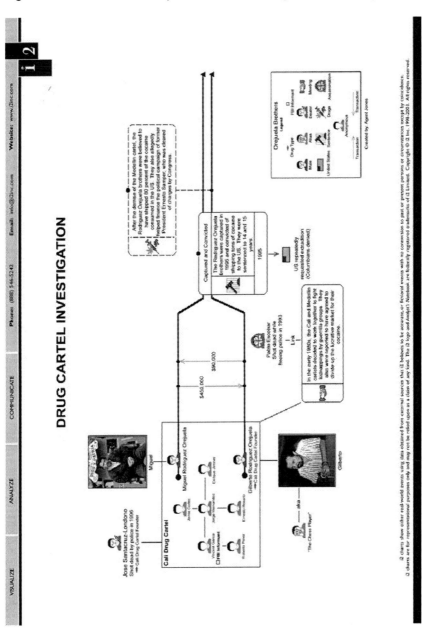

The association or network chart portrays relationships among suspects, patrons, and their connection to the criminal enterprise. The focus is on personalities, social histories, and patterns of social interaction. Association analysis creates opportunities for further investigative strategies, and analytical charting.

Telephone analysis and association analysis form the basis for electronic surveillance, to trace criminal suspects. Pablo Escobar was located based on association analysis of family members, and key cartel members of his criminal cocaine enterprise. The combination of a Colombian police lieutenant, U.S. intelligence officials, U.S. Army support teams, and cell telephone calls, fixed his position.

The pattern of cell telephone calls, led the Colombian police to his door, where he died of multiple gunshot wounds, while attempting to escape. Association analysis and HUMINT set the foundation for analyzing the human intelligence factor, i.e., human support systems. COMINT electronic communications can demonstrate links between suspected members, and known career criminals or terrorists. Refer to Figure 8-4 for an example of an association analysis chart.

Global association analysis is difficult when charting criminals because some organizations are loosely formed and have transient operations. After a particular operation, teams of specialists may disappear, only to reemerge for some other criminal enterprise, as part of the network structure.

Figure 8-4   Association Analysis: Refer to i2 Terrorism Plot

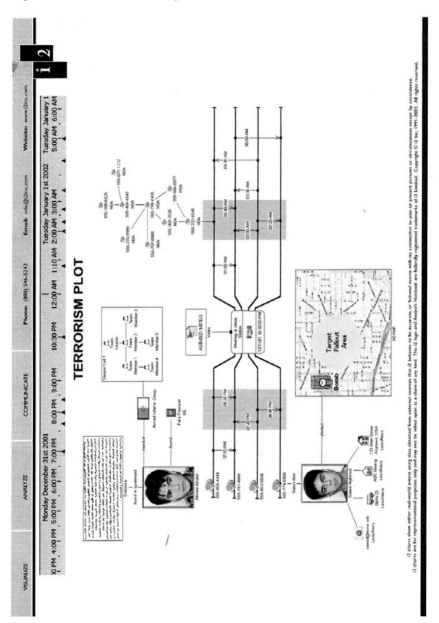

COMMODITY FLOW ANALYSIS

Commodity Flow Analysis identifies the distribution network, and money traced to key individuals. The process collects, complies, and organizes data that connects illegal contraband, currency, or illegal services, generally of an enterprise nature. The flow of these goods, monies, and services, serve investigators when depicted in a commodity flow chart format.

This chart depicts the flow of commodities and services. For example, commodity flow analysis would serve investigative objectives concerning enterprise crime. In addition, review a federal COPS publication, entitled Drug Dealing in Open-Air Markets for an unstated example of commodity flow analysis. [8] Refer to Figure 8-5 for a commodity flow chart.

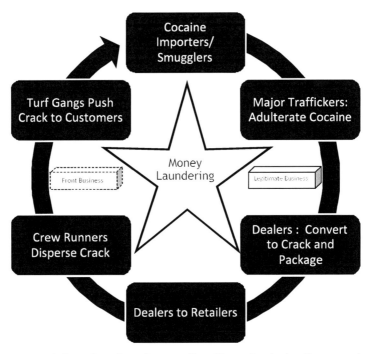

Figure 8-5   Cocaine Commodity Flow Analysis Chart and Intelligence Cycle

CASE ANALYSIS

Criminals carefully plan and execute enterprise crimes, unlike disorganized, spontaneous, or impulsive crimes. The primary objective is furtherance of the criminal organization, to enhance financial gain. Power and political influence insulate the enterprise from law enforcement investigations and prosecutions.

The enterprise may engage in both legal and illegal business ventures, to achieve financial supremacy and control over criminal activities. Visual Investigative Analysis (VIA) charting and analytical procedures assists in plotting an investigative examination, in complex cases. The sequencing of investigative strategies, assures progressions and priorities move smoothly to a logical conclusion. Refer to Figure 8-6 for an example of VIA charting.

There is an inclination to implement tactical strategies early in enterprise investigations. Early tactical operations may assist the criminal enterprise in recovering losses, and establishing a positive learning curve. The arrest of a few, low level participants, in the enterprise, is a dead end. Moreover, it ignores high-level leaders, and bankers that are central to the conspiracy case. The long-term strategic picture frames the whole system. The enterprise model and VIA chart systematically attack leadership, serving the demise of the entire enterprise.

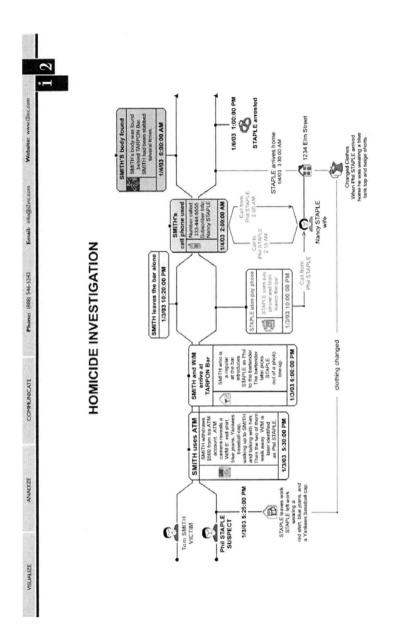

Figure 8-6   i2 Homicide Investigation/Event Flow and VIA Charting

FOCUS POINTS

Police senior leaders, middle managers and supervisors need timely, actionable intelligence, for the criminal targeting process. Analysts prefer to present intelligence products, and not become involved in the leadership decision-making process. Analysts produce intelligence products: (1) reports, (2) models, (3) and analytical charting, that support crime fighting endeavors and community solutions. Police leaders make decisions that lead to positive prevention and intervention outcomes.

Systems analysis involves structure, function, or process; combination models are possible. One superior example of structure, is the organized crime model, i.e., boss, underboss, and soldiers. Functional models deal with system functionality including: (1) systems maintenance, and (2) financial profits.

The visual presentation identifies an analytical overview of the facts, recommendations, and tactical applications. These analytical graphics clearly render the complex relationships in enterprise crime and their criminal networks for investigators. A visual charting diagram illustrates suspects, patrons, locations, and demonstrates criminal relationships.

Analytical charting and analysis offer strategic and tactical insight opportunities. Graphic and visual snapshots provide valuable insight into criminal enterprise strategies. Reviewing written reports may obscure important concepts and facts that could successfully conclude the investigation. Charting strategies address salient facts in an efficient manner.

The foundation for intelligence analysis is surveillance, informants and field interviews. The completed "intelligence product" may include brief biographical sketches, and charting analysis that illustrates the hierarchy leadership's strengths and vulnerabilities. Excellent intelligence analysis pieces together information that links the actions of criminals, to specific intelligence products, for field investigators.

The following intelligence products are applicable to ILP operations. The list is not inclusive; new strategies are constantly emerging. The main analytical charting strategies include: (1) event flow analysis, (2) association analysis, (3) commodity flow analysis, and (4) Visual Investigative Analysis (VIA). In addition, key graphic analysis include: (5) network analysis, (6) risk analysis, (7) financial analysis, (8) telephone record analysis and (9) other graphic visual formats.

Accurate intelligence analysis, reporting, models, and charting enterprise criminal operations, focuses a spotlight on criminals. Coordination and sharing of criminal intelligence counters enterprise crime threats, and can make a positive difference concerning prevention, intervention, and prosecution.

CONCLUSION

Investigators and intelligence analysts operate in similar ways. Criminal investigators lead the investigation; the analyst is supportive, planning and future oriented. Intelligence analysts offer strategic and tactical intelligence for field investigators; together they represent a formidable team. Intelligence-led policing and intelligence analysis products provide the criminal intelligence that allows both to function at optimal levels of performance.

ENDNOTES

1. Richard A. McFeely, "Enterprise Crime Theory of Investigation," FBI Law Enforcement Bulletin (May 2001), 19.

2. Oscar Newman, Defensible Space (New York: Macmillan, 1972), 3.

3. Newman, Defensible Space, 6.

4. James Lasley, U.S. Department of Justice, National Institute of Justice, Research in Brief, Designing Out Gang Homicides and Street Assaults (Washington, DC: GPO, 1998): 2.

5. Rana Sampson, U.S. Department of Justice, Office of Community Oriented Policing Services, Drug Dealing in Privately Owned Apartment Complexes (Washington, DC: GPO, 2002): 2-10.

6. Marilyn Peterson (Sommer), Applications in Criminal Analysis: A Source Book (Westport, CT: Praeger Publications Company, 1998), 44.

7. Frederick T. Martens, "An Enforcement Paradox: The Intelligence Dilemma in Narcotic Enforcement," Journal of Justice Issues, Volume 1, No. 2 (1986), 8.

8. Alex Harocopos and Mike Hough, U.S. Department of Justice, Office of Community Oriented Policing Services, Drug Dealing in Open-Air Markets (Washington, DC: GPO, 2005): 1-13.

CHAPTER 9
Investigative Strategies

They say that genius is an infinite capacity for taking pains. It is a very bad definition, but it does apply to detective work.
— Sir Arthur Conan Doyle

The investigator's professional responsibility is not simply to convict, but exonerate the innocent. Rigorous methods of investigation demand patience, discipline, and dedication. Investigations may require standing in freezing rain during a surveillance stakeout, or waiting long hours for a drug trafficker to emerge. In other cases, successful investigations require the boring and methodical search of a suspect's garbage can, attempting to locate evidence of an organized prostitution syndicate. Solving conspiracy enterprise crimes requires gathering, analyzing evidence, and taking great pains to close the investigation.

CHAPTER FOCUS

This chapter focuses on conspiracies associated with enterprise crime. In addition, emphasis is placed on career criminals and their organizations. Intelligence-Led Policing (ILP) targets career criminals and repeat offenders. ILP targets career felony offenders and their criminal organizations on the belief that they are responsible for significant amounts of serious crime.

The key basic ILP tools for investigating complex conspiracy crimes include: (1) human intelligence or HUMINT, primarily informants, undercover operations and surveillance procedures, (2) communications intelligence or COMINT, primarily electronic surveillance, i.e., wiretapping.

This chapter addresses: (1) analytic strategies for conspiracy crimes, (2) informants, (3) undercover operations, (4) physical surveillance tactics, and (5) electronic surveillance. Chapter topics emphasize the ILP connection to conspiracy crimes and related requirements. Refer to Table 9-1 for the chapter focus and basic concepts.

Table 9-1   Chapter Focus

Enterprise Crime	Investigative Tools
❖ Global concept ❖ White collar crime ❖ Organized crime ❖ Drug trafficking ❖ Cyber crimes ❖ Human trafficking ❖ Selling human body parts	❖ Human intelligence ❖ Communications intelligence ❖ Undercover operations ❖ Physical surveillance ❖ Informants ❖ Electronic surveillance ❖ Intelligence sharing
Informant Management	**Undercover Operations**
❖ Central ILP management ❖ Centralized database ❖ Control and corroboration ❖ Classifying informants ❖ Supervising informants ❖ Collecting and reporting ❖ Criminal information	❖ Personnel selection ❖ Planning ❖ Team training ❖ Team deployment ❖ Carrying out operations ❖ Operation termination ❖ Reintegration

(Intelligence-Led Policing)

ENTERPRISE CONSPIRACY CRIMES

Enterprise crime represents a wide-ranging concept, encompassing an expansive range of economic white collar, fraud, and organized crimes. The concept covers criminal activities other than traditional organized crime and drug trafficking. Criminal offenses are committed because both legal and illegal markets meet the laws of supply and demand.

Intelligence analysis provides the means to penetrate enterprise crime and dismantle the organizational structure.

According to the United Nations, world criminal enterprise activities include, but should not be limited to, corruption, arms trafficking, environmental crime, credit card fraud, cyber crime and trafficking in nuclear weapons. Trafficking in body parts, women, children, and other new forms of enterprise crimes may eventually render drug trafficking as a lesser law enforcement concern. [1]

For example, Asian criminals are involved in smuggling humans to the United States for the purpose of prostitution and involuntary servitude in brothels. Sex slave victims include underage children, especially from overseas source countries. Typical American front agencies include massage parlors, spas, and tanning parlors. Beauty salons may act as fronts for houses of prostitution. Brothels receive protection from Asian street gangs. These gangs may cross state lines and local jurisdictions to provide protection for front businesses. [2]

Global criminals and their conspiracy crimes are the most elusive and painstaking investigations that a law enforcement agency will encounter. Moreover, the array of emerging white-collar crimes, seem to illustrate the theory of *enterprise* crime, rather than the more restrictive term *organized* crime. *The Godfather* organized crime films portray these conspiracy crimes as an Italian problem. The enterprise model dispels this myth, and includes vast complex networks of diverse crimes comprising varied ethnic or racial groups.

The media can be misleading; however, occasionally, a well-written piece will appear in magazines depicting other ethnic or racial groups. Enterprise crime operates without a dominant group among numerous ethnic groups. These illegal transnational groups occasionally cooperate, and operate independently. Many criminal cartels have legitimate business fronts and government support.

The globalization and networking of a nation's economy has numerous systemic implications for enterprise criminals. Criminal opportunities have multiplied astronomically. Moreover, enhanced communications, world travel, and electronic options for transferring money have opened doors for complex white-collar criminals. Global requirements have altered the way traditional organized crime networks conduct business.

Enterprise crime varies in organizational structure; it is less traditional and related to function. A number of recent enterprise organizations have flexible, decentralized leadership structures. In some cases, the leadership may include a committee or confederation, with temporary ties to other criminal organizations. To avoid prosecution, some criminal organizations introduce additional layers of criminals to insulate leaders from direct participation. Leaders may simply communicate with trusted family members or confidants who relay orders to intermediaries. [3]

Professional criminals are adept at avoiding detection and apprehension. Moreover, enterprise criminals have protective insulation and hire the best legal defense teams. Enterprise or organized criminals represent the indefinable targets. Global crimes and international travel add to the difficulty of tracking vast amounts of sophisticated conspiracy crimes.

CONSPIRACY CRIMES

Criminal conspiracies form the foundation for enterprise crimes. A criminal conspiracy consists of two or more persons who engage in a criminal agreement. The crime of conspiracy at common law only involved the criminal agreement; one did not have to prove the act. The common law definition of conspiracy serves as the basic standard in the United States. The crime of conspiracy differs in many jurisdictions; many require some overt act, or more than an overt act, in the furtherance of the conspiracy.

For example, federal law requires a specific overt act committed by the conspirators for a conviction. Title 18 U. S. C. 371: "If two or more persons conspire either to commit any offense against the United States or to defraud the United States or any agency thereof in any manner or for any purpose and one or more of such persons do any act to effect the object of the conspiracy, each shall be fined not more than $10,000 or imprisoned not more than five years or both."

Investigating enterprise conspiracies involves considerable understanding of variable state statutes. Investigators should research the local statutes and understand the proof requirements. Even if there were no overt act requirement to further the goal of the conspiracy, it would be wise to wait for one to occur. Prosecutors prefer evidence beyond the mere meeting of minds to prove a criminal case.

The ideal prosecution is to have one of the members of the conspiracy withdraw and testify against the co-conspirators. The other opportunity is to give one conspirator immunity to testify against the others. The best-case scenario is to have evidence outside of verbal testimony under a plea bargain and immunity of one of the conspirators.

Intermediate objectives include the interdiction and prevention of criminal or terrorist activities. The related investigative strategies of surveillance, electronic monitoring of informants, and wiretapping endeavors provide additional intelligence regarding on-going conspiracies. An intervention

versus the continual flow of vital intelligence against the need
to prevent violence remains a recurring conflict.

The goal of conspiracy crimes investigation is to identify
the whole system and its related components. The criminal
membership is a starting point, but the leadership hierarchy
is the primary target. Investigations generally involve undercover officers, informants, and electronic surveillance to identify major participants, commodity trafficking and financial
patterns. Investigative objectives include the destruction of
terrorist or criminal enterprises and criminal prosecutions.

MANAGEMENT OF INFORMANTS

Informants remain central to ILP management criminal
information requirements. The ability to penetrate criminal
and terrorist organizations remains essential to achieving real
time intelligence requirements. The well-placed informant
who has access to the criminal leadership hierarchy is an
ideal investigative asset. Supportive management is vital to
maximizing the flow of essential criminal information. Refer
to Figure 9-1 for the fundamentals of an informant management program.

"The bread and butter of any effective law enforcement
agency enterprise control program remain a well-controlled
informant program. Enterprise investigations depend on a
successful informant recruitment program. Investigators rely
on informants to provide 'insider information' that provides
information on vulnerabilities or strengths. Informants provide the road map for law enforcement strategic and tactical
strategies. [4]

"Informant programs provide essential modus operandi
information that allows corroboration from other sources.
The agency, rather than individual investigators centrally

organize the control of informants. Managerial oversight ensures that the agency avoids informant manipulations that may include illegal activities or calculated attempts to eliminate competition. A coded number identifies informants and the monitoring of funds is rigorously scrutinized. Documentation of meetings with informants avoids accusations of misconduct and provide for the safety of investigators." [5]

Figure 9-1   Informant Management Program

CONTROLLING INFORMANTS

There will always be confidential informants who are not formally coordinated within the informant management program. Police agencies strive to avoid informants working independently with police officers and investigators. Failure to centralize and coordinate essential criminal information fosters an incomplete intelligence picture. Moreover, the failure to manage, supervise, and control informants properly can have tragic consequences.

Informant criminal information requires a central intelligence collation point. Moreover, one controller is the preferred mode of communication. Informants can disappear with multiple handlers or become "paranoid" when confronted with too many officers. Protection of an informant's identity remains the highest priority for informant management programs.

Informants remain anonymous; however, in some cases, they must testify in court because of prearranged plea agreements. Criminal informants "under the gun" have precondition agreements to testify against others, for a reduced sentence. Their identity cover remains undisclosed until discovery motions reveal their role in an upcoming trial. Informants of this nature are normally in protective custody or in the Witness Protection Program.

Informants are assigned code numbers; investigators avoid using their names in reports. Referring to informants in arrest reports and search warrants is not a good practice. Only the code number applies if the informant's information is crucial because of an emergency or investigative timing. Police officers are not required to identify informants unless the entire case bears on their testimony. Generally, the prosecutor will withdraw the case if the judge requires the identity of the informant.

Enterprise investigations may require the teaming of informants and undercover officers. This practice presents a delicate balance because of the danger associated with relying on a criminal informant to protect the officer's identity. Teaming works best when an informant is "under the gun" and facing serious criminal charges. The best enterprise informants are "under the gun" or revenge informants; they have a personal grudge or vendetta.

In some cases, informants may operate with an undercover officer; however, preferably not with a deep cover officer. This practice is high risk; the outcome may be a failed investigation or worse. The flow of criminal information from two sources enhances corroboration and cross validation. Informant information is operationally superior when corroborated through many sources.

Excellent undercover officers may only need an introduction, creating multiple opportunities for using unwitting informants. The best informants tend to be unwitting because they do not recognize the deep cover officer's identity. Informant status is a top-secret priority because it is a life and death issue for informants and undercover officers.

UNDERCOVER OPERATIONS

ILP management and intelligence analysis requirements directly support undercover police operations. Undercover sworn operatives perform best when there is intensive strategic planning, tactical and accurate intelligence support. The flow of criminal intelligence provides guidance and direction for undercover investigative teams. The targeting of criminals and their organization involves great risk; therefore, undercover operations require extensive planning.

Deep cover operations penetrate profoundly into the criminal organization, unlike street "buy-bust operations" that only snare a small segment of the operation. The objective of a deep cover officer is to dismantle the criminal enterprise leadership structure. The ultimate goal is the total destruction of the system, a very difficult goal to achieve. Accomplishing the related goals and objectives requires concise planning procedures. Refer to Figure 9-2 for an illustration of the planning process.

Figure 9-2   Deep Cover Planning

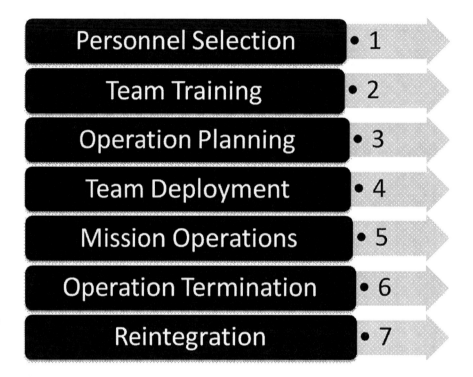

SELECTION CRITERIA

The starting point for successful undercover operations is the personnel selection process. The wrong person in the position can lead to the death of an officer, informant, or both. The criterion of selecting young officers because of their youthful appearance is not wise and could be perilous to the mission. The officer's sobriety, social maturity, and excellent judgment represent desirable personal qualities. Exceptional undercover officers are a rare commodity because of their experience, personality, and mind set.

Undercover operations are effective depending on the organization, support, and personnel selection process. The Federal Bureau selection of Special Agent Joseph D. Pistone, alias Donnie Brasco is an example of a successful mission. However, some undercover operations are not cost effective, and others are marginal at best.

Enterprise criminal organizations are very difficult to infiltrate with traditional undercover operations. Agent Pistone was the right person at the right time for his criminal targets. Match deep cover officers for target requirements on physical, cultural and personality requirements.

The basic attributes include the ability to work alone for long time intervals and dedication to the mission. The officer must have the temperament and investigative expertise. Moreover, *looking* the part does not suffice, *acting* the part is the essential requirement.

Successful deep cover officers have an uncanny ability to change, adapt, and play many roles, not unlike a chameleon. They understand that their guise is a temporary façade, not a real identity. The assignment requires great personal and professional risks and sacrifices. Inexperienced officers may imagine fame and become disillusioned because of hyped media images.

Stable officers with successful records for difficult assignments under stress, are often excellent candidates. Someone who understands the value of strategic intelligence is a real asset, including the ability to think outside the immediate tactical operation. Previous military experience, prior police service in a faraway municipality, and no family ties to the community, comprise positive attributes.

OPERATIONS PLANNING

The administration and supervision of deep cover officers needs to be close and personal. The officer should never feel isolated and alone. Moreover, the officer must never feel that he or she is a power unto himself or herself and not answerable to supervision. Deep cover officers are subject to criminal group pressure, psychological impairment and numerous temptations.

LEADERSHIP AND TEAM TRAINING

Deep cover officers historically learn on the job; however, an in-service training program serves as a fundamental requirement for the position. The basic in-service training normally includes a local course conducted by the unit. The best instructors are former vice, intelligence, and undercover operatives. The federal government has local training opportunities, and the Drug Enforcement Administration has a course for drug investigators.

Teams that train together prior to operations survive together. New members without team training do not engage in operations without understanding every facet of the operation. They require close supervision by experienced officers, regardless of past assignments. Excellent leadership, supervision, and organization increase undercover officer safety.

The deep cover officer requires several levels of supervision. A control officer who is an experienced investigator at the corporal level represents the first level. This level of supervision generally involves an on top-level investigator or plainclothes detective who may engage in temporary undercover operations. This individual meets the deep cover officer in the field, provides case information, and secures field intelligence and preliminary arrest reports. The control officer generally operates in a disguised façade, providing backup in minor or relatively safe operations.

The control officer is the deep cover officer's life support system, meeting officers in the field, on a regular basis. There may be a prearranged designated drop zone or pickup location for undercover field notes and less important communications. The control officer updates the officer on the latest criminal intelligence, and obtains intelligence feedback. Deep officers provide essential field intelligence reports.

The control officer meets his deep cover officer in remote locations, not in the back of the police station. The control supervisor is the only point of contact; secretaries and student interns are not appropriate alternatives. Deep cover officers or supervisors postpone appointments using a prearranged code by cell phone, if an emergency or a peak activity period arises. Moreover, every supervisory effort protects the deep cover officer's false identity and family.

The second level of supervision is central desk support; this position is a twenty-four hour service for deep cover personnel. This sergeant level position supervises the control officer and serves as a backup system for deep cover officers. Deep cover officers must never feel that they are a "lone-wolf" operation without support. However, these officers must function independently, cut all social ties to other officers, and think critically.

Depending on the size of the police department, the next level of supervision is that of lieutenant. This individual commands the Intelligence, Vice, and Organized Crime units and has direct contact with the Chief or Investigative Division Commander. In addition, the lieutenant should have direct access to the civilian ILP manager and real-time intelligence.

OPERATIONS PLANNING

During high-risk assignments, for example, high-level drug buys, team support, and planning save lives. The location and support requires current or real-time intelligence analysis. Contingency planning protects the officer's life first; mission operation success becomes the second priority. Contingency planning provides many courses of action and back-up plans. Planning, training, and deep cover deployment operations require feedback during the tour of duty.

Sinister drug deals may incorporate a "rip-off" transaction where the undercover officer dies or becomes wounded. Informants are always vulnerable and need protection on high level buys. Vast sums of money create opportunities and motivation for high-risk criminal behaviors. The police always control the terms of the transaction, not the criminals. If the police cannot control the location and tactical support team requirements, the deal does not take place. Dangerous high-level cash or drug transactions require detailed planning.

TERMINATION AND REINTEGRATION

Assignment requirements are preferably no longer than one or two years. Transfers to open supervisor positions serve as transition points to reintegration programs and uniformed service. Police officers may need counseling support for post-traumatic stress disorder and reintegration adjustment. Training and support programs assist family members; it is impossible to keep them in the dark. Acknowledge the reintegration process of deep cover officers, even in the euphoria of successful operations.

SAFETY PRECAUTIONS

We need the deep cover officers to take on extremely dangerous assignments, in this time of enterprise crime and terrorism. They are at great risk, more than they may realize. Police and federal agents operating in undercover capacities are ten times more likely to be shot or shoot someone else.[6] Therefore, it is important to plan, train and target criminals and their organizations prudently. Surveillance precedes undercover operations; it is essential to undercover officer safety.

PHYSICAL SURVEILLANCE

Excellent physical surveillance starts with in-depth planning procedures. Well executed planning requires research on the subject's background, personal habits, and acquaintances. Familiarity with the neighborhood and favorite haunts assures acknowledgment of subtle movements in the subject's surroundings. High-level members of a criminal enterprise may employ counter-surveillance strategies to detect police surveillance.

The principles of physical surveillance include two basic types: (1) fixed surveillance, and, (2) mobile, foot or vehicle surveillance. Fixed surveillance is a stationary stakeout from a predetermined blind, typically an apartment or vehicle. Surveillance mini-vans are fully equipped with cameras and electronic surveillance equipment. Mobile surveillance involves foot and vehicles, the latter being more difficult to implement. Both surveillance strategies require a team approach, not the endeavor of one person.

Vehicle surveillance requires three separate vehicles working as a team. Traffic turns are primary obstacles and the same vehicle cannot constantly remain in the subject's rearview mirror. One vehicle, not part of the team, stays behind the subject, creating a blind spot. One vehicle remains ahead of the suspect, the second vehicle alongside and the third to the rear. The three vehicles rotate positions on intersection turns. This kind of A-B-C surveillance works best in moderate traffic.

Foot surveillance, tailing or shadowing, follows some of the same principles, but is less complicated. The best technique involves the A-B-C system; two officers positioned across the street from the subject, the third officer in front of the subject. Officers rotate positions when the subject makes abrupt turns. Female officers should be part of the team, to authenticate representation of the local population. In addition, the subject may meet a female conspirator and transfer contraband.

Surveillance is the independent investigative mode of analysis and supports undercover operations. Moreover, physical surveillance is the precursor to electronic surveillance. The art of surveillance is a specialized craft best delegated to those who thoroughly comprehend the tactics. There is always the risk of "being burned or having your cover blown."

This brief description illustrates some coordination considerations involved as surveillance unfolds. Additional precursor coordination points include undercover operations and electronic surveillance requirements. Initiate electronic surveillance as the last investigative maneuver. Preconditions for electronic ex parte warrants require exhausting all informants, undercover and physical surveillance investigative remedies.

ELECTRONIC SURVEILLANCE

Wiretapping, eavesdropping, and associated technologies represent the most effective weapons against enterprise crime. However, issues of constitutional protections are not technicalities, but human rights safeguards. The Fourth Amendment and Bill of Rights provide strong constitutional foundations that protect against the invasion of privacy.

Law enforcement officers face serious legal consequences for violating the Omnibus Crime Control Bill, wiretapping and eavesdropping, Title III provisions. In addition, many state electronic surveillance laws include civil and criminal penalties, including loss of police pension programs.

Law enforcement personnel require excellent intelligence analysis that provides probable cause for obtaining and placing the electronic equipment. However, acquired intelligence may be so sensitive, that it precludes use in the application for ex parte. The decision to release confidential information depends on trust considerations that may influence on-going investigations.

The application of association analysis, link analysis and market analysis assists in identifying key members of criminal enterprise conspiracies. Links among members and enterprise entities assist in identifying credible locations for physical and electronic surveillance. However, enterprise counter-surveillance and other strategies may present surveillance placement obstacles. Intelligence from telephone record analysis, matrix, and record charts may identify enterprise conspirators' communication patterns and criminal violations.

Telephone record analysis is one superior approach in justifying probable cause and installation of electronic surveillance equipment. The telephone matrix and charts serve as preliminary tools for telephone analysis. Linking new or unknown suspects is useful when networking criminal relationships; multiple subscriber conversations are essential in criminal enterprise investigations.

The pen-register forms the foundation for ex parte authorization; technology intercepts telephone calls made or received and call duration. The pen register or number recorder is capable of copying telephone numbers, identifying conversation patterns, the identification of co-conspirators and the frequency of their conversations. A record of dialed telephone numbers from long distance telephone and cell phone companies is particularly useful in criminal investigations.

In summary, basic investigative strategies concerning enterprise crime involve contributions from: (1) informants, (2) deep cover officers, (3) physical surveillance, and (4) electronic surveillance. Refer to the following case study on Russian organized or enterprise crime and attempt to initiate opportunities to apply the investigative strategies.

CASE STUDY: RUSSIAN ENTERPRISE CRIME

"Russian criminals engage in enterprise or traditional organized crime depending on the preference for the terminology. Russian organized crime or enterprise operations consist of many diverse ethnic groups and nationalities from the former Soviet Union's satellite nations. Russian members appreciate the open markets and financial opportunities in America. This preference has an economic impact on state and local communities in the United States. [7]

"Russian organized crime operates in America's major cities including: Boston, Chicago, Cleveland, Dallas, Miami, New York, Philadelphia, San Francisco, and Seattle; less populated communities are experiencing the consequence of Russian enterprise crime encroachment. Many consider the threat from the former Soviet Union to be over; however, Russian criminals remain a formidable cold war legacy. [8]

"The former KGB deliberately released hard-core criminals from their prisons, including the infamous 'Vory criminals or thieves with a code of honor.' United States government intelligence agencies believe these Russian career criminals were interspersed among 200,000 Soviet citizens fleeing religious persecution. Once in the United States, Russian criminals practiced numerous enterprise crimes and exploited our free market system. These Russian criminals were not common criminals, but educated and innovative; their activities represent an economic threat to our economy. [9]

"Russian criminals prefer financial swindles based on complex fraudulent gas and fuel schemes. The swindles involve individuals in positions to further the criminal opportunities, i.e., the New York Italian mafia, Colombo Family. The swindle involved a 'daisy chain' with a vanishing point; transferring gasoline on paper from one bogus company to another delayed the opportunity for auditors and investigators to discover the violations. They would fraudulently avoid the tax paid to the government because the last 'burn company' only existed on paper. The 'burn company' would disappear with the records and assets, avoiding the taxes due when the gasoline arrived at the retail level. [10]

"Russian criminals primarily prey on business owners in their own communities; their extortion methods include the threat or actual practice of violence. These small gangs refer to themselves as 'brigades,' a military analogy. The exploitation creates a climate of fear in the small community of Brighton Beach, Brooklyn, New York, where the immigrants' fear of the police exceeds that of criminals." [11] Refer to Table 9-2 for an example of Russian illegal markets.

Table 9-2   Russian Traditional Crimes & Illegal Markets

Traditional Crimes	Enterprise Crimes
❖ Murder	❖ Money laundering
❖ Extortion	❖ Auto theft
❖ Weapons	❖ Counterfeiting currency
❖ Smuggling	❖ Credit card theft
❖ Narcotics trafficking	❖ Insurance fraud, staged accidents, etc.
❖ Immigration fraud	❖ False Medicare billing
❖ Prostitution	❖ Tax fraud in fuel and gas industry

The traditional organized crime structure and membership hierarchy facilitates dominance through fear and corruption. Organizational goals are well defined and members attempt to establish a monopoly over a criminal cartel. Crime members will not hesitate to use force, including murder. When corruption and compromise fail, violence is the likely course of action. For example, "the Red Mafiya employs former Army officers, KGB agents who are capable of intelligence and counter intelligence operations. In addition, they hire former Russian athletes as extortionists and enforcers." [12]

CRIMINAL ENTERPRISE STRUCTURE

Some enterprise criminal organizations are not highly structured, but loosely organized and may cooperate with other criminal groups. Enterprise crime varies in organizational structure; it is less traditional and related to function. Numerous global enterprise organizations have a flexible, decentralized leadership structure. In some cases, the leadership may include a committee or confederation, with temporary ties to other criminal organizations.

Criminal organizations introduce additional layers of criminals to insulate their leaders from direct participation and avoid prosecution. Leaders may simply communicate with trusted family members or confidants who relay orders to intermediaries. [13] Review Figure 9-3 for an illustration of Russian enterprise organizational structure:

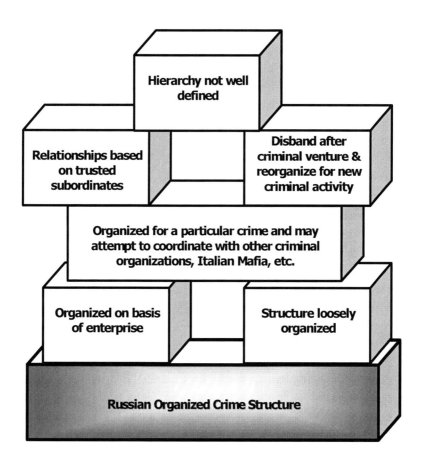

Figure 9-3 Russian Enterprise Structure

Intelligence analysis allows investigators to examine and understand every facet of the Russian criminal organization. Enterprise crime is a continuing criminal threat to the United States. Criminal organizations have the potential to subvert political, financial, and social institutions. Review the following case analysis for application of enterprise crime tools, intelligence analysis models, and charting strategies.

Russian Case Analysis

Infiltrating the conspiracy presents problems from the outside. Informants do not always have access to the inner circle and may exist on fringes of the enterprise. The fear of physical retaliation and death limit the numbers of those who act in the capacity of an informant.

Police undercover operations are very difficult for the same reasons informants experience. American law enforcement has difficulty infiltrating foreign national and ethnic groups because of cultural and language barriers. Physical and electronic surveillance offer the best opportunities in this case study.

The enterprise members' conversations provide the best evidence of participation in the conspiracy. The criminal membership communicates daily to further the business and execute the enterprise mission. Therefore, one of the best ways to penetrate the enterprise is electronic surveillance and technology. Telephone records and conversation analysis provides the tactical intelligence necessary for executing enforcement options.

Revisiting Analytical Models and Charting

Chapter 8 explores the applications of association analysis, event flow analysis, commodity flow analysis charting and describes how these analyses support investigations. The incorporation of these strategies provides a visual description of the enterprise model and analytical charting. The following ILP and intelligence analysis offers strategies to close an investigation successfully.

Association analysis helps define the principal co-conspirators of the enterprise, their roles in the power structure, and the organization as an entity. Criminal social interactions represent the primary goal of association analysis; personal histories may assist in the process. Association and network analysis may assist in this process. The end purpose is to define the enterprise system and all related subsystems.

Event flow analysis defines typical procedures and the chronological order of criminal events. The timing of criminal events allows for planned tactical intervention. Meeting times, frequency counts, and names of participants may reveal a patterned relationship. A connection exists among event flow analysis, association analysis and commodity analysis; nuances focus on different aspects of enterprise investigation.

Commodity flow analysis is particularly useful in tracking products and the money trail. It identifies the means of distribution and players, both overt and covert. Tracking the point of origin, flow, and destination facilitates interruption of the marketing cycle. Most importantly, evidence placement, before distribution, offers search and seizure opportunities.

FINANCIAL ANALYSIS

Economic analysis may reveal in what ways the operations of illegal businesses differ from legal business conditions. Money laundering has criminal origins; therefore, investigators may prove tax evasion on income. Criminal provisions include:

(1) filing a false income tax return, (2) failing to keep required records and (3) hiding assets with intent to defraud. [14]

Investigators followed the money in the Russian enterprise example. The basic investigative strategy of enterprise or organized crime is to follow the money trail from origination to final destination, including interval points along the way. Requiring purchasers to pay tax at the point of original distribution helps prevent enterprise fraud.

FOCUS POINTS: ENTERPRISE CRIME

Enterprise crime is an expansive concept; the definition continues to grow and operates outside the boundaries of traditional and organized crime. For example, enterprise crime offenses include environmental crime, and trafficking in body parts.

Targeting career felony offenders and their organizations can be a successful strategy for reducing repeat offenses and the level of crime. Opportunities for enterprise crime are abundant; including new global venues created for international criminals.

Undercover operations include high risks and rewards. Deep cover operations are expensive; however, when successful, the ultimate source of real-time criminal information. Undercover operations require excellent planning, management, and supervision. Intelligence sharing is a two-way endeavor, including field intelligence feedback from officers and intelligence analysis flowing to the undercover or deep cover operatives. Officers in the field cannot operate in a void or make cases without direction and adequate intelligence.

Informants are primary investigative tools; they operate in the criminal environment, have a trusted status, and intercept criminal information. The best informant is "under the gun," facing huge criminal charges and penalties, the second best is the revenge type. Excellent informant handlers control informants, place restrictions on informant behavior, and assist with possible betrayals.

Physical surveillance is the straightforward approach to assessing criminal patterns and interaction. Physical surveillance, informants, and pen registers of telephone calls serve as the foundation for the ultimate goal of wiretapping. Wiretapping and other forms of electronic surveillance are last resort investigative tools. Constitutional law regulates and dominates the application of electronic interceptions.

In summary, the basic keys for investigating enterprise crime are human intelligence (HUMINT) and communication intelligence (COMINT). Human intelligence includes, but is not limited to informants, undercover operations, and physical surveillance. Electronic communications include, but are not limited to wiretapping, and a host of other electronic tools.

CONCLUSION

ILP management forms the means of coordinating criminal intelligence. Intelligence analysis is the strategic strategy for organizing, reporting, and disseminating criminal intelligence. Career criminals exploit our society and represent a threat to our economic institutions. Enterprise criminals need to be this nation's first priority because they undermine our democracy. ILP management and criminal information sharing is the essential component of successful prevention, intervention and prosecution of enterprise criminals.

ENDNOTES

1. United Nations Economic and Social Council Report from the World Ministerial Conference on Organized Transnational Crime. National Legislation and its Adequacy to Deal with the Various Forms of Organized Transnational Crime: Appropriate Guidelines for Legislative and Other Measures to be taken at the National Level November 21-23, 1994, Item 5. (Excerpted in Trends in Organized Crime, Vol. 1, fall, 1995, 51-60.

2. Federal Bureau of Investigation, Asian Criminal Enterprise Unit, Trafficking of Asian Aliens, July 1998.

3. James W. Osterburg & Richard H. Ward, Criminal Investigation: A Method for Reconstructing the Past (Ohio: Anderson Publishing Company, 1997), 609.

4. Pennsylvania Crime Commission Report, Conshohocken, Pennsylvania, 1992, 46.

5. Pennsylvania Crime Commission, 46.

6. William A. Geller, "Put Friendly Fire Shootings in Perspective," Law Enforcement News, (1993), 18, 9.

7. James Q. Finckenauer and Yuri A. Voronin, U. S. Department of Justice, Office of Justice Programs, The Threat Of Russian Organized Crime, Washington, DC: GPO, 2001): 1-14.

8. Robert I. Friedman, Red Mafiya: How the Russian Mob has Invaded America (New York: Little Brown Company, 2000), 11.

9. Friedman, Red Mafiya, 13.

10. Petrus Van Duyne and Alan A. Block, "Organized Cross Atlantic Crime: Racketeering in Fuels," Crime and Social Change, 22, (1995), 127-147.

11. Friedman, Red Mafiya, 24.

12. Friedman, Red Mafiya, xv, 25.

13. James W. Osterburg and Richard H. Ward, 1997, 609.

14. Gerald Caiden and Herbert Alexander, The Politics and Economics of Organized Crime (New York: Lexington, 1986).

CHAPTER 10
Tactical Leadership: Training

Education never ends. It is a series of lessons with the greatest for last.   — Sir Arthur Conan Doyle

Intelligence-Led Policing (ILP) can provide real-time or near-time intelligence. The purpose of strategic and tactical intelligence is to educate and update leaders as to the essential criminal information necessary for effective decision making. Intelligence on criminals and terrorist activities provides valuable lessons, saves lives, avoiding the premature greatest last lesson.

CHAPTER FOCUS
The purpose of this chapter is to explore ILP support to field operations, and explore tactical operations. The role of intelligence is important; however, leadership and training are the essential requirements to successful missions and outcomes. This chapter addresses tactical leadership styles in the tactical environment.

Antiterrorism procedures are important leadership requirements for preventing terrorist operations. The proactive intelligence role requires denying terrorists intelligence on police operations and intelligence gathering methods. Areas of antiterrorism prevention include: (1) operations security, (2) personnel security, (3) physical security, and (4) crisis management planning. The goal of antiterrorism operations is to deny criminals and terrorist police information.

Once an incident occurs, police operations move to the reactive stage for performing crisis management and counterterrorism tactics. Excellent ILP and proactive prevention seeks to avoid tactical scenarios. Police, rescue, and fire team public safety training reduce injuries, fatalities and property damage. Excellent threat/risk management, crime prevention, and physical security programs assist in avoiding crisis management scenarios.

Dynamic planning articulates responsibilities and remedial responses for public safety agencies. Effective leadership, realistic training, and case study simulations, enhance tactical responses. Refer to the Chapter Focus, Table 10-1 for a chapter outline, and basic concepts.

Table 10-1   Chapter Focus

	ILP Police Strategies	ILP Intelligence Analyst Roles
Intelligence-Led Policing	❖ Antiterrorism strategies ❖ Counterterrorism strategies ❖ Intelligence summary ❖ Operations planning ❖ Threat analysis ❖ Swat teams ❖ Lessons learned	❖ Intelligence analysis ❖ Analytical charting ❖ Biographical sketches ❖ Terrorist profiling ❖ Terrorist group profile ❖ Model building ❖ Asymmetrical warfare intelligence
	ILP Antiterrorism Strategies	**ILP Counter Terrorism Leadership**
	❖ Proactive planning ❖ Police operations security ❖ Personnel security ❖ Physical security ❖ Crisis management ❖ OPSEC security measures ❖ Crime/physical security prevention surveys	❖ Tactical training ❖ Learning simulations ❖ Tactical leadership ❖ Frontline leadership ❖ Frontline behaviors ❖ Frontline feedback ❖ Field planning

ANTITERRORISM VERSUS COUNTERTERRORISM

Antiterrorism techniques include crime prevention surveys and related target hardening security procedures. This requires that crime or intelligence analysts think like terrorists, and anticipate possible terroristic acts before they take place. The Planning and Intelligence Cycle (refer to Chapter 1) is essential when gathering criminal information. Antiterrorism denotes the preventative stage of countering terrorism through the application of proactive prevention and security methods. Refer to Figure 10-1 for an illustration of differences between antiterrorism and counterterrorism models.

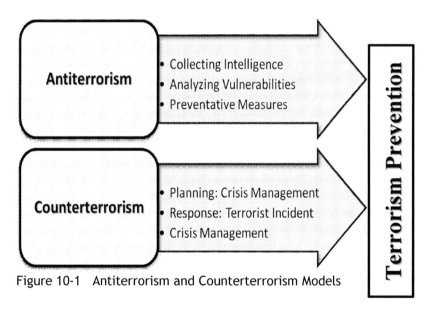

Figure 10-1   Antiterrorism and Counterterrorism Models

Counterterrorism techniques include the response to an immediate specific terrorist act. The response to a current terrorist incident requires the assignment of special reaction or SWAT teams, gathering intelligence information, and developing threat analysis intelligence to support the operation.

The success of tactical responses depends on planning antiterrorism proactive techniques and training methods.

Thus, prior training is important in the reactive counter-terrorism phase.

Counterterrorism planning includes: (1) intelligence summary collection of terrorist group intelligence, (2) threat analysis capabilities of the terrorist group, (3) force structure analysis (evaluation of friendly forces available), (4) stratify development (cooperative efforts among primary and secondary support agent), (5) requirements definition, (lessons learned), (6) operations plans (state of readiness), (7) plan validation (command center scenario training) and (8) plan implementation and review. [1]

INTELLIGENCE ANALYST: TERRORISM

The best tactic to prevail in a terrorist "asymmetrical warfare strategy" is accurate intelligence that provides the means to take the offense and avoid the defensive posture. Striking first takes the initiative away from the terrorists; attacking their base and organizational structure prevents future attacks. Intelligence and law enforcement operations have a significant role to play in antiterrorism and counterterrorism strategies. The United States is facing a national emergency and shadow war outside the limelight. American law enforcement, intelligence support and covert operations will play a significant battle in this long-term struggle. [2]

Information gathered by crime or intelligence analysts is important to countering terrorist activities. The collection, analysis, interpretation and timely dissemination of information remain essential to the effective response of field officers. Intelligence analysts gather information and intelligence on the terrorist threat from open sources of information, criminal information and covert sources.

Many analytical techniques discussed in Chapter 8 apply to terrorist organization investigations. For example, refer to: (1) event flow analysis, (2) commodity flow analysis, (3) association analysis, (4) financial analysis, (5) enterprise conspiracy, (6) electronic surveillance and (7) telephone record analysis. One form of analysis not discussed in Chapter 8, that has applications for both chapters, concerns biographical sketches.

BIOGRAPHICAL SKETCHES

Biographical sketches and photographs support the analytical techniques described above. The sketch proves useful in giving social and investigative histories to targeted suspects. It elaborates on their identities and assists in describing a rationale for their decision-making. The analyst reviews a variety of source documents; some are open files like news media accounts, while others are covert.

The biographical sketch identifies data particular to the suspect, for example, aliases, addresses, vehicles and business associations. A social history including cultural and ethnic heritage factors, proves helpful in terrorist investigations. Obvious details include: social security numbers, arrest numbers and convictions. Various national computer systems and regional intelligence projects may assist in this endeavor.

Terrorist groups are easier to profile than individuals. The format is similar to a biographical sketch; it offers terrorist motivation, group psychological, historical, and traditional value systems. The organizational profile describes strategic planning, tactics and past targets. The terrorists' religious, political, and ideological focus assists in threat analysis and assessment. The terrorist mission often defines symbolic targets and timetables. Pinpointing the terrorist organization and group characteristics focuses the investigative mission and technology applications.

INTELLIGENCE ANALYSIS: MODEL BUILDING

Terrorism definitions and profiles present problems for law enforcement officers; both represent an inferior means of analysis. There is the need to make the transition from definitions and personalities to models of terrorism. One researcher suggests that it may be possible to conceptualize a terrorism model that combines social structure and group psychology. [3] This approach may assist policy makers in developing improved counterterrorist responses.

There are five interconnected processes that are essential to understanding terrorism: (1) joining the group, (2) forming the activity, (3) remaining in the campaign, (4) leading the organization and (5) engaging in acts of terrorism. The emphasis on this model would include the social and psychological processes that produce and enhance terrorism. This model offers promise; however, there is the need for additional research and analytical models. [4]

PROACTIVE ANTITERRORISM STRATEGIES

Intelligence analysts and law enforcement officers can reduce the risk of becoming terrorist targets by understanding the nature of terrorism. Taking basic security precautions and developing antiterrorism (proactive) and counterterrorism (reactive) programs can reduce critical target vulnerability. Effective security measures require analytical strategies and field officers who conduct crime prevention and physical security surveys to counter terrorist incidents. Intelligence analysts target the dimensions of terrorism; organizational structure and individuals are of lesser importance.

Restricting the terrorists' ability to maneuver offensively requires constant vigilance. The best defense is a good offense, taking the initiative through proactive law enforcement. Making the mental transition to the second dimension to proactive prevention is not sufficient in the battle against terrorism. Countering terrorism requires thinking in several analysis dimensions.

When the police envision crime prevention, they think community, not self-protection or security. The trend is toward community involvement, designed to eliminate the opportunity and risk factors associated with street crime. Terrorists think in many dimensions; police and government officials represent symbolic targets of opportunity.

Street criminals tend to be impulsive and opportunistic; terrorists are well disciplined and organized. Moreover, terrorists are highly motivated and committed to a cause. They generally select ideological and symbolic targets; criminals are self-centered and committed to a lifestyle. While most criminals commit crimes of opportunity and avoid violence, terrorists create opportunities for violence. [5]

While law enforcement officers focus on protecting the public, they may fall prey to terrorist attacks. These attacks discredit government and police organizations as well as social institutions. The problem associated with second dimension thinking remains police officer and facility vulnerability. Police and security antiterrorism planning strategies include three additional considerations: (1) police operations security, (2) physical security and (3) personnel security.

POLICE OPERATIONS SECURITY

The main purpose of operations security is to reduce acts of terrorism with proactive measures, rather than reactive responses. Terrorist intelligence-gathering efforts focus on communications systems, and police personnel information. Police computer systems would be a primary target of cyber terrorists. Constant vigilance requires maintaining radio and telephone security; additional efforts on reporting, computer mapping and related plans, may necessitate special security procedures. Operations security denies information to terrorists, especially target vulnerability assessments.

Information Security (INFOSEC) is an important law enforcement issue; traditionally, enterprise or terrorist crime is the main concern. Law enforcement agencies face the significant threat of passive (public domain) and active (not in public's domain) information collection security challenges.

Police leaders stress the need for Operational Security (OPSEC). Operational Security denies potential information to individuals who are "not authorized" or "do not need to know" confidential information. Counterintelligence procedures guard sensitive information; the effectiveness of the program requires knowledgeable and trained personnel. [6]

POLICE PHYSICAL SECURITY

Terrorists dedicated to violent solutions are exceptionally capable and generally well-trained. They conduct recognizance, gather intelligence, and select a hard target, like a police station, if they deem it vulnerable. Physical security and target-hardening make it difficult to penetrate the target.

Well-trained security and police personnel are the best protection; humans are difficult to replace. Technology can enhance physical security; intrusion devices, closed circuit surveillance, and fences may improve access control. Physical security protects information, property, and police resources from terrorist criminal acts.

POLICE PERSONNEL SECURITY

Key personnel may be subject to attack, including high-ranking government and police personnel. Threat analysis may identify who is at risk; however, protection depends on planning, proactive plans, and personnel training. Personnel training programs include awareness and self-protection counter-measures. Analysts determine the need for increased patrols, or bodyguard assignments. Attacks on personnel and vehicles may be a diversionary technique to obscure an important target, or opportunity to gain access to the primary target.

THREAT ANALYSIS

Threat analysis is a tool to measure and analyze intelligence information. It requires the complete analysis of accessible intelligence, and assessment of security measures. Potential and vulnerable terrorist targets need identification. Crime prevention surveys identify weaknesses and vulnerabilities. Threat analysis has a basic equation:

> **ILP Management + Threat Analysis + Terrorist Information + Intelligence Analysis + Threat Assessment + Vulnerabilities = Assessment of Security Posture.**

The role of the intelligence analyst is to conduct threat analysis and assess the community's vulnerabilities to terrorist attack. Proactive steps identify community weaknesses; the starting point is police headquarters and related facilities. The preliminary assessment, analysis, and related efforts, improve vulnerabilities and the security posture. Threat analysis and the related planning process are not static, but constantly updated for security breaches.

Threat analysis is a timely process, coordinated by crime or intelligence analysts; however, patrol operations serve as the principle information-gathering source. Officers learn to think like a terrorist while analyzing the terrorists': (1) organizational structure and (2) possible methods deployed to attack community resources. Targets of opportunity might include: nuclear power plants, airports, bridges or flood control dams.

Terrorist threat assessments require compiling and evaluating terrorist information. The analysis of intelligence indicators, possible terrorist activities, and potential terrorist threats, require proactive remedial recommendations. Assessment requires moving beyond traditional individual criminal patterns. The assessment process includes: (1) potential targets, (2) group affiliations, and (3) analysis of terrorist profiles.

CRIME PREVENTION SURVEYS

Crime prevention and physical security surveys support the threat assessment process. Crime prevention surveys focus on the social fabric and human interaction. Physical security focuses on technology, lighting, locks, and access control. Mutual goals include target hardening and crime prevention strategies.

Police officers and prevention specialists collaborate in joint ventures to achieve those goals. Survey development includes: (1) defining the location through illustration, maps, drawings, photographs; (2) discussing the problem, number of offenses, times, places, and techniques; and (3) determining the causes, and formulating recommendations for remedial action. Refer to Table 10-2 for an example of crime prevention survey related strategies.

Table 10-2   Crime Prevention Survey: Related Strategies

Crime Prevention Surveys
- Formulate recommendations for remedial action
- Determine causes
- Supply detailed information
- Based on incident rate

Importance of Information
- Collection and evaluation of detailed information
- Exact types of crimes and offenses committed
- Methods of operations (offender)
- Targets of criminal attack

Crime Repression
- Reduction of crimes and offenses through the application of:
- Patrolling
- Physical security and crime prevention surveys
- Observation of persons and places

Crime Control
- Detection
- Investigation of crimes
- Apprehension
- Prosecution

CRISIS MANAGEMENT PLANNING

The analysis and planning mission begins once the threat assessment is accomplished. Preparedness requires ILP management and intelligence analysis to shape the foundation for the planning process. Terrorists have opportunities to select and prepare their operations well in advance. Targets are selected for maximum effect and casualties. The incident planning process is preventative and reactive. We as a nation, state, regional and local government must respond in an effective manner.

GEOGRAPHIC INFORMATION SYSTEMS (GIS) PLANNING

GIS mapping strategies offer numerous forms of criminal and terrorist analysis. Computer analysis supports a planning process that could not be imagined ten years ago; the integration of crisis planning and emergency response calculated in real-time scenarios.

Acts of terrorism and other crises happen without warning. Cities must respond quickly with coordinated efforts from many diverse agencies. However, integrated crisis management plans can greatly improve their emergency planning and response, with computer and geographic information systems (GIS) playing important roles in the development and implementation of these plans.

Examples of how integrated computer systems and GIS can assist in planning for terrorist attacks, and other possible disasters include: computer simulations and data mining techniques used to predict risks and decrease loss of life and property caused by terrorist attacks; target inventories developed and specific incident response scenarios rehearsed and included in crisis management plans; potential citizen evacuation routes mapped in advance; and then distributed to citizens in preparation for any emergency requiring evacuation; neighborhood notification systems and crisis management plans that include the automatic alerting of residents in the path of disasters, and direct them to the best evacuation routes, tailored to their particular location.

"Comprehensive crisis management plans can also include the development of command and control centers using integrated computer systems. Operational command and control centers that use crisis management plans, integrated computer systems, and GIS crime mapping are useful because: they identify available resources; and ensure the existence of effective and coordinated mechanisms that continuously assess and disseminate risk and threat information; and provide a forum for the general coordination and exchange of information among federal, state and local entities." [7]

IDENTIFYING SPECIFIC TARGETS

The SARA model (Scan-Analyze-Respond-Assess) scans the local environment and prepares a list of potential targets. Departments identify specific criteria for targets; prioritize planning and follow-up in the analysis stage. Police agencies pose practical questions, based on experience. Access to community survey information that indicates terrorism fears, should be noted, but not actively solicited from the community. This process focuses on the police agency, and other collaborating agencies, sharing local domestic preparedness information. [8]

Relevant questions to ask include: (1) *What type of terrorist incident would create a major disruption in the community?* (2) *What terrorist events would result in injuries and loss of life?* (3) *What kind of terrorist act would maximize the fear factor in the community?* and (4) *What kind of financial, and political impact would a terrorist act have on the community?* [9]

Crisis management planning remains the foundation for tactical leadership. Training for the execution of crisis management plans, is the means of achieving the purpose of the plan. Learning simulations require critical thinking and problem-solving skills that offer the opportunity to apply real world strategies.

CRISIS TRAINING STRATEGIES

A terrorist training requires maximizing six points:

(1) Finding resources, especially funding for training activities,
(2) Capitalizing on the minimal law enforcement resources available,
(3) Developing a new teaming process,
(4) Designing new types of training or modifying existing training, including team training,
(5) Using existing training facilities and programs and
(6) Building intra-agency team training. [10]

Excellent training and active learning methods assist officers in acquiring the terrorist training curriculum. The application of learning simulations originated in civil emergency preparedness, aviation, business and medicine. Learning simulations offer an ideal venue for critical thinking and application of newly acquired skills. Learning simulations are realistic applications that parallel many work environments and encourage opportunities to apply knowledge. Learning simulations create opportunities for the learner to practice complex skills, in positions of public safety responsibility.

CASE STUDY: TERRORIST SIMULATION

The terrorist response scenario is a time-phased, problem solving, training exercise, which requires critical thinking and crisis management skills. Officers receive additional facts as the problem progresses, the planning unfolds, and responses develop. Supplemental scenario information requires coordination, command post requirements and liaison with related public safety components. The document is layered to formulate hypothetical issues. Listed below is the first preliminary example narrative sheet, others will follow:

CASE STUDY EXAMPLE, (PHASE 1): TERRORIST SCENARIO:

Demonstrate the use of an Emergency Operations Plan (EOP) and informal Incident Action Plan (IAP), and consider the following scenario:

The time is 09:30 hours in Hometown, USA. There is an explosion originating from a parked gasoline truck on Monroe Street. Scattered bomb fragments resulted in 10 casualties, and 50 injured people. The first law enforcement units arrive at 09:32; fire and emergency medical services units arrive at 09:35. At 09:41, there is a massive explosion at a local university and Hometown Police Headquarters, including buildings immediately adjacent to the truck explosion site.

Several first responders are injured or killed. The University of Hometown, Baker Hall collapses (estimated occupancy 500 people). The Medical Emergency Center has admitted multiple injury patients from several bomb incidents. Multiple explosions threaten new secondary problems such as an area power failure, and loss of downtown communications. In addition, many patients appear to have chemical injuries in a combination explosive/chemical attack, (Scenario phase 2-5 of the case scenario intelligence reports continues).

LEARNER REQUIREMENTS

The terrorist project is a staff-learning scenario based on the above-mentioned case study. Learners analyze the scenario and apply the principles of planning, critical thinking and problem solving. This is an active learning project; groups present consensus-based solutions. In addition, simulation groups present individual solutions, and then compare and contrast remedial reactions.

The purpose is to conduct a briefing on the implementation of their EOP and IAP emergency response. Officers assume various roles in public safety organizations, i.e., police, fire and emergency service commanders. The remaining group members serve as the planning section. The composite solution of the five groups are compared and contrasted, providing feedback and the integration of a holistic response picture.

INSTRUCTOR REQUIREMENTS

The instructor acts as a group facilitator, guide and mentor. Officers provide feedback on the application of basic learning objectives and demonstrate competencies on the blackboard. The first assignment is a warm-up exercise where officers focus on course objectives and the mastery of specific first responder learning objectives. For example, students define the following terms: (1) first responder, (2) crisis management, (3) consequence management, and (4) incident management system.

Direct participation generally motivates learner involvement and small group activity. The ability to apply learning objectives is a basic step toward higher progressions and learning simulations. The primary goals of these instructional units are to build: (1) homeland security awareness, (2) scene control, (3) coordination and (4) safety considerations. The integration of passive learning, critical thinking and problem solving strategies provides the foundation for active learning scenarios.

TACTICAL LEADERSHIP

Sergeants serve as primary role models for officers in tactical or CompStat operations. Sergeants hold the most important rank in police agencies because of their quantity and quality of field contact with officers. Sergeants serve on the frontlines of supervision and the CompStat tactical planning process. Leadership style is essential to direction and influence in emergency and tactical scenarios.

There are four models of police supervision identified by the National Institute of Justice (NIJ): (1) traditional, (2) active, (3) innovative, and (4) supportive. The active leadership model likely serves the tactical or CompStat field operations effectively.

NIJ research cites advantages of being an active supervisor: "The police supervisors using the active leadership style of supervision emerged as having the most influence over patrol officers. Almost all active supervisors (95 percent) reported that they often go on their own initiative to incidents that their officers are handling, compared to 24 percent of traditional supervisors, 55 percent of innovative supervisors, and 68 percent of supportive supervisors." [11]

Clearly, traditional supervisors offer minimal field contact, support, and opportunities to influence police officers. The traditional and other leadership styles have positive and negative unintended consequences when compared to active supervision. Moreover, the integration of the Situational Leadership Approach may offer resources that compensate for NIJ assessed style weaknesses. For additional information on NIJ supervisory styles, refer to Tables 10-3 and 10-4.

Table 10-3   Frontline Supervisory Styles

1. Traditional Supervisors	3. Innovative Supervisors
❖ Expect aggressive enforcement from subordinates rather than engagement in community-oriented activities or policing of minor disorders. ❖ More likely than other types of supervisors to make decisions because they tend to take over encounters with citizens or tell officers how to handle those incidents. ❖ Traditional sergeants & lieutenants are highly task oriented & expect subordinates to produce measurable outcomes - particularly arrests & citations - along with paperwork and documentation.	❖ Characterized by the tendency to form relationships (i.e., they consider more officers to be friends). ❖ Low level of task orientation ❖ More positive views of subordinates ❖ Considered innovative because they generally encourage their officers to embrace new philosophies & methods of policing. ❖ Defined by their expectations for community policing & problem-solving efforts by subordinates.
2. Active Supervisors	**4. Supportive Supervisors**
❖ Embrace a philosophy of leading by example. ❖ Heavily involved in the field alongside subordinates while controlling patrol officer behavior. ❖ Perform duel function of street officer & supervisor. ❖ Give importance to engaging in patrol work themselves. ❖ Attempt to strike balance between being active in the field & controlling subordinate behavior through constant, direct supervision. ❖ Characterized by directive decision making, a strong sense of supervisory power, & relatively positive view of subordinates.	❖ Support subordinates by protecting them from discipline or punishment perceived as "unfair." ❖ Provide inspirational motivation. ❖ Serve as buffer between officers & management. ❖ Protect officers from criticism & discipline. ❖ Gives officers space to perform duties without constant worry of disciplinary action for honest mistakes. ❖ May not have strong ties to or positive relations with management. ❖ May attempt to shield patrol officers from administration. ❖ May function more as "protectors" than supporters.

Adapted from: Engel, R.S., How Police Supervisory Styles Influence Patrol Officer Behavior.
U.S. Department of Justice, National Institute of Justice (Washington DC: GPO, 2003): 1-6.

Table 10-4   Frontline Leadership Behaviors

1. Traditional Supervisors	3. Innovative Supervisors
❖ Less inclined toward developing relationships ❖ Give more instruction to subordinates ❖ Less likely to reward ❖ More likely to punish ❖ Ultimate concern is to control subordinate behavior ❖ More likely to support new policing initiatives if consistent with aggressive law enforcement ❖ More than 60 percent "agree strongly" that enforcing the law is by far a patrol officer's most important responsibility	❖ Help subordinates implement community policing and problem-solving strategies ❖ Coaching, mentoring and facilitating ❖ Less concerned with enforcing rules, regulations, report writing, or other task-oriented activities ❖ Do not tell officers how to handle situations ❖ Do not take over situation ❖ Delegate decision making ❖ Spend significantly more time dealing with public or other officers
2. Active Supervisors	**4. Supportive Supervisors**
❖ Engage in patrol work themselves ❖ Spend time per shift on general motor patrol ❖ Directive decision making ❖ Strong sense of supervisory power ❖ Relatively positive view of subordinates ❖ Believe they have influence over subordinates' decisions ❖ Not likely to encourage team building, coaching or mentoring	❖ Protection of officers from unfair criticism and punishment is important function ❖ Less concerned with enforcement of rules and regulations, paperwork, or ensuring that officers do their work ❖ Encourage officers through praise and recognition ❖ Act as counselors ❖ Display concern for personal and professional well-being

Adapted from: Engel, R.S., How Police Supervisory Styles Influence Patrol Officer Behavior. U.S. Department of Justice, National Institute of Justice (Washington DC: GPO, 2003): 1-6.

The NIJ study identified some interesting findings: (1) Officers with active supervisors spent more time on self-initiated activities, community-policing activities, and problem solving; and (2) The findings strongly suggest that

CompStat supervisory practices should involve a proactive frontline component that ensures the community and problem-oriented policing (COPPS) mission, goals and objectives are accomplished. [12] The evidence suggests that the results of active supervisors would function well in tactical scenarios and CompStat operations.

Limitations of the NIJ study include: (1) the study population came from urban police departments and the findings may not apply to smaller or rural police agencies; (2) this research did not measure long-term patterns of supervision; (3) the study did not address mixed supervisory styles or (4) explore whether supervisors adjust their leadership styles in response to an individual officer and the situation. [13]

FRONTLINE LEADERSHIP FEEDBACK

Frontline leaders seek field encounters, teachable moments, and support police officers. Excellent sergeants have situational leadership skills and are involved in feedback and coaching behaviors. They provide dual functions of back-up officer and supervisor. The presence of leaders is important because it demonstrates concern about the community and officers.

Leading from the frontlines is an effective approach to tactical or CompStat leadership; it allows leaders to encounter field problems directly. Moreover, field encounters provide direct feedback on officer performance, and provides data for policy changes. Direct observations are superior to reports that do not include all necessary information for conducting CompStat and other police strategies.

FIELD PLANNING OBJECTIVES

The first part of the terrorist planning stage is a critical phase of a counterterrorism program and information collection process. The planning stage determines the need for data collection required for a first-rate proactive and reactive program. Knowledge is power; the essential information about terrorists creates opportunities to deter terrorist operations and attacks. The old principle of "know thy enemy," including their strategies and tactics applies to terrorism planning.

Tactical leadership requires decisive leadership that requires direction for their officers. Commanders are responsible for implementing goals, objectives, and action plans for sergeants. Feedback from field commanders, lieutenants, sergeants and their officers provides the fine-tuning of the operational plans. Reviewing after-action reports on previous strategies assures previous errors will not affect future missions.

Experienced leaders and police officers know where the crime problems exist in their communities. Formulating measurable objectives may prove more difficult. When analysts provide accurate criminal intelligence on high visibility crimes, defining the problem is less burdensome. When the complete information is timely or in real time, it may require hasty field planning. In the field, limited objects are immediate, practical, readily recognizable, and flexible.

Operations Analysis provides information on police emergency operations. The analysis and information assists police leaders in planning patrol allocation, reserves, and logistical support. Analytical information improves decision-making and the quality of police service. The purpose is to examine workload responsibilities and deployment of law enforcement personnel.

Setting goals and objectives comprises the most practical system of motivation, an ideal method to motivate police officers that involves presenting officers with goals and objectives and convincing them that they can achieve positive outcomes. A winning attitude is cultivated and officers realize that they can achieve their objectives if they expend the effort. The leader evaluates task completion, and then praises the effort. Goals and objectives establish the "path to success" and sense of accomplishment. If the task is worth doing, it is worth doing well, especially when leaders evaluate it. [14]

Develop mission orders that tell officers what the mission requirements entail. Explain the order and related tasks, but not how to do it. The "how to" is left to the officers involved. Objectives must have a specific task, condition, and standard. Conditions are forces that officers operate under in the field. The standard allows for the proper evaluation of the task. Objectives are specific and measurable, but not quantitative percentages. [15] Leaders avoid specific quantitative measurements or percentages; it indicates finality. Arrest numbers and other fixed points of reference place caps on productivity.

Action plans are specific but flexible; they identify teams, steps, and procedures necessary to accomplish objectives. The sergeant assigns the action plans to individual teams or officers. Action plans help define who, what, where, when, how and why. At this point, leadership and motivational factors begin to influence productivity. [16]

The final incident action plan (IAP) may require informal modifications as the plan unfolds. Generally, first line supervisors are frontline leaders, responsible for tactical, terrorist or CompStat operations. Senior leader and middle manager roles defer from junior leaders, in tactical scenarios, and avoid micromanagement.

Focus Points: Training and Tactics

This chapter did not discuss a litany of terrorist organizations, nor attempt to examine terrorism from a historical, political, and social policy perspective. The chapter explores terrorism from a law enforcement, security and intelligence perspective. This text examines the analytical techniques of intelligence gathering and how ILP assists in that endeavor. The themes address the techniques of antiterrorism, counter-intelligence procedures, combating and detecting potential terrorist acts.

Antiterrorism is the first phase of the program; defensive measures include basic internal police and external target vulnerabilities. Threat assessment includes: (1) crime prevention and (2) physical security mandates.

Threat assessment leads to successful crime prevention, physical security goals and objectives. Effective threat analysis requires countering misinformation and deception, while determining trend lines and exact intelligence themes.

In the second phase, counterterrorism takes the offense and provides mechanisms to respond to terrorist initiatives. This phase implements sound planning procedures after a terrorist incident. The second phase response is timely and insures public safety. Special reaction or SWAT teams require integrated training programs, which are inter-jurisdictional in nature.

Law enforcement agencies plan and coordinate terrorism counter-measures. Counterterrorism planning requires constant revisions and real world applications. Excellent planning mandates learning simulations including active exercise scenarios, which require interagency coordination. The emphasis is on strategic and tactical flexibility to law enforcement operations.

Excellent intelligence analysis requires in-depth strategic and tactical planning. The planning cycle focuses on terrorists, and plans for the possibility of a direct assault on law enforcement operations. Planning avoids casualties and the possibility of reduced law enforcement services during a terrorist incident.

ILP and planning remain essentials to analyzing the terrorist threat; successful leadership applies the threat analysis equation. Excellent analysis requires constant review and assessment of security, crime prevention plans, and developing strategies addressing: crime prevention, operations security, physical security and personnel security. Superior proactive strategies include excellent planning, awareness and educational programs.

Tactical planning must be flexible, and includes commanders who adjust plans when conditions change. Planning can be effective in responding to emergency incidents, combating terrorism and the emergency response process. The combination of accurate and timely intelligence, rapid deployment, effective tactics and relentless follow-up, provides a foundation for terrorism, homeland security and unfolding criminal patterns.

Leadership implies being in control of *self, others*, and the *tactical mission*. Sergeants create a positive social climate by setting attainable objectives and clearly defined standards. Leadership by example and frontline presence remains the foremost requirement of influencing officers. High-quality leadership demonstrates the mature perspective of self-control and leads from the front-lines. Refer to tables located in Appendix C, Appendix D, and Appendix E for additional information concerning tactical planning.

CONCLUSION

Terrorism preparedness calls for a proactive approach that requires a different response from everyday criminal investigations. Traditional police incidents are considerably different from planned terrorist acts. The failure to plan, recognize, and capture the probability of a terrorist threat, can be catastrophic, the results deadly.

Law enforcement leaders identify the terrorist threat and address traditional goals. This balancing act is not easy; it requires intelligence analysis and vision. The new protocols, model policies and technical assistance may assist; however, the terrorist threat creates the need for additional applications of Intelligence-Led Policing (ILP).

ENDNOTES

1. Michael L. DeCapo, "Police Planning for Terrorism," Police Chief, April 1988, 31-33.

2. Michael Howard, "What's in a Name?: How to Fight Terrorism," Foreign Affairs, 81, January/February: 2002, 43-59.

3. Jeffery Ian Ross, "A Model of the Psychological Causes of Oppositional Political Terrorism," The Journal of Peace Psychology, Vol. 2, No. 2, 1996, 129-141.

4. Jeffery Ian Ross, "Beyond the Conceptualization of Terrorism: A Psychological - Structural Model of the Causes of This Activity," In Craig Summers and Eric Markusen, (eds.), Collective Violence: Harmful Behaviors in Groups and Governments (New York: Rowen and Littlefield, 1999), 27.

5. Douglas D. Bodrero, "State Roles, Community Assessment and Personality Profiles," Tallahassee, Florida: Institute for Intergovernmental Research, 2000.

6. David Cid, "Information Security in Law Enforcement," Police Chief, (February 2000), 15-19.

7. Robert Chapman, et al., U. S. Department of Justice, Office of Community Oriented Policing Services, Local Law Enforcement Responds to Terrorism: Lessons in Prevention and Preparedness (Washington, DC: GPO, 2002), 15-16.

8. Quint C. Thurman and J. D. Jamison, Police Problem-Solving (Lexis Nexis: Anderson Publishing, 2004), 135.

9. Quint C. Thurman and J. D. Jamison, 135.

10. M.K. Rehm and W.R. Rehm, "Terrorism Preparedness Calls for a Proactive Approach," Police Chief, (December 2000), 38-43.

11. R. S. Engel, U. S. Department of Justice, National Institute of Justice, How Police Supervisory Styles Influence Patrol Officer Behavior (Washington, DC: GPO, 2003): 1-6.

12. Engel, 1-6.

13. Engel, 1-6.

14. Thomas E. Baker, Effective Police Leadership: Moving Beyond Management (New York, New York: Looseleaf Law Publications, 2006), 105-107.

15. Baker, 105-107.

16. Baker, 105-107.

EPILOGUE
Concluding Focus Points

When you follow two separate chains of thought, you will find some point of intersection which should approximate the truth.   — Sir Arthur Conan Doyle

Intelligence-Led Policing (ILP) management philosophy allows police decision makers the opportunity to process two basic chains of thought. The flow of criminal information from ILP shapes one chain of thought. The second chain of thought is the leadership process, which permits effective decision-making. Intersections where the two basic chains of thought meet form the basis for truth, and scientific police operations.

The Epilogue's focus is on ILP leadership coordination and strategic planning requirements. Concluding focus points reiterate and further explain the ten basic Prologue strategies. The Epilogue discusses the integration of essential theories, concepts, and applications of the text's content. In addition, articulation points and synchronization of the planning and decision making process unfold for additional analysis. Refer to Table E-1, the Epilogue for 28 Focus Points.

The Epilogue reaffirms ten basic strategies and themes introduced in the Prologue. Ten chapters emphasize those strategies; the Epilogue integrates theories and concepts, summarizing essential themes. Replications enhance retention of successful leadership learning modalities and the application of the ten basic strategies.

Table E-1   Epilogue (28 Realignment Concepts)

	ILP Strategic Leadership	ILP Intelligence Cycle
Intelligence-Led Policing	❖ "Thin Blue" Line ❖ The "grand strategy" ❖ Influence process ❖ Decision-making ❖ Strategic planning ❖ Proactive operations ❖ Strike criminals & organizations	❖ Requirements & collection ❖ Planning & targeting ❖ Collection & collation ❖ Processing & analyzing ❖ Evaluation and production ❖ Dissemination ❖ Influence decision makers
	ILP Policing Strategies	**Eliminate Barriers**

	❖ Intelligence-led policing
	❖ Community-oriented
	  policing
	❖ Problem-oriented policing
	❖ SARA planning process
	❖ Strategic planning
	❖ CompStat
	❖ Strategies & tactics
		❖ Excellent communication
		❖ Johari window & feedback
		❖ Intelligence driven
		  analysis
		❖ Intelligence sharing
		  process
		❖ Regional & state
		  coordination
		❖ Federal coordination
		❖ Realignment sharing
		  process

STRATEGY 1: STRATEGIC LEADERSHIP

Excellent intelligence and leadership serve as the greatest defense against crime. "The Thin Blue Line" is the first line of defense within society. Intelligence is its first line of defense. Intelligence is often the last line of defense, as well." [1] ILP analytical reporting provides criminal information that supports proactive and offensive operations against criminals and their organizations.

Modern policing moves beyond the defensive position to offensive operations. O. W. Wilson, Father of Modern Policing, commented: "Next to total war the greatest threat to society is crime." [2] This statement is not zealous when one examines the causality rate for police officer deaths in the line of duty. The fatality rate continues to demonstrate unacceptable statistics.

Careful preparation for the strategic planning process remains a basic requirement; question all options. Effective leaders avoid "group think" and staff communicating what they think you want to hear. Listen to the department mavericks; they are innovative thinkers. Initiate offensive maneuvers, and strike at the core of criminal and terrorist organizations.

Strategic thinking requires flexible responses and the ability to plan. Leaders cannot become too complacent or comfortable; they must change with the times. Maintaining vigilance in the war against crime and terrorism requires discovering counterbalances to performance requirements under stressful circumstances.

> Strategic planning provides the counterbalances, and stability that enhance leadership's confidence.

Commanders understand that they are ultimately responsible for strategic decisions. Once the plan is in place, release the mind of any doubts, and stay the course. Ignore preliminary setbacks, learn from mistakes, and modify strategic or tactical plans. Move aggressively to the offensive attack, and take the defensive position only out of necessity.

We must know the criminal intimately, that is the role of ILP, intelligence analysis, and crime analysis. ILP strategies include striking and enveloping criminals at their organizational center of gravity. Successful ILP leaders understand criminal patterns and how offenders think, the perfect scenario to controlling crime.

STRATEGY 2: INTELLIGENCE-LED POLICING

ILP represents the new organizational nomenclature and management philosophy for meeting criminal intelligence requirements. Successful leadership requires accurate intelligence, strategic planning, and informed decision-making. ILP is the vehicle and pathway for successful leadership. ILP drives excellent leadership, and formulates the correct strategic and tactical destinations.

ILP focuses intelligence and crime analysis on career repeat offenders. Moreover, the intelligence attempts to infiltrate criminal organizations and their conspiracy crimes. Seven basic tenets include:

(1) targeting career criminals,
(2) using offender interviews,
(3) analyzing repeat victimization and hot spots,
(4) informants,
(5) undercover operations,
(6) physical and electronic surveillance and
(7) intelligence sharing.

ILP derives its power from the logic that supports the philosophy and criminal information systems.

The strategic formula is:

> **ILP** Organization + Intelligence Analysis **(IA)** + Crime Analysis **(CA)** + Collection **(C)** + Storage **(S)** + Computer Analysis **(CA)** + Dissemination **(D)** = Criminal Intelligence **(CI)**.

Critical thinking, analysis, and timely dissemination to those who need the information, define the Intelligence Cycle core. Accurate criminal intelligence/information is ultimately applied to successful prevention and intervention strategies.

STRATEGY 3: REMOVING THE BARRIERS

Excellent communication and feedback represent essential ingredients for removing barriers to social change. When examining impediments to successful ILP operations, two obvious factors surface: (1) poor communication and (2) poor feedback. Johari Window analysis remedies both negative communication factors. Positive communication helps resolve negative issues.

Social change impediments may emerge from the: (1) community, (2) civilian staff, and (3) police missions. Related to that problem is the police organizational structure and diverse areas of specialization. The issues of police, civilian turf, and social group dynamics need not contribute to maintaining the status quo. Adequate training, communication, and feedback can reduce fear associated with anticipated social change.

Communication issues evolve from the human component of the ILP equation. The human relations impediment, between police officers and civilian groups, is first on the priority list. The Johari Window, candor, and superior communication, assist police leaders in achieving quality human relations and bonus related positive outcomes. Mutual respect and equality among police officers and civilian analysts serves as a transition point.

Human interpersonal communication remains the primary facilitator in the *diffusion* and *adoption* of any innovation. The innovation of merging intelligence and crime analysis will ultimately take place on the reorganizational level. Joining both operations in the same office is the starting point, however, not the absolute solution. Communication,

openness, and feedback may provide essential social adjustments. Decentralized analyst access to police patrol operations and investigators, is a logical conclusion when viewed
through the Johari Window.

Direct access to the chief and senior commanders by
analysts is controversial, but necessary after viewing Johari
dynamics. However, it will likely evolve with the assistance
of Johari communication analysis. The need to be open and
candid with analysts and other members of the department,
becomes evident when examining the four quadrants of the
Johari Window.

STRATEGY 4: SYNCHRONIZATION COP & POP

The consolidation and synthesis of **Community-Oriented
Policing (COP) + Problem-Oriented Policing (POP) + SARA
planning model = COPPS**. The most recent component of the
equation would include CompStat, a form of focused policing,
plus the leadership and technology components.

Therefore, the new intelligence-led policing approach
would include **ILP + COPPS + CompStat + Quality Leadership
= Police Excellence**. The updated formula serves as a pathway
and necessary progression to the evolution and development
of an intelligence-led policing grand strategy. ILP should
have a strong affinity for the COPPS philosophy strategy in
the United States. Refer to Figure E-1 for an analytical
analysis of the ILP management philosophy.

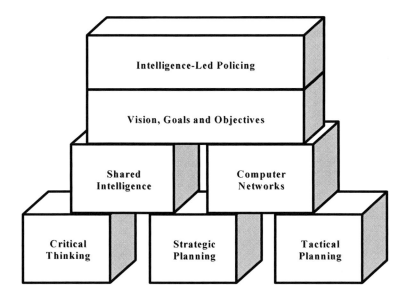

Figure E-1   Intelligence-Led Policing Management Philosophy

STRATEGY 5: STRATEGIC PLANNING

ILP is the umbrella management philosophy for planning strategies and criminal information coordination requirements. Planning is a means to an end; it engages the mind. Strategic planning is the centerpiece of the planning process, and is directly related to problem oriented policing (POP) and long-term planning. In addition, there are two other contingency feedback planning models: (1) intelligence analysis, and (2) crime analysis. Refer to Figure E-2 for the planning model that centralizes and coordinates the planning process.

In large departments, coordination and liaison functions represent major components of mission requirements. In smaller police agencies, a few individuals may coordinate informally, or one officer or civilian may accomplish the intelligence and planning responsibilities. Regardless of agency size, someone needs to address intelligence and planning issues.

Figure E-2 Intelligence-Led Policing and Strategic Planning
Centralized Planning Model

STRATEGY 6: INTELLIGENCE ANALYSIS

Law enforcement operates best when intelligence and crime analysis support line supervisors, officers, and investigators. Coordination and dissemination of actionable intelligence plays a significant role in successful crime prevention and intervention. The Intelligence Cycle is the collection, dissemination, and sharing of criminal information, which benefits law enforcement agencies, and the nation.

The strategic intelligence process is shifting from criminal outcomes to criminal intelligence, analysis, and logic. The Intelligence Cycle provides the means to organize criminal information, and identify potential targets. Intelligence analysis serves as the principle strategy to achieve enterprise criminal targeting objectives.

Crime analysis forms the foundation for the analysis of street crimes and CompStat operations. Intelligence analysis is the twin process for analyzing conspiracy enterprise crimes and strategic intelligence. Intelligence analysis is strategic and long-term; crime analysis is tactical and short-term.

Crime and intelligence analysis must combine forces to achieve intelligence harmony. Crime and intelligence analysts, who cooperate and exchange data, enhance ILP operations. In fact, this liaison intelligence and coordination demonstrates the essence of the ILP management function.

ILP management operations and intelligence analyst responsibilities do not survive disconnected and apart from crime analyst responsibilities. Most importantly, senior leadership must support intelligence and crime analyst collaboration, integration and synchronization. In addition, logical ILP solutions require formal and informal intelligence and crime analyst coordination. Moreover, ILP integration and consolidation policies support COP, POP, and CompStat operations.

Logic and inferences drawn without preconceptions, suggests the need for a central location, shared office space, and technology. ILP management depends on analysis and strategic coordination of criminal information. The ability to draw inferences from data and evidence remains an indispensable analyst prerequisite. Therefore, the evidence suggests that shared information facilitates collaboration between partners and improved decision-making.

Crime is an endless battle, police leaders need to identify and trace criminals. Once police leaders have criminals or terrorists within target zones, the purpose, direction, and course(s) of action integrate well in the strategic or tactical planning process. Defining problem(s) and related criminal target(s) or organization(s), assures that the goals and objectives will unfold successfully. Intelligence analysis improves strategic planning and decision-making. Refer to Table E-2 for an example of ILP intelligence support.

Table E-2   Intelligence Support

Intelligence-Led Policing Decision-Making Process	Strategic Policing and Planning
• Identify the problems(s) • Identify intervention opportunities	• **Intelligence Phase I:** Collection/Collation
• Identify and explore alternative courses of action	• **Identification Phase II:** Analysis
• Evaluate intervention and prevention alternatives	• **Intelligence Phase III:** Design Feasibility
• Choose alternative courses of action	• **Selection Phase IV:** Actionable Intelligence
• Implement the decision	• **Implementation Phase V:** Decision Makers Implement Choice
• Evaluate results of the decision-making remedy	• **Evaluation Phase VI:** Assessment

STRATEGY 7: CRIME ANALYSIS

Crime analysts are less interested in random crime or independent incidents; practitioners identify street crimes by trend, pattern, or series. Crime analysts focus on repeat crimes, distinctive offender patterns, and hot spot locations. Crime analysts identify patterns and trends and promptly support police leaders, investigators and police officers. [3]

CRIME PREVENTION SURVEYS

Crime prevention surveys provide core information concerning criminal behavior for police patrol and tactical applications. Crime prevention surveys gather information that can help police officers eliminate the motives, opportunities, and means for individuals to commit crimes. This information provides officers with the approximate temporal factors, kinds of offense, and methods of operation.

Most importantly, crime analysis identifies targets of attack, crime generators, and hot spot locations. Crime prevention surveys can determine the underlying causes of crime, and aid in eliminating opportunities for offenders to select victims or criminal targets. Refer to Figure E-3 for an example of the Crime Prevention Planning Model.

Figure E-3   Crime Prevention Planning Model/Cycle

Crime prevention surveys assist in developing pattern information on offenders, travel distance and related hot spot activities. Crime analysts conduct formal observations regarding offender behaviors. The analyst employs a field approach; observations include a crime prevention survey and assessment instrument. The crime analyst and field officers implement the crime prevention surveys. Refer to Figure E-4 for an example of crime prevention survey requirements.

Figure E-4   Crime Prevention Survey Requirements

PLANNING AND COLLECTION PHASE

After gathering information and carefully analyzing the problem and causative factors, officers can implement appropriate responses. For example, they can pinpoint hot spot locations through computer GIS mapping. Then they can outline the problem by numbering the offenses, plotting times and places crimes occurred, and noting techniques used to commit the crimes. Leaders establish goals and priorities to determine where they need police patrols. Then, officers can attack these hot spots in an effective and efficient manner.

A crime cannot occur without the presence of three elements that form a crime triangle: the *offender*, the *victim*, and the *crime scene* or *location*. [4] Accordingly, crime analysts must discover as much as possible about all three sides, while examining the links between each. By asking *who, what, when, where, how, why* and *why not* about each side of the triangle, as well as observing the way these elements interact, analysts can understand what prompts certain crime problems. [5]

CRIME-SPECIFIC PLANNING

Similar to problem-oriented policing, crime-specific planning approaches crime problems by considering underlying factors that characterize each type of offense. Crime-specific planning aids problem-oriented policing by using proactive measures aimed at protecting citizens and property. For example, law enforcement agencies task police personnel and allocate equipment based on crime analysis results and crime-specific programming. [6]

Crime analysis can improve CompStat tactical planning by graphically illustrating criminal patterns to senior leaders, managers, and sergeants. Crime analysis assists in these early CompStat strategies by examining the geographic, statistical, and economic aspects of the hot spot locations, along with the relationship between the victim and the offender. Crime analysis supports CompStat tactical operations.

Strategy 8: Criminal Investigative Analysis

Another form of crime analysis is Criminal Investigative Analysis (CIA). The term *criminal investigative analysis* concerns violent serial crimes. The CIA groups offenders by applying the criminal profiling process and crime scene reconstruction. This investigative analysis focuses on serial crimes that have case linkage patterns.

A missing piece of the puzzle can be solved with **Criminal Geographic Targeting** (CGT) techniques. This model generates a three-dimensional geographic probability surface; which represents the relative probability that a given point is the residence or workplace of the offender. In addition, possible offender travel routes can be generated by applying analytical techniques to the computer jeopardy surface. The basic formula for the model is that there must have been a basic intersection of the following elements for a crime to occur:

> **Time (T) + Place (P) + Victim (V) + Offender (O) = Crime Opportunity (CO)**

The offender seeks a predatory space and calculates the risk, opportunity and victim vulnerability. Most offenders tend to commit crimes in places where they feel comfortable. They may return to their original haunts to feel comfortable and relive former fantasies. [7]

Searching the residence of registered sex offenders, and those on probation for violent crimes, remains the initial point of investigation. "The proclivity of chronic serial offenders to use repeatedly the same geographic and ecological space...the geographical and ecological patterning of the serial offender may be tangible information which is discerned by police investigators and utilized in apprehensions." [8]

Violent serial crimes represent a minuscule percentage of reported crimes. However, violent crimes generate immediate media coverage, an outraged public response, and concern. Effective investigative options include coordination with the Federal Bureau of Investigation, State Bureau of Investigation, or outside consultants. CIA requires crime scene reconstruction and criminal profiling specialists, skilled beyond the assets of many local police agencies.

STRATEGY 9: ANALYTICAL REPORTING

Intelligence reporting is the heart of ILP management. Analytical reporting, models and charting, keep police commanders informed. Key decision-makers have influence over operations, tactics, and logistical resources. In addition, analytical reports assist police leadership with staff planning, patrol allocations and deployments.

Developing criminal information from intelligence products assists in suppressing criminal activity, through successful police prevention and intervention strategies. Intelligence reporting represents superior analytical criminal intelligence, after processing raw data or information. The finished intelligence report and related analytical products frequently contain actionable criminal intelligence.

STRATEGY 10: INTELLIGENCE SHARING

ILP management derives criminal information from numerous sources: (1) coordination and sharing information with other agencies, (2) field intelligence reports, and (3) GIS crime mapping. ILP deploys many digital and computer regional, state, and federal network strategies.

Individual states determine local protocols concerning the exchange and dissemination, of mutual intelligence requirements. Regional Intelligence Centers (RIC) respond to local crime priorities within a region or state. The convincing reason for RIC, is their proactive response to the threat of organized crime, drug trafficking and terrorism.

FUSION CENTERS

The purpose of "fusion centers" is to coordinate resources across overlapping local jurisdictional boundaries. The RIC or "fusion center" concept may involve local county jurisdictions, or encompass an entire state. The RIC may coordinate with other intelligence centers, i.e., El Paso Intelligence Center, National Operations Center, and National Joint Terrorism Task Force, etc.

REGIONAL INTELLIGENCE SHARING

Many small agencies cannot fund full-time intelligence units; however, intelligence sharing is possible under the Regional Information Sharing System (RISS) Program. Typical RISS activities include targeting: (1) drug trafficking, (2) terrorism, (3) violent crime, (4) cyber crime, (5) gangs and (6) organized crime activities. The Department of Justice and Bureau of Justice Assistance administer the RISS Program that includes over 6300 member agencies. RISS represents six regional centers that share intelligence, and coordinate efforts against criminal networks, that operate across jurisdictional lines.

LOCAL AND REGIONAL COORDINATION

Small and some mid-sized police departments are at a disadvantage, relatively few of the 30,000+ law enforcement agencies in the United States, can afford a crime analyst or crime analysis section. One solution is to participate in a regional Crime Analysis Unit (CAU), or contract to share the crime analyst position. [9] The regional crime analysis approach may serve as a reasonable solution.

For a crime analysis unit to be effective, strategies must reflect the vision of the department's leaders and top management. It should support a collaborative effort among the region's law enforcement agencies, and the communities they serve. In addition, provide a unit-level crime management plan. The regional crime analysis program provides the means to inform citizens of the community, of the level of crime. The collaborative efforts must reduce the level of crime in their neighborhoods and demonstrate the effectiveness of the program. [10]

Key to the operation is a region-wide digital platform that links all law enforcement agencies together, for efficient and secure data sharing. This collaborative effort of developing regional crime analysis zones is an essential part of the planning process and program development. Crime analysis zones are contiguous geographic areas with crime rates, criminals, crime targets and crime patterns. These zones should be developed throughout the region to reflect a focused analysis of criminological, sociological and psychological variables that influence crime trends. [11]

Zone steering committees, an essential element of crime analysis zones, bring together key community elements. Collaborative efforts include police staff officers, representatives of the political or municipal entities, business representatives and other appropriate partners. Crime analysis and strategic and tactical planning serve the community-oriented policing (COP), and problem-oriented policing (POP) SARA model planning process. Steering committees provide oversight functions and participate in program evaluation. [12]

FEDERAL AGENCIES

A myriad of federal agencies and related intelligence liaison requirements challenge State, Local, and Tribal Law Enforcement (SLTLE) agencies. The FBI, the lead anti-terrorism agency, is most noticeable and actively involved. Federal agencies supply more intelligence/criminal information to SLTLE officers; however, an information/intelligence gap remains. Proper access demands precise security clearance considerations, and accurate background investigations. The critical flow of terrorist intelligence and related sensitive investigations, requires trust and security clearances.

DRUG INTELLIGENCE

The EL Paso Intelligence Center (EPIC) is a cooperative effort among federal agencies, which includes information-sharing agreements with law enforcement agencies across the United States. Representatives of the Immigration and Naturalization Service, the U.S. Customs Service, and the DEA, staff this intelligence service center. EPIC's jurisdiction includes the United States and Western Hemisphere, where drug and alien movements influence the United States.

In addition, other regional databases include High Intensity Drug Trafficking Areas (HIDTA). This database enhances and coordinates drug control efforts among local, state, and federal law enforcement agencies. HIDTA provides coordination, equipment, technology, and additional resources to combat drug trafficking, and its harmful consequences in critical regions of the United States. The primary mission is reduction of drug trafficking; however, HIDTA serves as a valuable intelligence gathering organization. The collection, gathering, and analysis activities may have implications for additional related investigations.

TECHNOLOGICAL APPLICATIONS

Several forms of advanced technology help compensate for terrorist technological applications, and assist intelligence analysts. Unraveling coded and ambiguous message assignments are demanding for analysts; it takes considerable persistence and dedication. Several technological advanced programs assist in that endeavor: ECHELON and DCS-1000 represent exceptional examples.

The United States government applies the latest technology to the war on crime and terrorism; it incorporates a variety of methods to capture criminal intelligence. The National Security Agency operates a global spy system, entitled ECHELON. The spy program can capture and analyze telephone calls, faxes, and telecommunications messages worldwide.

The codeword ECHELON stands for a computer program that has the ability to search descriptors, code words, and phrases. In addition, voice recognition capabilities include optical scanner recognition to select and flag questionable messages. Analysts transcribe key word messages from satellite, microwave, cellular and fiber optics communications traffic; messages are then isolated for analysis and investigative follow-up procedures.

According to the Federal Bureau of Investigation, DCS-1000 is a sophisticated computerized-based system (protocol decoder) designed to capture e-mail or electronic communications. The FBI obtains a court order to intercept the communication. DCS-1000 reviews all network data, but only selects information authorized by the court order. The FBI computer system cooperates with the Internet Service Provider (ISP) to collect precise information from a specific user, the target of the investigation. The system also has the ability to conduct "content-wiretap" and pen-register applications.

FOCUS POINTS: EPILOGUE SUMMARY

ILP and successful policing strategies determine much of what transpires. The synchronization of strategies is preferable to competing strategies. Moreover, blending strategies requires cooperation and assimilation into the ILP management philosophy. Refer to figure E-5 for the synchronization of law enforcement strategies.

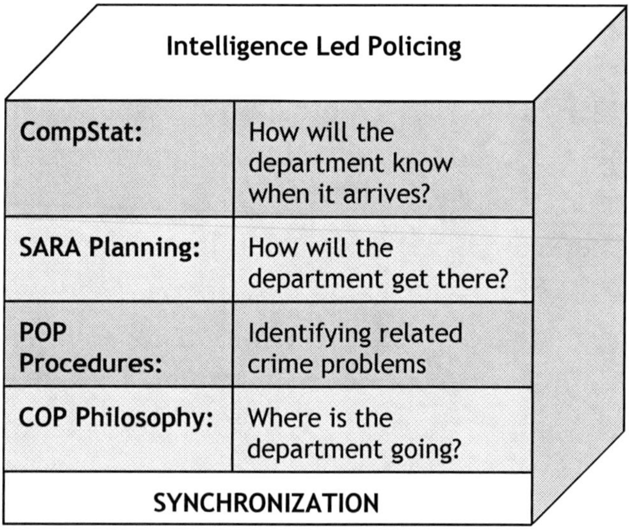

Intelligence Led Policing	
CompStat:	How will the department know when it arrives?
SARA Planning:	How will the department get there?
POP Procedures:	Identifying related crime problems
COP Philosophy:	Where is the department going?
SYNCHRONIZATION	

Figure E-5   Synchronization of Strategies

Integration and synchronization requires superior planning to achieve the goal of effective administration. Leaders must seize opportunities to implement effective strategies. The following four equations support the "grand theory" of ILP and much of what transpires:

---

(1) The consolidation and synthesis of **Community-Oriented Policing (COP) + Problem-Oriented Policing (POP) + SARA planning model = COPPS.**

(2) The new intelligence-led policing approach would include: **ILP + COPPS + CompStat + Quality Leadership = Police Excellence.**

(3) The strategic formula is: **ILP Organization + Intelligence Analysis (IA) + Crime Analysis (CA) + Collection (C) + Storage (S) + Computer Analysis (CA) + Dissemination (D) = Criminal Intelligence (CI).**

(4) Finally, the new intelligence-led policing *grand strategy* would include: **ILP + COPPS + CompStat + Quality Leadership = Police Excellence.**

A clear sense of vision enables us to understand the importance of diverse strategies, which allow police agencies to "arrive" and achieve improved crime control, prevention and homeland security. The formidable goal becomes possible with proactive ILP strategic and tactical intelligence planning, supported by excellent police strategic leadership.

Conclusion

Crime is a moral crusade that involves commitment to a "grand strategy." Our survival as a nation depends on superior strategy implementation. The "grand strategy" is INTELLI-GENCE-LED POLICING. Therefore, we should apply ILP, and carefully pick our battles, if we want to win the war. We can afford to lose some battles, but not the war against crime and terrorism. ILP is the leadership "grand strategy," and mortal enemy of criminals and terrorists. However, the "grand strategy" calls for excellent leadership and vision.

ENDNOTES

1. Lawrence B. Sulc, Law Enforcement Counter Intelligence (Kansas: Varro Press, 1996), xiii.

2. O. W. Wilson and Roy Clinton McLaren, Police Administration (New York: McGraw-Hill, 1977).

3. Steven Gottlieb, Sheldon Arenberg, and Raj Singh, Crime Analysis: From First Report to Final Arrest, 301.

4. W. Spellman and J. E. Eck, "Sitting Ducks, Ravenous Wolves, and Helping Hands: New Approaches to Urban Policing," Public Affairs Comment (Austin, Texas: School of Public Affairs, University of Texas, 1989).

5. Spellman and Eck.

6. B. D. Cummings, "Problem-Oriented Policing and Crime-Specific Planning," The Chief of Police, (March 1990), 63.

7. Kim Rossmo, Geographic Profiling (New York: CRC Press, 2000).

8. James L. LeBeau, "Rape and Racial Patterns," The Journal of Offender Counseling, Services and Rehabilitation, (Volume 9, 1984). 125-148.

9. Mike Woods, Crime Analysis: "A Key Tool in any Crime Reduction Strategy," The Police Chief, (April 1999), 17-30.

10. Woods, 17-30.

11. Woods, 17-30.

12. Woods, 17-30.

APPENDIX A

An International Intelligence Network

CRIMINAL INTELLIGENCE
FILE GUIDELINES

Prepared by LEIU

Reprinted July 2004

LAW ENFORCEMENT INTELLIGENCE UNIT

FOREWORD

These guidelines are provided to member agencies as an ongoing effort by your Executive Board to promote professionalism, provide protection for citizens' privacy, and yet enable law enforcement agencies to collect information in their pursuit of organized crime entities. It has long been established that agencies engaged in the collection, storage, analysis, and dissemination of criminal intelligence information must operate under specified guidelines to ensure abuses to this process do not occur. Along with operational guidelines, it is essential that member agencies adopt file procedures as a check and balance against inappropriate activities.

Each member agency is encouraged to have a written policy regarding its file procedures. A member may wish to adopt these guidelines or modify them to meet its particular state or local policies, laws, or ordinances. Member agencies with existing written file policies are commended and are encouraged to examine this document for any ideas that may augment their guidelines.

L.E.I.U. and its member agencies are in the forefront in promoting the value of the criminal intelligence function as a tool on combating organized crime and terrorism. Please do not hesitate to contact members of your Executive Board if you have questions, wish to discuss new ideas, or have suggestions for training.

Sincerely,

Russell "Russ" Porter
General Chairperson
Law Enforcement Intelligence Unit

CRIMINAL INTELLIGENCE FILE GUIDELINES

I. CRIMINAL INTELLIGENCE FILE GUIDELINES

These guidelines were established to provide the law enforcement agency with an information base that meets the needs of the agency in carrying out its efforts to protect the public and suppress criminal operations. These standards are designed to bring about an equitable balance between the civil rights and liberties of citizens and the needs of law enforcement to collect and disseminate criminal intelligence on the conduct of persons and groups who may be engaged in systematic criminal activity.

II. CRIMINAL INTELLIGENCE FILE DEFINED

A criminal intelligence file consists of stored information on the activities and associations of:

A. Individuals who:

1. Are suspected of being involved in the actual or attempted planning, organizing, financing, or commission of criminal acts; or

2. Are suspected of being involved in criminal activities with known or suspected crime figures.

B. Organizations, businesses, and groups that:

1. Are suspected of being involved in the actual or attempted planning, organizing, financing, or commission of criminal acts; or

2. Are suspected of being operated, controlled, financed, or infiltrated by known or suspected crime figures for use in an illegal manner.

III. FILE CONTENT

Only information with a criminal predicate and which meets the agency's criteria for file input should be stored in the criminal intelligence file. Specifically excluded material includes:

A. Information on an individual or group merely on the basis that such individual or group supports unpopular causes.

B. Information on an individual or group merely on the basis of ethnic background.

C. Information on any individual or group merely on the basis of religious or political affiliations.

D. Information on an individual or group merely on the basis of non-criminal personal habits.

E. Criminal Offender Record Information (CORI), should be excluded from an intelligence file. This is because CORI may be subject to specific audit and dissemination restrictions which are designed to protect an individual's right to privacy and to ensure accuracy.

F. Also excluded are associations with individuals that are not of a criminal nature.

State law or local regulations may dictate whether or not public record and intelligence information should be kept in separate files or commingled. Some agencies believe that separating their files will prevent the release of intelligence information in the event a subpoena is issued. This belief is unfounded, as all information requested in the subpoena (both public and intelligence) must be turned over to the court. The judge then makes the determination on what information will be released.

The decision to commingle or separate public and intelligence documents is strictly a management decision. In determining this policy, administrators should consider the following:

A. Records relating to the conduct of the public's business that are prepared by a state or local agency, regardless of physical form or characteristics, may be considered public and the public has access to these records.

B. Specific types of records (including intelligence information) may be exempt from public disclosure.

C. Regardless of whether public record information is separated from or commingled with intelligence data, the public may have access to public records.

D. The separation of public information from criminal intelligence information may better protect the confidentiality of the criminal file. If a request is made for public records, an agency can release the public file and leave the intelligence file intact (thus less apt to accidentally disclose intelligence information).

E. Separating of files is the best theoretical approach to maintaining files; however, it is not easy to do. Most intelligence reports either reference public record information or else contain a combination of intelligence and public record data. Thus, it is difficult to isolate them from each other. Maintaining separate public and intelligence files also increases the amount of effort required to index, store, and retrieve information.

IV. FILE CRITERIA

All information retained in the criminal intelligence file should meet file criteria prescribed by the agency. These criteria should outline the agency's crime categories and provide specifics for determining whether subjects involved in these crimes are suitable for file inclusion.

File input criteria will vary among agencies because of differences in size, functions, resources, geographical location, crime problems, etc. The categories listed in the suggested model below are not exhaustive.

A. Permanent Status

1. Information that relates an individual, organization, business, or group is suspected of being involved in the actual or attempted planning, organizing, financing, or committing of one or more of the following criminal acts:

- Narcotic trafficking/manufacturing
- Unlawful gambling
- Loan sharking
- Extortion
- Vice and pornography
- Infiltration of legitimate business for illegitimate purposes
- Stolen securities
- Bribery
- Major crime including homicide, sexual assault, burglary, auto theft, kidnapping, destruction of property, robbery, fraud, fencing stolen property, and arson
- Manufacture, us of, or possession of explosive devices for purposes of fraud, intimidation, or political motivation

2. In addition to falling within the confines of one or more of the above criminal activities, the subject/entity to be given permanent status must be identifiable-distinguished by a name and unique identifying characteristics (e.g., date of birth, criminal identification number, driver's license number, address). Identification at the time of file input is necessary to distinguish the subject/entity from existing file entries and those that may be entered at a later time. NOTE: The exception to this rule involves modus operandi (MO) files. MO files describe a unique method of operation for a specific type of crime (homicide, fraud) and may not be immediately linked to an identifiable suspect. MO files may be retained indefinitely while additional identifiers are sought.

B. Temporary Status:

Information that does not meet the criteria for permanent storage but may be pertinent to an investigation involving one of the categories previously listed should be given "temporary" status. It is recommended the retention of temporary information not exceed one year unless a compelling reason exists to extend this time period. (An example of a compelling reason is if several pieces of information indicate that a crime has been committed, but more than a year is needed to identify a suspect.) During this period, efforts should be made to identify the subject/entity or validate the information so that its final status may be determined. If the information is still classified temporary at the end of the one-year period, and a compelling reason for its retention is not evident, the information should be purged. An individual, organization, business, or group may be given temporary status in the following cases:

1. **Subject/entity is unidentifiable** - subject/entity (although suspected of being engaged in criminal activities) has no known physical descriptors, identification numbers, or distinguishing characteristics available.

2. **Involvement is questionable** - involvement in criminal activities is suspected by a subject/entity which has either:

    - **Possible criminal associations** - individual, organization, business, or group (not currently reported to be criminally active) associates with a known criminal and appears to be jointly involved in illegal activities.

    - **Criminal history** - individual, organization, business, or group (not currently reported to be criminally active) that has a history of criminal conduct, and the circumstances currently being reported (i.e., new position or ownership in a business) indicates they may again become criminally active.

3. **Reliability/validity unknown** - the reliability of the information sources and/or the validity of the information cannot be determined at the time of receipt; however, the information appears to be significant and merits temporary storage while verification attempts are made.

V. INFORMATION EVALUATION

Information to be retained in the criminal intelligence file should be evaluated and designated for reliability and content validity prior to filing.

The bulk of the data an intelligence unit receives consists of unverified allegations or information. Evaluating the information's source and content indicates to future users the information's worth and usefulness. Circulating information which may not have been evaluated, where the source reliability is poor or the content validity is doubtful, is detrimental to the agency's operations and contrary to the individual's right to privacy.

To ensure uniformity with the intelligence community, it is strongly recommended that stored information be evaluated according to the criteria set forth below.

Source Reliability:

   (A) **Reliable** - The reliability of the source is unquestioned or has been well tested in the past.

   (B) **Usually Reliable** - The reliability of the source can usually be relied upon as factual. The majority of information provided in the past has proven to be reliable.

   (C) **Unreliable** - The reliability of the source has been sporadic in the past.

   (D) **Unknown** -The reliability of the source cannot be judged. Its authenticity or trustworthiness has not yet been determined by either experience or investigation.

Content Validity:

   (1) **Confirmed** - The information has been corroborated by an investigator or another independent, reliable source.

   (2) **Probable** - The information is consistent with past accounts.

   (3) **Doubtful** - The information is inconsistent with past accounts.

(4) **Cannot Be Judged** - The information cannot be judged. Its authenticity has not yet been determined by either experience or investigation.

VI. INFORMATION CLASSIFICATION

Information retained in the criminal intelligence file should be classified in order to protect sources, investigations, and the individual's right to privacy. Classification also indicates the internal approval which must be completed prior to the release of the information to persons outside the agency. However, the classification of information in itself is not a defense against a subpoena duces tecum.

The classification of criminal intelligence information is subject to continual change. The passage of time, the conclusion of investigations, and other factors may affect the security classification assigned to particular documents. Documents within the intelligence files should be reviewed on an ongoing basis to ascertain whether a higher or lesser degree of document security is required to ensure that information is released only when and if appropriate.

Classification systems may differ among agencies as to the number of levels of security and release authority. In establishing a classification system, agencies should define the types of information for each security level, dissemination criteria, and release authority. The system listed below classifies data maintained in the Criminal Intelligence File according to one of the following categories:

Sensitive

1. Information pertaining to significant law enforcement cases currently under investigation.

2. Corruption (police or other government officials), or other sensitive information.

3. Informant identification information.

4. Criminal intelligence reports which require strict dissemination and release criteria.

Confidential

1. Criminal intelligence reports not designated as sensitive.

2. Information obtained through intelligence unit channels that is not classified as sensitive and is for law enforcement use only.

Restricted

1. Reports that at an earlier date were classified sensitive or confidential and the need for high-level security no longer exists.

2. Non-confidential information prepared for/by law enforcement agencies.

Unclassified

1. Civic-related information to which, in its original form, the general public had direct access (i.e., public record data).

2. News media information - newspaper, magazine, and periodical clippings dealing with specified criminal categories.

VII. INFORMATION SOURCE

In all cases, source identification should be available in some form. The true identify of the source should be used unless there is a need to protect the source. Accordingly, each law enforcement agency should establish criteria that would indicate when source identification would be appropriate.

The value of information stored in a criminal intelligence file is often directly related to the source of such information. Some factors to consider in determining whether source identification is warranted include:

- The nature of the information reported.

- The potential need to refer to the source's identity for further or prosecutorial activity.

- The reliability of the source.

Whether or not confidential source identification is warranted, reports should reflect the name of the agency and the reporting individual. In those cases when identifying the source by name is not practical for internal security reasons, a code number may be used. A confidential listing of coded sources of information can then be retained by the intelligence unit commander. In addition to identifying the source, it may be appropriate in a particular case to describe how the source obtained the information (for example "S-60, a reliable police informant heard" or "a reliable law enforcement source of the police department saw" a particular event at a particular time).

VIII. INFORMATION QUALITY CONTROL

Information to be stored in the criminal intelligence file should undergo a thorough review for compliance with established file input guidelines and agency policy prior to being filed. The quality control reviewer is responsible for seeing that all information entered into the criminal intelligence files conforms with the agency's file criteria and has been properly evaluated and classified.

IX. FILE DISSEMINATION

Agencies should adopt sound procedures for disseminating stored information. These procedures will protect the individual's right to privacy as well as maintain the confidentiality of the sources and the file itself.

Information from a criminal intelligence report can only be released to an individual who has demonstrated both a "need-to-know" and a "right-to-know."

"Right-to-know" Requestor has official capacity and statutory authority to the information being sought.

"Need-to-know" Requested information is pertinent and necessary to the requestor agency in initiating, furthering, or completing an investigation.

No "original document" which has been obtained from an outside agency is to be released to a third agency. Should such a request be received, the requesting agency will be referred to the submitting agency for further assistance.

Information classification and evaluation are, in part, dissemination controls. They denote who may receive the information as well as the internal approval level(s) required for release of the information. In order to encourage conformity within the intelligence community, it is recommended that stored information be classified according to a system similar to the following.

Security Level	Dissemination Criteria	Release Authority
Sensitive	Restricted to law enforcement personnel having a specific need-to-know and right-to-know	Intelligence Unit Commander
Confidential	Same as for sensitive	Intelligence Unit Manager or designee
Restricted	Same as for Sensitive	Intelligence Unit Supervisor or designee
Unclassified	Not restricted Personnel	Intelligence Unit

The integrity of the criminal intelligence file can be maintained only by strict adherence to proper dissemination guidelines. To eliminate unauthorized use and abuses of the system, a department should utilize a dissemination control form that could be maintained with each stored document. This control form would record the date of the request, the name of the agency and individual requesting the information, the need-to-know, the information provided, and the name of the employee handling the request. Depending upon the needs of the agency, the control form also may be designed to record other items useful to the agency in the management of its operations. This control form also may be subject to discovery.

X. FILE REVIEW AND PURGE

Information stored in the criminal intelligence file should be reviewed periodically for reclassification or purge in order to: ensure that the file is current, accurate, and relevant to the needs and objective of the agency; safeguard the individual's right of privacy as guaranteed under federal and state laws; and, ensure that the security classification level remains appropriate.

Law enforcement agencies have an obligation to keep stored information on subjects current and accurate. Reviewing of criminal intelligence should be done on a continual basis as agency personnel use the material in carrying out day-to-day activities. In this manner, information that is no longer useful or that cannot be validated can immediately be purged or reclassified where necessary.

To ensure that all files are reviewed and purged systematically, agencies should develop purge criteria and schedules. Operational procedures for the purge and the method of destruction for purged materials should be established.

A. Purge Criteria:

General considerations for reviewing and purging of information stored in the criminal intelligence file are as follows:

1. Utility

How often is the information used?
For what purpose is the information being used?
Who uses the information?

2. Timeliness and Appropriateness

Is this investigation still ongoing?
Is the information outdated?
Is the information relevant to the needs and objectives of the agency?
Is the information relevant to the purpose for which it was collected and stored?

3. Accuracy and Completeness

Is the information still valid?
Is the information adequate for identification purposes?
Can the validity of the data be determined through investigative techniques?

B. Review and Purge Time Schedule:

Reclassifying and purging information in the intelligence file should be done on an ongoing basis as documents are reviewed. In addition, a complete review of the criminal intelligence file for purging purposes should be undertaken periodically. This review and purge schedule can vary from once each year for documents with temporary status to once every five years for permanent documents. Agencies should develop a schedule best suited to their needs and should contact their legal counsel for guidance.

C. Manner of Destruction:

Material purged from the criminal intelligence file should be destroyed. Disposal is used for all records or papers that identify a person by name. It is the responsibility of each agency to determine that their obsolete records are destroyed in accordance with applicable laws, rules, and state or local policy.

XI. FILE SECURITY

The criminal intelligence file should be located in a secured area with file access restricted to authorized personnel.

Physical security of the criminal intelligence file is imperative to maintain the confidentiality of the information stored in the file and to ensure the protection of the individual's right to privacy.

Glossary

PUBLIC RECORD

Public record includes any writing containing information relating to the conduct of the public's business prepared, owned, used, or retained by any state or local agency regardless of physical form or characteristics.

"Member of the public" means any person, except a member, agent, officer, or employee of a federal, state, or local agency acting within the scope of his or her membership in an agency, office, or employment.

For purposes of these guidelines, public record information includes only that information to which the general public normally has direct access, (i.e., birth or death certificates, county recorder's information, incorporation information, etc.)

CRIMINAL OFFENDER RECORD INFORMATION (CORI)

CORI is defined as summary information to arrests, pretrial proceedings, sentencing information, incarcerations, parole and probation.

   a. Summary criminal history records are commonly referred to as "rap sheets." Data submitted on fingerprint cards, disposition of arrest and citation forms and probation flash notices create the entries on the rap sheet.

APPENDIX B

28 CFR PART 23 GUIDELINE

Executive Order 12291

These regulations are not a "major rule" as defined by section 1(b) of Executive Order No. 12291, 3 CFR part 127 (1981), because they do not result in: (a) An effect on the economy of $100 million or more, (b) a major increase in any costs or prices, or (c) adverse effects on competition, employment, investment, productivity, or innovation among American enterprises.

Regulatory Flexibility Act

These regulations are not a rule within the meaning of the Regulatory Flexibility Act, 5 U.S.C. 601-612. These regulations, if promulgated, will not have a "significant" economic impact on a substantial number of small "entities," as defined by the Regulatory Flexibility Act.

Paperwork Reduction Act

There are no collection of information requirements contained in the proposed regulation.

List of Subjects in 28 CFR Part 23

Administrative practice and procedure, Grant programs, Intelligence, Law Enforcement.

For the reasons set out in the preamble, title 28, part 23 of the Code of Federal Regulations is revised to read as follows:

PART 23–CRIMINAL INTELLIGENCE SYSTEMS OPERATING POLICIES
Sec.

- Purpose.
- Background.
- Applicability.
- Operating principles.
- Funding guidelines.
- Monitoring and auditing of grants for the funding of intelligence systems.

Authority: 42 U.S.C. 3782(a); 42 U.S.C. 3789g(c).

§ 23.1 Purpose.

The purpose of this regulation is to assure that all criminal intelligence systems operating through support under the Omnibus Crime Control and Safe Streets Act of 1968, 42 U.S.C. 3711, et seq., as amended (Pub. L. 90-351, as amended by Pub. L. 91-644, Pub. L. 93-83, Pub. L. 93-415, Pub. L. 94-430, Pub. L. 94-503, Pub. L. 95-115, Pub. L. 96-157, Pub. L. 98-473, Pub. L. 99-570, Pub. L. 100-690, and Pub. L. 101-647), are utilized in conformance with the privacy and constitutional rights of individuals.

§ 23.2 Background.

It is recognized that certain criminal activities including but not limited to loan sharking, drug trafficking, trafficking in stolen property, gambling, extortion, smuggling, bribery, and corruption of public officials often involve some degree of regular coordination and permanent organization involving a large number of participants over a broad geographical area. The exposure of such ongoing networks of criminal activity can be aided by the pooling of information about such activities. However, because the collection and exchange of intelligence data necessary to support control of serious criminal activity may represent potential threats to the privacy of individuals to whom such data relates, policy guidelines for Federally funded projects are required.

§ 23.3 Applicability.

(a) These policy standards are applicable to all criminal intelligence systems operating through support under the Omnibus Crime Control and Safe Streets Act of 1968, 42 U.S.C. 3711, et seq., as amended (Pub. L. 90-351, as amended by Pub. L. 91-644, Pub. L. 93-83, Pub. L. 93-415, Pub. L. 94-430, Pub. L. 94-503, Pub. L. 95-115, Pub. L. 96-157, Pub. L. 98-473, Pub. L. 99-570, Pub. L. 100-690, and Pub. L. 101-647).

(b) As used in these policies: (1) Criminal Intelligence System or Intelligence System means the arrangements, equipment, facilities, and procedures used for the receipt, storage, inter-agency exchange or dissemination, and analysis of criminal intelligence information; (2) Interjurisdictional Intelligence

System means an intelligence system which involves two or more participating agencies representing different governmental units or jurisdictions; (3) Criminal Intelligence Information means data which has been evaluated to determine that it: (i) is relevant to the identification of and the criminal activity engaged in by an individual who or organization which is reasonably suspected of involvement in criminal activity, and (ii) meets criminal intelligence system submission criteria; (4) Participating Agency means an agency of local, county, State, Federal, or other governmental unit which exercises law enforcement or criminal investigation authority and which is authorized to submit and receive criminal intelligence information through an interjurisdictional intelligence system. A participating agency may be a member or a nonmember of an interjurisdictional intelligence system; (5) Intelligence Project or Project means the organizational unit which operates an intelligence system on behalf of and for the benefit of a single agency or the organization which operates an interjurisdictional intelligence system on behalf of a group of participating agencies; and (6) Validation of Information means the procedures governing the periodic review of criminal intelligence information to assure its continuing compliance with system submission criteria established by regulation or program policy.

§ 23.20 Operating principles.

(a) A project shall collect and maintain criminal intelligence information concerning an individual only if there is reasonable suspicion that the individual is involved in criminal conduct or activity and the information is relevant to that criminal conduct or activity.

(b) A project shall not collect or maintain criminal intelligence information about the political, religious or social views, associations, or activities of any individual or any group, association, corporation, business, partnership, or other organization unless such information directly relates to criminal conduct or activity and there is reasonable suspicion that the subject of the information is or may be involved in criminal conduct or activity.

(c) Reasonable Suspicion or Criminal Predicate is established when information exists which establishes sufficient facts to give a trained law enforcement or criminal investigative agency officer, investigator, or employee a basis to believe that there is a reasonable possibility that an individual or organization is involved in a definable criminal activity or enterprise. In an interjurisdictional intelligence system, the project is responsible for establishing the existence of reasonable suspicion of criminal activity either through examination of supporting information submitted by a participating agency or by delegation of this responsibility to a properly trained participating agency which is subject to routine inspection and audit procedures established by the project.

(d) A project shall not include in any criminal intelligence system information which has been obtained in violation of any applicable Federal, State, or local law or ordinance. In an interjurisdictional intelligence system, the project is responsible for establishing that no information is entered in violation of Federal, State, or local laws, either through examination of supporting information submitted by a participating agency or by delegation of this responsibility to a properly trained participating agency which is subject to routine inspection and audit procedures established by the project.

(e) A project or authorized recipient shall disseminate criminal intelligence information only where there is a need to know and a right to know the information in the performance of a law enforcement activity.

(f) (1) Except as noted in paragraph (f) (2) of this section, a project shall disseminate criminal intelligence information only to law enforcement authorities who shall agree to follow procedures regarding information receipt, maintenance, security, and dissemination which are consistent with these principles.
(2) Paragraph (f) (1) of this section shall not limit the dissemination of an assessment of criminal intelligence information to a government official or to any other individual, when necessary, to avoid imminent danger to life or property.

(g) A project maintaining criminal intelligence information shall ensure that administrative, technical, and physical safeguards (including audit trails) are adopted to insure against unauthorized access and against intentional or unintentional damage. A record indicating who has been given information, the reason for release of the information, and the date of each dissemination outside the project shall be kept. Information shall be labeled to indicate levels of sensitivity, levels of confidence, and the identity of submitting agencies and control officials. Each project must establish written definitions for the need to know and right to know standards for dissemination to other agencies as provided in paragraph (e) of this section. The project is responsible for establishing the existence of an inquirer's need to know and right to know the information being requested either through inquiry or by delegation of this responsibility to a properly trained participating agency which is subject to routine inspection and audit procedures established by the project. Each intelligence project shall assure that the following security requirements are implemented:

(1) Where appropriate, projects must adopt effective and technologically advanced computer software and hardware designs to prevent unauthorized access to the information contained in the system;

(2) The project must restrict access to its facilities, operating environment and documentation to organizations and personnel authorized by the project;

(3) The project must store information in the system in a manner such that it cannot be modified, destroyed, accessed, or purged without authorization;

(4) The project must institute procedures to protect criminal intelligence information from unauthorized access, theft, sabotage, fire, flood, or other natural or manmade disaster;

(5) The project must promulgate rules and regulations based on good cause for implementing its authority to screen, reject for employment, transfer, or remove personnel authorized to have direct access to the system; and

(6) A project may authorize and utilize remote (off-premises) system data bases to the extent that they comply with these security requirements.

(h) All projects shall adopt procedures to assure that all information which is retained by a project has relevancy and importance. Such procedures shall provide for the periodic review of information and the destruction of any information which is misleading, obsolete or otherwise unreliable and shall require that any recipient agencies be advised of such changes which involve errors or corrections. All information retained as a result of this review must reflect the name of the reviewer, date of review and explanation of decision to retain. Information retained in the system must be reviewed and validated for continuing compliance with system submission criteria before the expiration of its retention period, which in no event shall be longer than five (5) years.

(i) If funds awarded under the Act are used to support the operation of an intelligence system, then:

(1) No project shall make direct remote terminal access to intelligence information available to system participants, except as specifically approved by the Office of Justice Programs (OJP) based on a determination that the system has adequate policies and procedures in place to insure that it is accessible only to authorized systems users; and
(2) A project shall undertake no major modifications to system design without prior grantor agency approval.

(j) A project shall notify the grantor agency prior to initiation of formal information exchange procedures with any Federal, State, regional, or other information systems not indicated in the grant documents as initially approved at time of award.

(k) A project shall make assurances that there will be no purchase or use in the course of the project of any electronic, mechanical, or other device for surveillance purposes that is in violation of the provisions of the Electronic Communications Privacy Act of 1986, Public Law 99-508, 18 U.S.C. 2510-2520, 2701-2709 and 3121-3125, or any applicable State statute related to wiretapping and surveillance.

(*l*) A project shall make assurances that there will be no harassment or interference with any lawful political activities as part of the intelligence operation.

(m) A project shall adopt sanctions for unauthorized access, utilization, or disclosure of information contained in the system.

(n) A participating agency of an interjurisdictional intelligence system must maintain in its agency files information which documents each submission to the system and supports compliance with project entry criteria. Participating agency files supporting system submissions must be made available for reasonable audit and inspection by project representatives. Project representatives will conduct participating agency inspection and audit in such a manner so as to protect the confidentiality and sensitivity of participating agency intelligence records.

(o) The Attorney General or designee may waive, in whole or in part, the applicability of a particular requirement or requirements contained in this part with respect to a criminal intelligence system, or for a class of submitters or users of such system, upon a clear and convincing showing that such waiver would enhance the collection, maintenance or dis-semination of information in the criminal intelligence system, while ensuring that such system would not be utilized in violation of the privacy and constitutional rights of indi-viduals or any applicable state or federal law.

§ 23.30 Funding guidelines.

The following funding guidelines shall apply to all Crime Control Act funded discretionary assistance awards and Bureau of Justice Assistance (BJA) formula grant program subgrants, a purpose of which is to support the operation of an intelligence system. Intelligence systems shall only be funded where a grantee/subgrantee agrees to adhere to the principles set forth above and the project meets the following criteria:

(a) The proposed collection and exchange of criminal intelligence information has been coordinated with and will support ongoing or proposed investigatory or prosecutorial activities relating to specific areas of criminal activity.

(b) The areas of criminal activity for which intelligence information is to be utilized represent a significant and recognized threat to the population and:

(1) Are either undertaken for the purpose of seeking illegal power or profits or pose a threat to the life and property of citizens; and

(2) Involve a significant degree of permanent criminal organization; or

(3) Are not limited to one jurisdiction.

(c) The head of a government agency or an individual with general policy making authority who has been expressly delegated such control and supervision by the head of the agency will retain control and supervision of information collection and dissemination for the criminal intelligence system. This official shall certify in writing that he or she takes full responsibility and will be accountable for the information maintained by and disseminated from the system and that the operation of the system will be in compliance with the principles set forth in § 23.20.

(d) Where the system is an interjurisdictional criminal intelligence system, the governmental agency which exercises control and supervision over the operation of the system shall require that the head of that agency or an individual with general policymaking authority who has been expressly delegated such control and supervision by the head of the agency:

(1) assume official responsibility and accountability for actions taken in the name of the joint entity, and

(2) certify in writing that the official takes full responsibility and will be accountable for insuring that the information transmitted to the interjurisdictional system or to participating agencies will be in compliance with the principles set forth in § 23.20.

The principles set forth in § 23.20 shall be made part of the by-laws or operating procedures for that system. Each participating agency, as a condition of participation, must accept in writing those principles which govern the submission, maintenance and dissemination of information included as part of the interjurisdictional system.

(e) Intelligence information will be collected, maintained and disseminated primarily for State and local law enforcement efforts, including efforts involving Federal participation.

§ 23.40   Monitoring and auditing of grants for the funding of intelligence systems.

(a) Awards for the funding of intelligence systems will receive specialized monitoring and audit in accordance with a plan designed to insure compliance with operating principles as set forth in § 23.20. The plan shall be approved prior to award of funds.

(b) All such awards shall be subject to a special condition requiring compliance with the principles set forth in § 23.20.

(c) An annual notice will be published by OJP which will indicate the existence and the objective of all systems for the continuing interjurisdictional exchange of criminal intelligence information which are subject to the 28 CFR Part 23 Criminal Intelligence Systems Policies.

1993 Revision and Commentary

DEPARTMENT OF JUSTICE
Office of Justice Programs
28 CFR Part 23
Final Revision to the Office of Justice Programs, Criminal Intelligence Systems Operating Policies

AGENCY: Office of Justice Programs, Justice.

ACTION: Final Rule

SUMMARY: The regulation governing criminal intelligence systems operating through support under Title I of the Omnibus Crime Control and Safe Streets Act of 1968, as amended, is being revised to update basic authority citations and nomenclature, to clarify the applicability of the regulation, to define terms, and to modify a number of the regulation's operating policies and funding guidelines.

EFFECTIVE DATE: September 16, 1993

FOR FURTHER INFORMATION CONTACT: Paul Kendall, Esquire, General Counsel, Office of Justice Programs, 633 Indiana Ave., NW., Suite 1245-E, Washington, DC 20531, Telephone (202) 307-6235 http://www.ojp.usdoj.gov/.

SUPPLEMENTARY INFORMATION: The rule which this rule supersedes had been in effect and unchanged since September 17, 1980. A notice of proposed rulemaking for 28 CFR part 23, was published in the Federal Register on February 27, 1992, (57 FR 6691).

The statutory authorities for this regulation are section 801(a) and section 812(c) of title I of the Omnibus Crime Control and Safe Streets Act of 1968, as amended, (the Act), 42 U.S.C. 3782(a) and 3789g(c). 42 U.S.C. 3789g (c) and (d) provide as follows:

Confidentiality of Information

Sec. 812....

(c) All criminal intelligence systems operating through support under this title shall collect, maintain, and disseminate criminal intelligence information in conformance with policy standards which are prescribed by the Office of Justice Programs and which are written to assure that the funding and operation of these systems furthers the purpose of this title and to assure that such systems are not utilized in violation of the privacy and constitutional rights of individuals.

(d) Any person violating the provisions of this section, or of any rule, regulation, or order issued thereunder, shall be fined not to exceed $10,000, in addition to any other penalty imposed by law.

Policy Clarification
[Federal Register: December 30, 1998 (Volume 63, Number 250)]

[Page 71752-71753]
From the Federal Register Online via GPO Access
[wais.access.gpo.gov]

DEPARTMENT OF JUSTICE
http://usdoj.gov/
28 CFR Part 23
[OJP(BJA)-1177B]
RIN 1121-ZB40
Criminal Intelligence Sharing Systems; Policy Clarification

AGENCY: Bureau of Justice Assistance (BJA), Office of Justice Programs (OJP), Justice. http://ojp.usdoj.gov/

ACTION: Clarification of policy.

SUMMARY: The current policy governing the entry of identifying information into criminal intelligence sharing systems requires clarification. This policy clarification is to make clear that the entry of individuals, entities and organizations, and locations that do not otherwise meet the requirements of reasonable suspicion is appropriate when it is done solely for the purposes of criminal identification or is germane to the criminal subject's criminal activity. Further, the definition of "criminal intelligence system" is clarified.

EFFECTIVE DATE: This clarification is effective December 30, 1998.

FOR FURTHER INFORMATION CONTACT: Paul Kendall, General Counsel, Office of Justice Programs, 810 7th Street N.W., Washington, DC 20531, (202) 307-6235.

SUPPLEMENTARY INFORMATION: The operation of criminal intelligence information systems is governed by 28 CFR Part 23. This regulation was written to both protect the privacy rights of individuals and to encourage and expedite the exchange of criminal intelligence information between and among law enforcement agencies of different jurisdictions. Frequent interpretations of the regulation, in the form of policy guidance and correspondence, have been the primary method of ensuring that advances in technology did not hamper its effectiveness.

Comments

The clarification was opened to public comment. Comments expressing unreserved support for the clarification were received from two Regional Intelligence Sharing Systems (RISS) and five states. A comment from the Chairperson of a RISS, relating to the use of identifying information to begin new investigations, has been incorporated. A single negative comment was received, but was not addressed to the subject of this clarification.

Use of Identifying Information

28 CFR 23.3(b)(3) states that criminal intelligence information that can be put into a criminal intelligence sharing system is "information relevant to the identification of and the criminal activity engaged in by an individual who or organization which is reasonably suspected of involvement in criminal activity, and *** [m]eets criminal intelligence system submission criteria." Further, 28 CFR 23.20(a) states that a system shall only collect information on an individual if "there is reasonable suspicion that the individual is

involved in criminal conduct or activity and the information is relevant to that criminal conduct or activity." 28 CFR 23.20(b) extends that limitation to collecting information on groups and corporate entities.

In an effort to protect individuals and organizations from the possible taint of having their names in intelligence systems (as defined at 28 C.F.R. Sec. 23.3(b)(1)), the Office of Justice Programs has previously interpreted this section to allow information to be placed in a system only if that information independently meets the requirements of the regulation. Information that might be vital to identifying potential criminals, such as favored locations and companions, or names of family members, has been excluded from the systems. This policy has hampered the effectiveness of many criminal intelligence sharing systems.

Given the swiftly changing nature of modern technology and the expansion of the size and complexity of criminal organizations, the Bureau of Justice Assistance (BJA) has determined that it is necessary to clarify this element of 28 CFR Part 23. Many criminal intelligence databases are now employing "Comment" or "Modus Operandi" fields whose value would be greatly enhanced by the ability to store more detailed and wide-ranging identifying information. This may include names and limited data about people and organizations that are not suspected of any criminal activity or involvement, but merely aid in the identification and investigation of a criminal suspect who independently satisfies the reasonable suspicion standard.

Therefore, BJA issues the following clarification to the rules applying to the use of identifying information. Information that is relevant to the identification of a criminal suspect or to the criminal activity in which the suspect is engaged may be placed in a criminal intelligence database, provided that (1) appropriate disclaimers accompany the information noting that is strictly identifying information, carrying no criminal connotations; (2) identifying information may not be used as an independent basis to meet the requirement of reasonable suspicion of involvement in criminal activity necessary to create a record or file in a criminal intelligence system; and (3) the individual who is the criminal suspect identified by this information otherwise meets all requirements of 28 CFR Part 23. This information may be a searchable field in the intelligence system.

For example: A person reasonably suspected of being a drug dealer is known to conduct his criminal activities at the fictional "Northwest Market." An agency may wish to note this information in a criminal intelligence database, as it may be important to future identification of the suspect. Under the previous interpretation of the regulation, the entry of "Northwest Market" would not be permitted, because there was no reasonable suspicion that the "Northwest Market" was a criminal organization. Given the current clarification of the regulation, this will be permissible, provided that the information regarding the "Northwest Market" was clearly noted to be non-criminal in nature. For example, the data field in which "Northwest Market" was entered could be marked "Non-Criminal Identifying Information," or the words "Northwest Market" could be followed by a parenthetical comment such as "This organization has been entered into the system for identification purposes only-it is not suspected of any criminal activity or involvement." A criminal intelligence system record or file could not be created for "Northwest Market" solely on the basis of information provided, for example, in a comment field on the suspected drug dealer. Independent information would have to be obtained as a basis for the opening of a new criminal intelligence file or record based on reasonable suspicion on "Northwest Market." Further, the fact that other individuals frequent "Northwest Market" would not necessarily establish reasonable suspicion for those other individuals, as it relates to criminal intelligence systems.

The Definition of a "Criminal Intelligence System"

The definition of a "criminal intelligence system" is given in 28 CFR 23.3(b)(1) as the "arrangements, equipment, facilities, and procedures used for the receipt, storage, interagency exchange or dissemination, and analysis of criminal intelligence information ***." Given the fact that cross-database searching techniques are now common-place, and given the fact that multiple databases may be contained on the same computer system, BJA has determined that this definition needs clarification, specifically to differentiate between criminal intelligence systems and non-intelligence systems.

The comments to the 1993 revision of 28 CFR Part 23 noted that "[t]he term 'intelligence system' is redefined to clarify the fact that historical telephone toll files, analytical information, and work products that are not either retained, stored, or exchanged and criminal history record information or identification (fingerprint) systems are excluded from the

definition, and hence are not covered by the regulation ***."
58 FR 48448-48449 (Sept. 16, 1993.) The comments further
noted that materials that "may assist an agency to produce
investigative or other information for an intelligence system
***" do not necessarily fall under the regulation. Id.

The above rationale for the exclusion of non-intelligence
information sources from the definition of "criminal intelligence system," suggests now that, given the availability of
more modern non-intelligence information sources such as
the Internet, newspapers, motor vehicle administration
records, and other public record information on-line, such
sources shall not be considered part of criminal intelligence
systems, and shall not be covered by this regulation, even if
criminal intelligence systems access such sources during
searches on criminal suspects. Therefore, criminal intelligence systems may conduct searches across the spectrum of
non-intelligence systems without those systems being
brought under 28 CFR Part 23. There is also no limitation on
such non-intelligence information being stored on the same
computer system as criminal intelligence information,
provided that sufficient precautions are in place to separate
the two types of information and to make it clear to operators
and users of the information that two different types of
information are being accessed.

Such precautions should be consistent with the above
clarification of the rule governing the use of identifying
information. This could be accomplished, for example,
through the use of multiple windows, differing colors of data
or clear labeling of the nature of information displayed.

APPENDIX C

Table C-1 Tactical Planning

Tactical Planning	
	■ Tactical and Action Planning
	■ What is the mission?
	■ What are the possible alternatives?
	■ Why must the mission be accomplished?
	■ When?
	■ Where?
	■ Who?
	■ Required officer skills and abilities?
	■ Tactical and Action Planning
	■ Where should the officers assemble?
	■ Planning and execution?
	■ Methods and procedures?
	■ Innovative techniques?
	■ Logistical support and weapons?
	■ Tactical teams?
	■ Evaluation and after action report?
	■ Decision Making
	■ Is the decision:
	■ Consistent with the agency's mission, goals and objectives?
	■ A long-term solution?
	■ Cost effective?
	■ Legal?`
	■ Ethical?
	■ Practical?
	■ Acceptable to those responsible?

APPENDIX D

Table D-1   Basic Planning Steps

Basic Training Steps
■ 7 Basic Planning Steps: Step 1
■ Consider the task:
■ What has to be done?
■ Who does what?
■ When?
■ Where?
■ How?
■ Planning: Step 2
■ Consider the resources:
■ What time is available?
■ What are the skills of the group?
■ What equipment and supplies are needed and available?
■ What other items should be considered?
■ Planning: Step 3
■ Consider alternatives:
■ What happens if something goes wrong?
■ What are the emergency procedures?
■ What is the alternate plan?
■ Could the alternate plan be better than the original plan?
■ Planning: Step 4
■ Reach a decision:
■ Who has the responsibility?
■ Is a poor decision better than no decision?
■ Is no decision a decision?
■ Is a group decision best?
■ A decision usually is needed at every step in the process.
■ Planning: Step 5
■ Write down the plan:
■ The act of writing down an action plan may cause it be revised or refined.
■ The final plan might need considerable discussion.
■ Planning: Step 6
■ Put the plan into action:
■ All too often great plans are formed but never followed.
■ Planning: Step 7
■ Evaluate
■ Evaluation must take place all during this process.
■ The plan is evaluated against the previous steps to assure that the original task is still being considered.

APPENDIX E

Table E-1   Evaluation & Assessment

■ Where Are We Now?
■ Evaluation:
■ Compares impact of completed goals and objectives
■ Judges program efforts critically
■ Describes and interprets action plans in a wider context of the mission and values statement
■ What Is The Problem?
■ A problem is any situation that a police department may need or want to address.
■ A clear understanding of the problem is needed before the department can set a goal.
■ Define Goals
■ A goal redefines the problem into a positive statement that answers the question:
■ What do we want?
■ Define Related Objectives
■ Must be important to the officers
■ Must be realistic
■ Not based on wishful thinking
■ Should require the officers' best effort
■ Officers should feel good after reaching goal.
■ Stop and Think
■ Allow officers to examine the problem and goal before continuing to the next step.
■ First suggestion may not be best.
■ Make a Plan
■ Look for options
■ Examine consequences of particular course of action
■ Each alternative has pros and cons
■ Decision made on a start-to-finish plan
■ Persistence
■ Achievement demands excellence and endurance.
■ Officers must recognize that before a plan is abandoned, sustained effort is needed.
■ Sometimes only a small adjustment in the plan is required to achieve success.
■ Evaluation and Assessment
■ Was the goal attained?
■ Objectives completed?
■ Did we do our best?
■ What might have been changed?
■ Evaluate the entire problem-solving process.
■ Reassess where the department goes next.

INDEX